THE EVERLASTING CIRCLE

` BUXOM LASS !

As I was walking out one morning, I met a
  buxom lass,
Going to a dairyman, she had a field of grass,
It grew between two mountains, at the foot
  of a spring,
She hired me to cut it down, while the birds
  did sweetly sing.

I said my pretty fair Maid, what wages do
  you give,
For mowing is hard labour, unless my scythe
  is good,
She said if you do please me, I solemnly do swear
I'll give a crown an acre, & plenty of strong beer
I said my pretty fair Maid, I like your wages
  well,
If I mow your grass down, you shall say it
  is done well,
My scythe is in good order, and lately has
  been ground,
My bonny lass I'll cut your grass, close upon
  the ground.

She said my lusty young man when will you
  begin,
My grass is in good order, I long to have it in,
It is such pleasant weather, I long to clear
  the ground,
So get your scythe in order, to mow your
  meadow down,

With courage like a lion, he entered in the field,
I'll mow your meadow down, before that I do
  yield,
Before I'd mowed a rood of grass, my scythe
  it bent and broke,
She said my man, you must give in you're
  tired of your work.

She said my man you must give in, you are
  tired of your work,
For mowing is hard labour, and weakening to
  the back,
For mowing is hard labour, and you must it
  forsake,
And round my little meadow you may use
  your rake,

I said my handsome fair Maid, do not on me
  frown,
For if I stop the summer through, I cannot
  mow it down,
It is such pleasant weather, and bears such
  crops of grass,
It's watered by a spring, that makes it grow
  so fast.

THE

ROSE

IN

JUNE!

Some idly throughout spend their time,
Not to enjoy their rose in prime.

CHORUS.

Let it be early late or soon,
I will enjoy my rose in June.

The violets make the meadows smell sweet
None with my roses can compete,

Primroses make the meadows look neat,
None with my roses can compete,

Cowslips make the meadows look fair,
None with my roses can compare,

Of every sweet flower that grows,
None can compare to my blooming rose.

Let it be early late or soon,
I will enjoy my rose in June.

Jackson and Son, (late Russell,) Printers,
      Moor street,) Birmingham.

A broadside in the Baring-Gould collection

James Reeves

★

THE EVERLASTING CIRCLE

★

English Traditional Verse

EDITED

WITH AN INTRODUCTION

AND NOTES

FROM THE MANUSCRIPTS OF

S. BARING-GOULD, H. E. D. HAMMOND

AND GEORGE B. GARDINER

THE MACMILLAN COMPANY

NEW YORK

821.08
R

TO

PAT SHULDHAM-SHAW

For singing English songs in English
'God send you prosperation
all the days of your life'

CONTENTS

LIST OF ILLUSTRATIONS

INDEX OF SONGS

xi

ACKNOWLEDGMENTS

I wish to acknowledge my indebtedness to the following, and to express my sincere thanks for their co-operation: to the Plymouth Public Libraries Committee for their kind permission to transcribe and reprint the texts of songs in the Baring-Gould mss., and especially to the City Librarian, Mr W. Best Harris, for most generously extending to me the hospitality of the Central Library, Plymouth; to Messrs Novello and Co. Ltd and the English Folk Dance and Song Society, for permission to quote from the Gardiner Collection at Cecil Sharp House; to Miss Sara E. Jackson, Librarian of the English Folk Dance and Song Society, for her invaluable help; to Messrs Methuen and Co. Ltd for permission to quote from copyright works by S. Baring-Gould, and to reproduce the illustrations on page 294; to the Registrar of the Edinburgh Academy for information about George B. Gardiner; to Mr H. M. Sherry, County Librarian of Hampshire, for information about *The Owslebury Lads*; to Mr Peter Kennedy for permission to quote the version of *Betsy* collected by him; to Mrs Glenys Roberts for an English rendering of the Welsh version of *The Everlasting Circle*; to Miss Valerie Little for help in transcription and research; and to Mrs Heather Karolyi and to my wife for seeing the book through the press. For help and advice on a variety of matters I wish to thank Miss Margaret Dean-Smith once more; and Miss Violet Alford, whose *Introduction to English Folklore* (Bell) offers a valuable background for the study of traditional song. I must emphasize, however, that for errors of fact or interpretation in this book I alone am responsible. Finally, for permission to reprint texts from the Hammond Collection at Cecil Sharp House I have to acknowledge the kindness of the late Dr Ralph Vaughan Williams.

J. R.

Chalfont St Giles,
1959

Introduction

BARING-GOULD AS FOLK SONG COLLECTOR

O F THE THREE folk song collectors whose work is here represented, Sabine Baring-Gould had by far the greatest influence.
Indeed, the other two were comparatively late followers of a movement in which Baring-Gould was a pioneer. He was born in Exeter
in 1834 and remained all his life a West Country man with strong
local prejudices. Like Cecil Sharp a generation later, he graduated
at Clare College, Cambridge. He entered the Church of England
and obtained a living first in Yorkshire and later in Essex. In 1881
he returned to his native county, and was for the rest of his life
Rector of Lew Trenchard in North Devon. He died in 1924 at the
age of ninety.

A man of varied but erratic intellectual gifts and of abounding
creative energy, he interested himself in popular religion, mythology
and folk-lore, travel, topography and the writing of fiction. The
titles of his romantic novels, his volumes of sermons, his antiquarian
and local studies, and the rest of his miscellaneous output occupy
twelve columns in the catalogue of the British Museum. Despite the
somewhat undirected character of his labours, he must be accounted
one of the last of the great line of English country parsons who were
amateurs of art and learning. A recluse rather than an eccentric, he
spanned the Victorian age, preferring to employ in the pursuit of his
changing personal interests the industry and talent which might have
served to advance him in the Church.

In 1887, when he was over fifty, and had settled in his native
Devon, Baring-Gould turned his attention to the collection and
publication of folk songs. In noting the melodies he was obliged to
enlist the help of two musical collaborators, the Rev. H. Fleetwood
Sheppard and the Rev. F. W. Bussell, since he himself was unable
to take down music except at a piano. Together they would make
excursions to the inns and farmsteads of Dartmoor and persuade the

old, usually illiterate, country singers to give them their songs. The fruits of these expeditions appeared, first in four parts and then in a single volume, between 1889 and 1891, as *Songs and Ballads of the West: A Collection made from the Mouths of the People*. The melodies were 'Harmonized and Arranged for Voice and Pianoforte' by Fleetwood Sheppard. The texts were edited and annotated by Baring-Gould. A further revised edition, under the musical editorship of Cecil Sharp, was issued in 1905. *Songs of the West* contained 110 (ultimately 121) songs recovered in Devon and Cornwall. In 1895 appeared *A Garland of Country Song*, by Baring-Gould and Fleetwood Sheppard, containing fifty songs, mostly from other counties. In these collections the texts are drastically emended, abridged, restored, expurgated or wholly re-written. In the prefaces Baring-Gould expounds his views on folk song, and in the copious notes he displays a wide but unsystematic knowledge of rural lore and traditional balladry.

What prompted Baring-Gould in the late eighties to undertake the recovery of folk song 'from the mouths of the people' was, first, a local and national patriotism which, in cultural matters, amounted almost to xenophobia. The singers of traditional songs were old, and fast dying out; a mere handful of collectors were at work in the field. Soon it would be too late: the heritage would be lost for ever —a belief which has animated collectors from the eighteenth century to the present day. Secondly, English music, especially vocal, was in a parlous condition and needed to be re-vitalized and saved from the all-pervasive influence of Germany. 'The professional musician of today knows nothing, absolutely nothing, of English folk music' (1895).[1] Baring-Gould admitted that his main purpose was to rescue the melodies: 'The melodies are far more precious than the words, and we have been more concerned to rescue these than the words, which are often commonplace, and may frequently be found on broadside ballad sheets' (1905). His interest in modal tunes sprang partly from religious antiquarianism, and was influential in creating the later musical revolution associated with the names of Holst and Vaughan Williams.

He approached folk song, then, first as a West Country Briton, secondly as an amateur of music, and thirdly as a historian. He

[1] In quoting from Baring-Gould's prefaces I have in each case given the date, since his views changed somewhat between 1891 and 1905.

believed that the survival of folk song in rural districts was due in the first place to the laws against itinerant gleemen and ballad-singers during the reign of Elizabeth I and later the Common-wealth. These singers, deprived of their accustomed livelihood, had settled down in country towns and villages and taken up rural trades. They had acquired a certain recognized but unofficial status as local singers, and had come to be in demand at May games, wakes and Christmas feasts, Whitsun-ales, harvest suppers, weddings and other local occasions. Their skill and their stock of songs had been handed down from father to son. But latterly the occupation of 'singing man' had fallen on bad days: the decline of cottage industries and agricultural depression had impoverished rural life and put an end to the seasonal festivities. The girls who sang at their milking and the women who sang in their kitchens now preferred hymns to ballads. The young men regarded the modal music of their fathers as behind the times and preferred the productions of the music hall.[1] Evangelical religion frowned upon the wantonness and licence of the songs which, as a boy, Baring-Gould had heard in the parlours of Dartmoor taverns. 'One of my old singers, James Olver,' wrote Baring-Gould, 'was the son of very strict Wesleyans. When he was a boy, he was allowed to hear no music save psalm and hymn tunes. But he was wont to creep out of his window at night, and start away to the tavern where the miners congregated, and listen to and heap up in his memory the songs he there heard. As these were forbidden fruit they were all the more dearly prized and surely remembered, and when he was a white-haired old man, he poured them out to us' (1905).

It was a matter of urgent importance for the cultural life of the nation that this heritage should be saved before it perished with the old singers. There were not enough collectors in the field. 'Few counties of England have been worked', Baring-Gould could write as late as 1905. 'Sussex has been well explored by the late Rev. John Broadwood, and then by Miss Lucy Broadwood; Yorkshire, by Mr Frank Kidson; Northumberland, by Dr Collingwood Bruce and Mr John Stokoe. Mr Cecil Sharp is now engaged on Somerset-shire, and Dr Vaughan Williams on Essex. Who will undertake Lincolnshire, Dorset, Hampshire, and other counties?'

[1] See also Appendix III.

3

For his part in the stirring up of enlightened interest which culminated, ten years after *Songs of the West* began to appear, in the inauguration of the Folk-Song Society, Baring-Gould's credit is secure. His handling of the material he recovered is more questionable. He has been praised for his knowledge of folk songs in other European countries, and for his wide acquaintance with the printed literature of the subject. His allusions to these in the notes to his published songs, in the form of detailed references to broadsides, garlands, chapbooks and mss. in the British Museum, from the later middle ages to the mid-nineteenth century—these are indeed helpful to students and editors. But in a sense all this scholarship was a handicap to Baring-Gould in his assessment of the value of the texts he noted. He did indeed amass a considerable private collection of printed broadsides, and this material is now in the British Museum in ten bulky volumes. Anyone who has read through a large and haphazard collection of broadsides, early and late, must admit that the experience is, aesthetically speaking, tedious and even depressing. Along with the hack productions of purveyors of street ballads in Seven Dials and elsewhere, there are comparatively few songs which appear to have been drawn from the oral tradition of genuine 'folk' balladry. That there *was* such a tradition—and that it still persists in the outlying parts of Britain among relatively illiterate people— independently of written records, there can be no doubt. But when it was used by town printers to replenish their supply of 'new' ballads of hack composition, the versions printed were often garbled, confused or fragmentary. 'The broadside is the echo, not the original', as Baring-Gould wrote (1895). But his study of these and other printed texts inclined him to conclude that *all* traditional songs were, so far as the words went, irretrievably corrupt and virtually worthless. Either they were, from a literary point of view, feeble and commonplace, or they were gross and indelicate. He felt himself obliged to re-write them in order to make them suitable for the drawing-room of a gentleman's house or for a respectable concert hall. He had as precedent the example of previous collectors. Burns and Allan Ramsay had similarly cleaned up and restored the rough songs of the Scottish peasantry when contributing to Johnson's *Scots Musical Museum*. Baring-Gould, moreover, like A. P. Graves a little later, was a fluent versifier in his own right, and the temptation to replace unsuitable traditional words by more appropriate ones of his own composition was irresistible. The practice of fabricating pseudo-folk songs for publication with the old melodies was already established. As they stand, the texts which accompany the tunes in Baring-Gould's published collections are almost worthless. What of the words as he took them down 'from the mouths of the people'?

2

BARING-GOULD'S MANUSCRIPTS

In his 1891 preface Baring-Gould says:

> In some instances the ballads reveal a rudeness of manner and moral that make it impossible for me to publish the words exactly. We have endeavoured to obtain three or four versions of the same ballads and tunes, and are by this means enabled to arrive at what we believe to be the most correct form of both. But as to the antiquary everything is important exactly as obtained, uncleansed from rust and unpolished, it is the intention of Mr Sheppard and myself to deposit a couple of copies of the songs and ballads, with their music *exactly as taken down*, one in the library of the Exeter, the other in that of the Plymouth Institution, for reference. [Italics by B-G.]

In the 1905 preface this last clause is altered to:

> I have deposited a copy of the songs and ballads with their music exactly as taken down, for reference, in the Municipal Free Library, Plymouth.

Nothing more in fact was heard of the Exeter proposal, but the City Library at Plymouth possesses two manuscript volumes, one of tunes and the other of words. It is not at all clear from this whether the phrase 'exactly as taken down' is intended to apply to the words as well as to the music. The pages of the music volume do indeed appear to be working sheets. They have been written at various times, and some of them are stained. But the volume of words is a very different matter. It is in fact a fair copy, all of it in Baring-Gould's small, neat autograph. Presumably these fair copies were made from working-sheets or notebooks. What has happened to these no one knows. But if any student expects to find in the Plymouth mss. complete and undoctored transcriptions, such as are found in the ms. notebooks of Cecil Sharp, he will be disappointed. The volume of words contains 202 songs numbered in Roman figures. Baring-Gould includes not only versions recovered from local singers, but also copies sent by correspondents, and transcriptions from broadsides and other scarce printed sources. He does not often include more than one or two versions from oral communication. Anyone who pays particular attention to these oral versions cannot help noticing how many of them have been censored or restored. For instance, the transcription of *As I went down to Salisbury* (Ms. No. XC), 'taken down from William Setter at Postbridge, January 1890', consists of three stanzas followed by the words '*Rest coarse*'. In other transcriptions too such expressions as 'indecent' and 'omitted as gross' indicate *lacunae*. Moreover, some of the songs in *Songs of the West* have no counterpart whatever in the mss. Such are *The Queen of Hearts* (No. 114, stated to be 'sung by workmen engaged on the Burrow-Tor reservoir at Sheepstor' in 1894), *The Mole Catcher* (No. 45, 'taken down from J. Hockin, South Brent, by H. Fleetwood Sheppard in 1888. The original words were very gross and I did not note them') and *The Keeper* (No. 113, 'taken down from Peter Sandry, St Ervan's. He had a bad cold and could not reach the upper notes'). Again, some of the songs in *Songs of the West* are ascribed to singers whose words are not recorded anywhere in the mss. What appears to have happened in such cases is that Baring-Gould or his musical collaborator recovered the melody and if, for one reason or another, they did not wish to note the words, they obtained them from a printed source, and if necessary adapted them for publication. But it is clear that Baring-Gould's statement that he 'deposited a copy of the songs and ballads with their music exactly as taken down' must be accepted with reservations.

Of the 202 songs in the mss., I have included fifty-three in the present volume.

It is not easy to assess the contribution made by Baring-Gould to the study of English folk song. It must be admitted that in comparison with those of Sharp or of either of the other two collectors represented here, his mss. are disappointing. Considering his opportunities—those of a newcomer in an almost virgin field—the record

XL The Forsaken Maiden,

1. A maiden sat a weeping
   Down by the sea-shore.
   What ails my pretty Sally?
   What ails my pretty Sally?
   And makes her heart sore.

2. Because I am a-weary
   Aweary in my mind..
   No comfort, & no pleasure
   No comfort & no pleasure
   Henceforth can I find.

3. I'll spread my sail of silver
   I'll loose my rope of silk.
   My mast is of the cypress tree
   My mast is &c
   My track is white as milk.

4. I'll spread my sail of silver,
   I'll steer toward the sun.
   And then, false love, will weep for me
   And then &c
   For me when I'm gone.

Taken down from James Parsons, Oct. 1888.

THE FORSAKEN MAIDEN (No. 44)

Facsimile from the Baring-Gould Mss.

LXVIII. Strawberry Fair.

As I was agoing to Strawberry Fair,
  Ri-tol-ri-tol, riddle-tol-de-lido
I saw a fair maiden of beauty rare
      Tol-de-les!
I saw a fair maid go selling her ware
As she went on to Strawberry Fair,
  Ri-tol-ri-tol, riddle-tol-de-lido.

O pretty fair maiden I prithee tell,
My pretty fair maid, what do you sell?
O come, tell me truly (my) sweet damsel.
As you go on to Strawberry Fair.

O I have a lock that doth lack a key.
O I have a lock sir, she did say,
If you have a key then come this way,
As we go on to Strawberry Fair

Between us, I reckon, that when we met
The key to the lock it was well set;
The key to the lock it well did fit
As we went on to Strawberry fair.

O would that my lock had been a ....
I'd shoot the Blackamoor, for I'm unsure,
And wares to carry I now have some
.... I should go to Strawberry Fair.

Taken down from J. Masters, Bradstone, by H.F.S.

STRAWBERRY FAIR (No. 125)
Facsimile from the Baring-Gould Mss.

of his actual discoveries in the midst of a living tradition is meagre. He began with certain prejudices which stood in his way from the start. First, his conviction that the tradition was moribund evidently prevented him from trying to get songs from any but the extremely old—in case they died before he could reach them. 'The singers are nearly all old, illiterate—their lives not worth five years' purchase, and when they die the traditions will be lost' (1891).

Now it is true that later collectors—Sharp, for instance—got their best songs from the elderly; but if the collectors of the first decade of the twentieth century and later got genuine folk songs from men and women in their sixties, it is obvious that Baring-Gould, working a generation earlier, could have got a wealth of material from singers of fifty and less. Yet he seems not to have tried; but rather to have assumed that, like the swan of mythology, the Dartmoor peasant sang only on his deathbed. His collecting was unsystematic, and it seems certain that he missed opportunities which a man of greater pertinacity and thoroughness would have taken.

A more serious handicap was his belief that the words of folk songs had been hopelessly corrupted by their contact with broadsides. He never seems to have been fully aware that the oral tradition, as regards words as well as tunes, existed independently of the printed text.[1] 'The broadside is the echo, not the original'—so he had written, but he did not draw the obvious inference, that the task of the student of folk song is to establish the original and as far as possible ignore the echo. Instead, wherever the words as recollected by ancient and infirm singers were confused or fragmentary, he went to a printed source and found a version which was necessarily at some remove from the original. It must be remembered that Baring-Gould did not like folk song words. The verses he composed himself are by contrast anaemic and pretty-pretty. He collected songs with an eye to popular publication, and the words as he heard them did not suit his purpose. They were at best a necessary adjunct to the melodies.

Nevertheless he did take down, for the record, a number of texts he could not hope to publish, among them *The Barley Rakings*, *The Ragged Beggar Man*, *Strawberry Fair*, *What did your Sailor Leave?* and

[1] An exception is the remark quoted in my notes to *The Carpenter's Wife* (No. 19), where he points out the superiority of one of his recovered versions to its counterpart in Child.

7

an important version of *The Everlasting Circle*. He also preserved unique versions of such ballads as *The Silly Doe, The Unquiet Grave, The Trees they are so High* and *The Raggle-Taggle Gypsies*. For this we must be grateful.

His knowledge of out-of-the-way printed sources was large; even if it acted against him as a student of oral tradition, it was of value in itself, and helped towards making his annotations some of the most interesting in any published collections. Another factor which adds value to these notes is his genuine interest in the local conditions and customs connected with singing. His notes to the *Garland* and to *Songs of the West* are a mass of miscellaneous information about printed texts, history and folk-lore which, despite some inaccuracies, is of considerable use to students, and I have been glad to draw upon it for the purposes of this volume. There is also much speculation which, if not always well supported by evidence, is often suggestive.

It is impossible to sum up in any simple formula the achievement of a man of such diverse, and often contradictory, qualities as Baring-Gould. He is not to be blamed for being unscientific at a time when there was no such thing in England as the scientific study of folk song. He was an individualist working largely in isolation. His field-work was finished some years before the foundation of the Folk-Song Society, though he joined it early in its history. He had strong aesthetic and moral prejudices; while the former were perhaps his principal incentive towards collecting, the latter made it impossible for him to accept what he found in a spirit of detached enquiry. He was an amateur in both the best and the worst senses. He had the natural curiosity and the feeling for history without which antiquarian research is pedantic and uninspired; yet he lacked the patience and the detachment which mark the true scholar. But we must accept the achievements of our forefathers for what they were; and it is incontestable that without Baring-Gould's contribution the study of folk song in England would be the poorer.

H. E. D. HAMMOND AND
GEORGE B. GARDINER

As if in answer to Baring-Gould's appeal to folk song collectors to 'undertake' other counties, two brothers, H. E. D. and R. Hammond, began collecting in 1905 in Dorset, and George B. Gardiner simultaneously in Hampshire. Henry Hammond, though he tells us (*FSJ* 11, 1907) that his brother noted the words and he the tunes, is credited with the collection of the published and ms. songs which exist in his name. He was born in 1866 and became a scholar of Corpus Christi College, Oxford. He then joined the staff of the Edinburgh Academy. He was a classical scholar of wide and varied interests. In 1899 he was appointed Director-General of Education in Rhodesia, but his health broke down and he returned to England a year later. In 1905 he became one of the most active members of the Folk-Song Society. His cycling expeditions with his brother took him through Somerset, Worcestershire and Wiltshire, but principally through Dorset. Between 1905 and 1908 he collected 600 songs and variants. He died in 1910.

He was noted for his modesty and his avoidance of publicity. He printed a collection of forty of his songs as No. 11 of the Journal of the Folk-Song Society in 1907; and in 1908 Novello published *Folk-Songs from Dorset* as Book I of a projected comprehensive collection called *Folk-Songs of England*, under the general editorship of Cecil Sharp. This contains sixteen songs collected by Hammond, with piano accompaniments and a preface by Sharp, but no editorial matter by Hammond. We have thus virtually no statement of any views or theories Hammond may have formed about folk songs. Sharp's preface contains the usual proviso about the necessity for emending the texts.

In 1948 a booklet containing twenty-six songs from the Hammond mss., edited by Joan Brocklebank and Biddy Kindersley, was issued by the English Folk Dance and Song Society under the title *A Dorset Book of Folk Songs*. This is remarkable as being one of the first folk song publications to give authentic and unamended texts.

Apart from these modest paper-covered productions no publication has ever been made from the large and unique treasury of mss.

which has remained in the library at Cecil Sharp House ever since it was amassed half a century ago. I have included fifty-two of Hammond's texts in the present collection.

The relation of Hammond to the folk song movement is on strangely parallel lines to that of Gardiner. George B. Gardiner, the son of an Edinburgh clergyman, was born at Kincardine-on-Forth, probably in 1852, and graduated at Edinburgh University; then, like Hammond, he taught classics at the Edinburgh Academy. He became an active collector only towards the end of his life. In the summer of 1905, at the suggestion of Lucy Broadwood, then Secretary of the Folk-Song Society, he undertook Hampshire. He died in 1910.

Although personally interested in music, Gardiner confined his field-work to the recovery of texts, his tunes being noted for him by three musical colleagues, including H. Balfour Gardiner. His ms. collection of over 700 songs and variants, now at Cecil Sharp House, is thus of especial importance for the purpose of this book. I have included sixty-six of Gardiner's texts. His contribution to folk song publication is even smaller than Hammond's. A selection of forty-five songs from Hampshire constitutes No. 13 of the Society's journal, 1909; and Book III of Cecil Sharp's *Folk-Songs of England* consists of fourteen of Gardiner's songs, published by Novello under the title *Folk-Songs from Hampshire*. There is a brief introduction by Gardiner and the same general preface by Sharp reprinted from Book I of the series. All Gardiner's printed texts were expurgated or emended in conformity with Edwardian practice.

The ms., or rather typescript, collections of Hammond and Gardiner are an extremely valuable record of traditional song as it existed in the memories of the old country singers of Dorset and Hampshire in the first decade of this century. Gardiner did, it is true, send to the Secretary of the Folk-Song Society a few melodies with an accompanying note to say that the words were 'Too broad to be sent in'. But generally speaking his transcriptions, like Hammond's, are remarkably free from emendation or censorship. In point of magnitude, and of the wealth of the variants, Cecil Sharp's mss. are superior, but not in other respects.

In my choice of texts from all three collectors here represented I have been guided by (1) literary or social interest, (2) fullness and absence of confusion, (3) unfamiliarity. Both Hammond's and

Gardiner's mss. contain dozens of commonplace songs, as well as many which are already sufficiently familiar through ballad and folk song collections. This is less true of Baring-Gould's mss., which are far less copious. A great many ms. versions of well-known or previously published songs prove to be simply the standard versions, and are of no special interest. A good many are confused or fragmentary.

I have included thirty-six songs already published in *The Idiom of the People*, because the versions now given are fuller or have some other peculiar interest. Of the other 110 songs most are not now in print in authentic versions, and an indeterminate number have probably never before appeared in print.

4

THE VARIETIES OF FOLK SONG

The 146 texts and fragments here given represent a selection from the repertoire of a number of singers, mostly old, living between 1887 and 1908 in the south-western counties of Devon, Dorset and Hampshire. They are a part of the unwritten inheritance of song possessed until recent years by the country people all over Britain, and still surviving in outlying districts.

This inheritance is far from homogeneous, and many of the items in it survive only in fragmentary or confused forms. Even when the music hall ditties and other 'composed' songs in the repertoire of a country singer are ignored, the remainder exhibit a bewildering variety of style, period and theme. The only qualities one can discern running through the whole stock are, on the one hand, anonymity, and on the other the absence of literary art—which is perhaps only another way of saying the same thing. Even then there is a considerable gulf between the traditional song or ballad of known antiquity, such as *I will Give my Love an Apple* or *The Golden Vanity*, and a late broadside ballad such as *The Croppy Boy* or *The Death of Parker*. It is easier to imagine an author for the latter than for the former, but that may be because they are nearer to our own time. The communal conventions change—the medieval song, perhaps the creation of a monk or a minstrel; the Elizabethan ballad composed by a London tavern singer; the eighteenth-century love song of a travelling ballad-singer; the nineteenth-century street song of a town printer's hack: each has its distinctive style. Yet each is a part of one rich and many-sided tradition. Nothing is more difficult than to be certain of the age of an apparently ageless folk song. Those of the impersonal May-song category, usually beginning 'As I walked out', appear to be much older in theme than in language; but this may well be because the language has changed with the handing on of the song. This may also be the reason for so many imperfect rhymes and lines of irregular or defective rhythm. The process of adaptation, which has never ceased from what we loosely call medieval times to the present day, has all but obliterated the origins of folk song.

While a collection such as this is therefore inevitably an anthology of diverse styles and periods, it is possible to suggest certain rough categories into which the songs may be grouped.

First we may notice a number of songs which can be traced, through ms. or printed sources, to early Tudor times or before. Versions of *I will Give my Love an Apple* and *The Foolish Boy* appear in late medieval mss. *Death and the Lady*, recalling as it does the atmosphere of Chaucer's *Pardoner's Tale*, has the air of a morality of even earlier date. *Go from my Window* is of Tudor origin, and *Gossip Joan* belongs to the eighteenth century or earlier. *Sing Ovy, Sing Ivy* is probably derived from an earlier ballad in Child.

The following twelve songs in the present collection are versions of ballads found in Child:

Barbara Allen	*The Gypsy Countess*
Blow Away ye Morning Breezes	*Lamkin*
The Carpenter's Wife	*The Maid freed from the Gallows*
Georgie	*Sir Hugh*
The Golden Vanity	*The Unquiet Grave*
The Grey Cock	*Willie o' Winsbury*

While most of these, as was to be expected, are far less full than the best versions in Child, some offer interesting and unique variants. One, *The Gypsy Countess*, contains a long section not in Child; of the authenticity of this Child was himself sceptical, on what seem to me inadequate grounds. Admittedly Part I of *The Gypsy Countess* bears traces of literary influence; but if it was not a forgery on the part of Baring-Gould, as there is no reason to suspect, where did

Baring-Gould's singer get it? If we accept it as genuine, it entirely alters the purport of the ballad as we know it.

Students of folk song are becoming increasingly aware of certain limitations to Child's great collection, of which we have to admit that, exhaustive as it is in some respects, it is after all only an anthology. Either Child was ignorant of the oral tradition as it existed in some vigour during his time, or he undervalued it, relying too exclusively on the printed collections of previous editors. The esteem in which Child has been held has led to certain general beliefs which must be questioned in the light of the work done by 'oral' collectors during and since his time. One is that a good ballad is necessarily Scottish; another is that ballads are 'dead' and belong to an irrevocable age some three or more centuries past; a third error is that there is something canonical about Child's collection—that anything not in it is not a real ballad. This is clearly untrue, as is evidenced by at least one ballad now printed but not to be found in Child—*The Trees they are so High*. If we accept Child as the canon in balladry, there is no definition of the ballad which can exclude a large proportion of folk songs; yet even now a reviewer can give expression to a preference for ballads over folk songs. All that can be said is there are better ballads and inferior ballads, both inside and outside Child.

A small but important group of songs which lie outside the province of balladry as understood by Child consists of songs such as the Padstow and Helston May Songs, *Poor Old Horse* and *The Derby Ram*, which have a known relation to some piece of seasonal ritual or mummery. Admittedly it is difficult to be sure how authentic are the versions here given: by 'authentic' is here meant 'without modern additions, adaptations, confusions and excisions'. That the *songs* are authentic is certain; that they are 'of great antiquity' is certain (to use, *faute de mieux*, the phrase once favoured by antiquarians); but of the precise or even the approximate age of, say, the Padstow May Song it is impossible to write with authority. Students of folk song can and do dig a little further into the past and find traces which imply a remoter origin than had hitherto been suspected. We may say, then, that the Padstow May Song had its origin in an almost unrecorded epoch; but since we know that songs grow and change as time passes, we cannot say that any particular *form* of the song now preserved is of greater antiquity than,

13

say, the time of Elizabeth I. What is clear is that the singers of any period are inclined to replace what they do not understand by something they do understand, which approximates in sound, but not necessarily in meaning, to the earlier form.[1] In particular, symbolic and metaphorical, local and topical elements tend to lose their significance and become blurred or altered. The more vigorous the tradition at any one time or place, the more active and inventive the singers, the greater is likely to be the change. While it seems, therefore, that the forms of many of the songs current during the nineteenth century became more or less fixed in the late seventeenth and early eighteenth centuries, the songs themselves may have gone back to much earlier periods. Another circumstance which makes it difficult to be sure about the age of any particular song is that certain stock lines and stanzas are readily transferable from one song to another where the context is similar. The line 'The youth arose, put on his clothes', which occurs in *Abroad as I was Walking* and elsewhere, is found also among the ballad scraps sung by the mad Ophelia; but it is not to be inferred that the song as a whole is necessarily as old as *Hamlet*.

Whether or not the song whose title I have borrowed for the present volume, *The Everlasting Circle*, should be classed as of ritual origin I do not know. Possibly it was once part of a singing game, as were *Ripest Apples* and *The Twelve Days of Christmas*. What a former scholar of great and deserved repute, Anne Gilchrist, described as a 'rigmarole', and what still exists among children as a pretty cumulative song and among adults as a vulgar parody, must once have been something of vitality and significance. Baring-Gould alone, it seems, preserved out of the oral tradition a version which goes back beyond the period of broadside degeneration.[2] It

[1] That this process continues to some extent so long as a song remains in the oral tradition is evidenced by an example noted as late as 1953. (See notes to *Betsy*, No. 7.)

[2] In using this expression here, I do not subscribe to what seems to me the error of Kidson, Baring-Gould, Sharp and others of their time in assuming that 'broadside' inevitably spells degeneracy. Essentially a broadside is not a *kind* of poem, as is frequently implied, but a method of communication. To approve or disapprove of broadsides as such is analogous to approving or disapproving of etchings. Just as 'etchings' in common parlance tends to mean the artistically undistinguished landscapes purveyed by picture-dealers in cathedral cities, so 'broadside' is taken to mean crude and popular doggerel. But it should be

is only when one reads this version, which makes the 'circle' complete and lifts the song out of the regions of bawdry, vulgarity and prettiness, that one sees something of the real quality of the folk song. Man, woman and child are contained in the predestinate life-cycle which is intimately and organically related to the life of nature—the oak or 'tree of life' and the bird that builds and breeds among its leaves.

History—political, social, naval and military—forms the subject of many folk songs. Two of the oldest, *The Golden Vanity* and *Sir Hugh*, have already been noted as Child ballads. These belong rather to the region where history merges into legend. *Farewell to Kingsbridge*, *The Croppy Boy*, *The Death of Parker*, *Me and Five More* and *The Greenland Whale Fishery* belong to a later period. *The Owslebury Lads* is, I am told, the best extant version of a ballad or broadside of strictly local and topical origin, a documentary footnote to the history of agricultural revolt immediately preceding the passing of the Reform Acts.

By far the largest category of songs in any collection is likely to be concerned with amorous, domestic and pathetic situations. In tone they range from the realistic and sensual to the sentimental or humorous. In period they range from the fifteenth to the nineteenth centuries. *A Bold Dragoon* deals with the subject of the woman seducer, once common but later banished from sentimental literature. *May and December* is a humorous reflection on marriage between youth and age. *A Sailor Cut Down in his Prime*, which in its present form appears to belong to the middle of the eighteenth century, is the only song I know which deals directly with the social evil of venereal disease, and in two distinct versions the victim is now a young man and now a young woman. *Farewell He* and *Fare*

remembered that there are etchings by Rembrandt and broadsides of worth and vitality. In general, I would say that up to the end of the seventeenth century many excellent as well as many dull ballads were preserved on broadsides, some of them on broadsides alone. During the eighteenth and nineteenth centuries it is easier to distinguish between texts composed especially for broadside circulation, many of them topical, and texts circulated on broadsides but recovered from singers in the oral tradition. Printers of broadsides had little regard for authenticity, and on the whole served the oral tradition badly. It is only on this limited sense that I would write of 'broadside degeneration'. That many songs composed for broadside circulation were lively and vigorous, and possessed their own special virtues, is not to be denied.

Thee Well, Cold Winter lament the theme of 'Men were deceivers ever', and *The Green Bushes* and *Some Rival has Stolen my True Love Away* are variations on the complementary theme of '*La donna è mobile*'. The foolish virgin, treated now realistically and now pathetically, is the subject of *Seventeen Come Sunday* and *Sweet William*. *Oh as I was a Walking* and *Our Ship she lies in Harbour* are concerned with true love rewarded at the altar. *Died of Love, Deep in Love* and *The Seeds of Love*, in which the theme of betrayal is raised from pathos to tragedy, are among the best known and finest of all folk songs.

Three songs—*As I set off to Turkey, I'm Going up to London* and *The Red Herring*—may be grouped under the heading of 'lies and marvels', and demonstrate the Englishman's fondness for a tall story or a solemn leg-pull. This is a taste he has, or had, in common with the people of many other countries. It arises from a kind of naïve sophistication in the peasant character which recognizes that it takes imagination to appreciate a really monstrous hyperbole or an audacious lie.

Jolly Old Hawk and the *Farmyard Song* are cumulative rhymes of a class probably once connected with singing games, in which failure to repeat the lines correctly involves the payment of a forfeit. *Jinny Jan* is part of a mime of death and rebirth which must once have been enacted by adults but which had become a children's game, and evidently an inappropriate one, by the mid-nineteenth century.

Finally there is a not very numerous group of ribald, comic or grotesque songs, of which *Mathew the Miller* and *O Shepherd, O Shepherd* are typical. Others are *The Tailor and the Crow* and *Tailor and Louse*, examples of a class of popular tales and rhymes in which this particular tradesman is always a figure of ridicule. Allusions to tailors in popular tradition are invariably malicious, the usual charge being that of cowardice, due no doubt to the effeminacy of their occupation; on the other hand, the unenviable reputation of tailors probably owes something to their supposed possession of unusual opportunities for adventures with women.

5

THE THEME OF FERTILITY

Despite the heterogeneity of the traditional heritage, it is possible to discern certain characteristics running through many, if not all, of its components. I will say nothing here of the poetic style of folk songs, for that has been dealt with very frequently by writers on the ballad. I do not think it is possible to draw a hard-and-fast line between ballads and folk songs, though such a line is often assumed. After all, 'ballad', as understood by readers of Percy, Scott and Child, is a literary category analogous to 'lyric', 'essay' or 'verse drama', not an exclusive and self-defining natural form of expression. No definition of 'ballad' can be framed so as to exclude folk songs: fragments or versions of many indubitable folk songs (for instance, *The Seeds of Love*) are embedded in unimpeachable Child ballads. Popularly a ballad is often thought of as being concerned with action, expressed in the third person, longer than a folk song, and devoid of subjective elements. But both ballad and song belong essentially to the same tradition, though they may have served different social functions. In style certainly, if not in content, the song is of the same kind as the ballad.

It will be more pertinent to say something about what seems inescapably to be the commonest element found throughout the folk song heritage—the theme of fertility. To call this 'sex', as is now common, is to ignore the fact that folk songs originate in a pastoral and agricultural society. It is true that the sole remaining repository of traditional song in an active and popular form in Britain today is the student group or military unit.[1] A college athletic club or Forces' mess, usually but not always an exclusively male group, possesses a stock-in-trade of songs used in celebrating a holiday, a victory or simply its sense of group cohesion; the motive for many of these songs is the sense of temporary freedom from the restraints of civilized behaviour, and the observance of the saturnalia by means

---

[1] It is too soon to be sure that the present 'revival', admirably described in an article in *The Times* of January 10, 1959, is more than a passing vogue. If it grows, then we may yet see social gatherings of both sexes in public houses and elsewhere singing the old songs and inventing new ones.

of bawdy songs, especially on sexual themes, appears to be a necessary outlet for natural spirits normally under control. That human fertility, or sex, is the exclusive concern of such songs, rather than fertility in the wider sense, is due to the fact that we are no longer an agricultural community.

The decay of folk song as a communal activity enjoyed by men and women alike went step by step with the decay of agriculture. A society which lives by manufacture and commerce is apt to forget its roots in the activities of the soil; the fertility of crops and herds is of no pressing concern. Human fertility alone becomes important. A city community, a town-dwelling and largely middle-class society whose relations are governed by politeness and restraint, takes human fertility for granted, and may even regard it as an inconvenience. Accordingly sex can become a joke, and the bawdy sex song may form the only recognized outlet for superfluous natural spirits.

To read the conditions of today into the past, then, is to miss the point and purpose of folk song: to say that many folk songs have to do with sex is only a half-truth. It is nearer the truth to say that folk song stems from a civilization, now long superseded in Britain, in which natural fertility was always a pressing and urgent concern.

The communities which populated Europe at the break-up of the Roman Empire were pastoral and agricultural. It is almost a truism to say that the recurrent basic need of such peoples was for the continued productivity of the soil and of the creatures it supported. Winter meant the death of men, animals and vegetation; summer meant re-birth. Even so, a drought or flood could spell disaster. Not only rain was necessary, so also was sun. All primitive religion was concerned, in one way or another, with ensuring man's continued existence through the fertility of himself, his herds and his crops. Religious observances were concerned with the propitiation of the tutelary gods, and with the celebration of the seasonal activities of the community.

When the Christian missionaries came to Britain, they found themselves, as all Christian churches have done, at odds with the pagan religions of the natives. Towards these observances, which were in the main concerned with the basic theme of fertility, they adopted an attitude which veered now towards suppression and now

18

towards absorption. It was the policy of the pre-Reformation Church to absorb and adapt and overlay the pagan practices which had survived from pre-Christian times. Churches were built on the sites of pagan temples; the seasonal feasts and practices were adapted to the Christian calendar; the saints, and later the Virgin Mary, took over the functions of the tutelary gods. From time to time, as one policy succeeded another at Rome, the attitude of the Church altered; and the official attitude was often interpreted in different ways by the parish priests. The Church did indeed at all times attempt to suppress the more licentious and uninhibited expressions of pagan belief. The essential ideals of the Church could not but be, after all, fundamentally in conflict with the worship of the gods of fertility. Whitsun-ales, the festivals of the plough, and especially the May games were vigorously opposed by the Church. As the Church established itself with ever greater strength and authority, the various rituals associated with May Day and the coming of summer became the focus for popular resistance to ecclesiastical domination. May Day was the great central event in the traditional agricultural and pastoral calendar; it was celebrated with dancing and singing, with the decoration of streets and houses with green boughs in honour of the gods of vegetation; the mayers performed in the villages, and the hobby horse pranced joyfully through the streets for the induction of fertility in man and nature. The pre-Reformation Church never accepted the May games; on the other hand, so great was its success in at least living side by side with, and in part assimilating pagan practices, that after the Reformation the Church authorities, and especially the Puritans, were able to make propaganda by condemning pagan customs such as dancing round the maypole as Romish. They swept away Roman Catholic and pre-Christian practices indiscriminately. The Royalist, Herrick, combined in his poems a love for 'the old religion' with respect for the old country customs that went back to times before the first Christians came to Britain.

After the Reformation the country people clung obstinately to their songs and their superstitions, as the reformers called them; and the Church continued to waver between tolerance and suppression. The Evangelical Churches of the eighteenth and nineteenth centuries were unremitting in their efforts to suppress what they erroneously condemned as the remnants of Popish superstition; and the

Methodists of the early nineteenth century attempted to substitute hymn-singing for the singing of profane and indecorous ballads.[1]

The singing of songs whose basic theme was fertility continued long into the nineteenth century as part of the seasonal feasts of the agricultural communities. Love songs, always regarded by Puritans and reformers as socially dangerous because they tended to wantonness and the lowering of communal morality, were sung by the milkmaids and the women engaged in cottage industries, 'the spinsters and the knitters in the sun, and the free maids that weave their thread with bones'. Such songs, whether restrained or licentious—and the country singer was less obsessed by the difference than were parsons and gentlemen antiquaries—were treasured by the people even after they were felt to be no longer respectable. Typical of the atmosphere prevailing in the nineteenth century is the boyhood experience of the Dartmoor singer, James Olver, described by Baring-Gould.[2]

Gradually, as the cottage industries died out, folk songs tended to be sung mainly at harvest suppers and other seasonal gatherings, or on festive occasions at village inns. But education, respectability and the decline of agriculture drove them out of common use and back into the memories of the older, less sophisticated country people, whose children preferred more up-to-date ditties from the music halls and concert rooms of the towns. This was the situation when the pioneer collectors began their work of recovering the oral tradition of English song.

Some who were brought up in the atmosphere of the 'revived' folk song of Cecil Sharp and his contemporaries have been tempted to think that sex does not appear in folk song except in the most idyllic and innocent form; those who have become acquainted at first hand, or through ms. or other inaccessible sources, with the

---

[1] It should be remembered that from Elizabethan times itinerant ballad-singers were regarded as tramps and as such were liable to prosecution by the law. A notice in faded characters on a once white board, still to be seen on the wall of a cottage near where I live, reads:

24 June 1811

The Magistrates acting for this Hundred have given peremptory Orders to the Constables and other Peace Officers to apprehend all Common Beggars, Ballad Singers and other Vagrants so that they may be dealt with according to Law.

[2] See p. 292.

genuine thing may have been tempted to think there is nothing but sex in folk song. Neither conclusion is correct. I have tried to indicate how in the folk song tradition sex is connected with the primitive theme of fertility as it permeated the religious and social customs of our ancestors.

6

THE *LINGUA FRANCA*

It remains to be discussed how this theme permeates English traditional song, not indeed to the exclusion of other themes, but rather as a unifying factor in the diverse strands which compose it. In turning from revived to restored folk song, some have been struck by what they regard as its indelicacy. 'Indelicate' was a word commonly used by the editors of fifty years ago—and even later. Yet I think it would be equally relevant to remark on the delicacy of folk song. I do not deny that what is variously called grossness, coarseness or indecency occurs often. It would be as idle to deny it in Shakespeare. The peasant who treasured, adapted and transmitted the songs of his ancestors was a whole man: he had occasion for coarseness, as for delicacy; like other men of refinement, he could be unrefined. He could enjoy the broad as well as the subtle; he never spoke of an agricultural implement, but he had at least some appreciation of a metaphorical system of expression which was in part euphemistic. This is what I mean when I speak of the delicacy of folk song, a delicacy which consists not in avoiding some of the major facts of life but in accommodating them to an idiom both civilized and expressive. The peasant's attitude to sex is half naïve, half sophisticated, and has nothing in common with the attitude of middle-class propriety and Nonconformism.

Until the decadence of folk song in the nineteenth century, and dating how far back no one knows, there existed a *lingua franca* which must have been accepted and understood between singer and audience. The symbolism of the garden as the locality of love is, of course, much older than western European literature, and the extension of this symbolism into other fields is also of universal application. The metaphorical significance of a song on the fertility theme must have been generally understood; where it was not, then no offence was given. The existence of a *lingua franca* is a proof of delicacy. In *Strawberry Fair* the phallophoric intention of the 'key in the lock' is clear enough. Commenting on this song, Baring-Gould noted with pleasure that some of the Dartmoor singers of his time did not understand it. Evidently, then, some at least did, despite the late date of writing—a date by which it must be supposed that the *lingua franca* was becoming less widely understood. It is reasonable to assume that in relevant contexts the 'key' image would always have this significance.[1] In the curious traditional sequence known as *The Key of the Kingdom* (repeated in reverse so that the sequence 'unwinds'), such a meaning is to be assumed, since the key opens the way first to the city, then to a street, a lane, a house, a room and a bed, and on the bed is 'a basket of sweet flowers'. The sexual application of this final image is a commonplace in the traditional idiom. But of course it is open to anyone who so prefers to take the poem as a mystical allegory relating to the Kingdom of Heaven. Even so, there is evidence that 'Heaven' itself was sometimes endued with metaphorical significance, as in the song variously called *The Keys of Heaven*, *The Keys of Canterbury*, and so on.

There is ground for thinking that Shakespeare intended Ophelia's mental derangement to be due to sexual frustration, touched off by the shock of her father's death, a parallel to Hamlet's assumed madness in similar circumstances. In Ophelia's case the subconscious found expression in ballad snatches, many of them bawdy.

In the song *The Loyal Lover* the collocation of 'arrow', 'sparrow', 'fish', 'reaper' and the hunting 'keeper' is of unmistakable sexual import; and if, as seems certain, the song is a version of *Bedlam*, here is another example of mental derangement expressing itself in erotic symbolism. The phenomenon of an innocent girl's relapsing into obscenity under the stress of a mental breakdown is well known to psychiatry. The importance of Ophelia's balladry in the study of folk lore has often been remarked on. Now it seems to me that the fertility theme, expressed either directly or under the euphemistic guise of the *lingua franca*, acted as a safety valve which helped to preserve the mental health of the community; and that the absence of such an outlet in any artistic form may have bad social effects, such as the popularity of sensational sex journalism.

[1] cf. Herrick: *Corinna's Going a Maying*, 4, 14.

The most universal communal activity which supplied a vocabulary of fertility was that of ploughing and sowing, the work of the husbandman. 'Husband' originally meant no more than a 'householder', and the extension of the word to apply to agriculture came later. Thus, the function of the husband towards a wife was regarded as analogous to that of a husbandman towards his land. 'He ploughed her, and she cropped' is Agrippa's summary of Caesar's adventure with Cleopatra which resulted in the birth of Cesarion. Thus the ploughshare, the 'coulter', acquires phallophoric significance.

> 'Twas Cupid was this ploughing boy
> His furrows deep did plough,
> He brake the clods that hard he found
> The seeds that he might sow.
> I wish that pretty ploughing boy
> My eyes had never seen.
> O Cupid was that ploughing boy
> With coulter sharp and keen.
>
> (*Cupid the Ploughboy*)

In another version of the song 'coulter' becomes 'arrows'.

Green Besoms describes the adventures of a broom gatherer with, first, a farmer, then a miller, a squire and a parson.

> One day as I was trudging
> Down by my native cot
> I saw a jolly farmer,
> O happy is his lot.
> He ploughs his furrows deep,
> The seeds he layeth low,
> And there it bides asleep
> Until the green broom blow.
> O come and buy my besoms,
> Bonny green besoms,
> Besoms fine and new,
> Bonny green-broom besoms,
> Better never grew.

Of the significance of broom gathering the final stanza leaves no doubt:

> O when the yellow broom is ripe
> Upon its native soil

> It's like a pretty baby bright
> With sweet and wavily smile.

The Molecatcher is concerned with a man living 'at the sign of the Plough', whose wife takes advantage of his nocturnal absences to entertain a young farmer. The molecatcher promises to make the seducer 'pay dear for tilling my ground'.

The metaphorical intention of sowing and reaping[1] may indeed be taken for granted, and is frequently extended to cover such words as 'grove', 'field' and 'meadow'.

> In yonder grove I sowed my seed,
> In yonder grove I fared away
> And for to reap it I could not stay
> For I being a stranger, I fell in danger,
> I ran away, I ran away.
>
>   (*I Sowed some Seeds*)

Common synonyms for 'seed' in the *lingua franca* are 'corn', 'barley' and 'grain'.

> As I walked out one morning fair
> To view the fields and take the air
> There I heard a pretty maid making her complain
> And all she wanted was the chiefest grain
>   Chiefest grain,
> And all she wanted was the chiefest grain.
>
> I said, My pretty maid, what do you stand in need.
> Oh yes, kind sir, you're the man that can do my deed,
> For to sow my meadow with the wanting seed
>   Wanting seed,
> For to sow my meadow with the wanting seed.
>
>   (*The Wanton Seed*)

The symbolism of husbandry is very clearly and fully exemplified in a broadside, *The Little Farm*,[2] in which the natural imagery of the

---

[1] It is perhaps worth pointing out that 'reap' would formerly have been pronounced 'rape'. Except in Ireland this once general pronunciation of the diphthong 'ea' has survived only in a very few words such as 'great', 'break' and 'steak'.

[2] Pinto and Rodway, *The Common Muse*. Appendix A No. 27. Bodleian: Firth Collection of Original Broadsides.

popular idiom is elaborated into a sophisticated composition. Not only is the symbolism of husbandry worked out with some skill, but there is ingenuity in the introduction of what may be called physio-topographical imagery.

You husbandmen and ploughmen, of every degree,
I pray you give attention and listen unto me,
I hope it will offend not, not meaning any harm
But concerning of a bonny lass who kept a little farm.
    Chorus. I was both weak and weary by daylight in the morn
    I thought it young and growing but to stubble it was worn.

I stept up to this blooming lass thinking to get employ,
She said Young man be civil and do not me annoy,
My farm though in the lowlands was never overflown,
I've made a resolution to keep it as my own.

I said My charming fair maid I am a husbandman,
And have had great experience in cultivating land,
There's nothing comes amiss to me in the farming line I vow,
You'll find me likewise useful in working at your plough.

She said No longer time delay, your mind shall be at ease,
My farm-house lies in the valley between two poplar trees,
Surrounded too with rushes I've long kept in store,
There is a tree you'll see growing each side the door.

I said with your permission I there will enter in,
Command me at your leisure my labour to begin,
You'll find me use to ploughing, likewise my seed to sow,
If we agree you soon will see it for to thrive and grow.

With courage in good order she said come try your skill,
The plow is near the furrough at the bottom of the hill
Above the hill two milking-pails [orig. maids] resemble cocks of hay
If you feel weak no further seek a pillow for to seek [? stay]

At length with toil being weary I laid my head between
Those milking-pails that were so white although the grass was green,
The land being in bad order it made me sweat and groan,
I was forc'd to yield and quit the field for it was overflown.

She said when you have rested your strength for to regain,
If it's your intention commence ploughing again,
No said I excuse me and do not on me frown
Although I'm young and in my prime my courage is pull'd down.

It is clear that 'mowing a meadow', like 'ploughing', has a precise and generally accepted meaning in the *lingua franca*. The cumulative song *One Man Shall Mow my Meadow*, now innocently enjoyed as *One Man and his Dog*, was evidently once ribald; the number of mowers, determined only by the length of time the singers' breath would hold out, being equivalent to the number of lovers. A more sophisticated version of the mowing theme appears in a broadside in the Baring-Gould collection.[1] In *Buxom Lass* the metaphor is exploited in some detail.

As I was walking out one morning, I met a buxom lass,
Going to a dairyman, she had a field of grass,
It grew between two mountains, at the foot of a spring,
She hired me to cut it down, while the birds did sweetly sing.

I said my pretty fair Maid, what wages do you give,
For mowing is hard labour, unless my scythe is good,
She said if you do please me, I solemnly do swear
I'll give a crown an acre, & plenty of strong beer

I said my pretty fair Maid, I like your wages well,
If I mow your grass down, you shall say it is done well,
My scythe is in good order, and lately has been ground,
My bonny lass I'll cut your grass, close upon the ground.

She said my lusty young man when will you begin,
My grass is in good order, I long to have it in,
It is such pleasant weather, I long to clear the ground,
So get your scythe in order, to mow your meadow down,

With courage like a lion, he entered in the field,
I'll mow your meadow down, before that I do yield,
Before I'd mowed a rood of grass, my scythe it bent and broke,
She said my man, you must give in you're tired of your work.

---

[1] British Museum L.R. 271 a. 1. Vol. 2, p. 111. Jackson and Son. n.d.

She said my man you must give in, you are tired of your work,
For mowing is hard labour, and weakening to the back,
For mowing is hard labour, and you must it forsake,
And round my little meadow you may use your rake,

I said my handsome fair Maid, do not on me frown,
For if I stop the summer through, I cannot mow it down,
It is such pleasant weather, and bears such crops of grass,
It's watered by a spring, that makes it grow so fast.

It is difficult to date such a production as this. It has none of the convivial spontaneity of the cumulative hay-making song. The latter, I imagine, belongs to a date not earlier than the beginning of the seventeenth century, while *Buxom Lass* can hardly be earlier than the end of that century. By the early eighteenth century 'mowing' had become an accepted euphemism, requiring no agricultural context, as is clear from the anonymous Scots ballad entitled *Jockey's Deliverance. Being the Valiant Escape from* Dundee, *and the Parson's Daughter, whom he had mow'd. To an Excellent Tune, call'd* Bonny Dundee.[1]

> Since *Jenny* the fair was willing and kind,
>   And came to my Arms with ready good Will,
> A Token of Love Ise leave her behind,
>   That I have requited her Kindness still,
> Tho' *Jenny* the fair I often have mow'd,
> Another may reap the Harvest I sow'd,
>   *Then open the Gates and let me go free,*
>   *She's ken me no more in bonny Dundee.*

The kind of physio-topographical reference which abounds both in *The Little Farm* and *Buxom Lass* evidently had the advantage of esoteric appeal. There was no need for anyone to understand it, or be offended by it, who did not choose to. A recent case in point is that of Henry Reed's war poem *Movement of Bodies* which was reprinted in all innocence by the lady editor of a school poetry anthology. This ingenious poem is written as an army lecture on tactics, in which the lecturer is evidently unaware of the way in which a military assault on a carefully described position suggests to

[1] *A Collection of Old Ballads, &c.* London, 1723, Vol. I. Editorship ascribed to Ambrose Phillips.

his sex-starved audience an erotic assault. A similar *jeu d'esprit* by E. E. Cummings, beginning *She being brand new*, extracts the maximum of metaphorical suggestion from an account of running-in a new car; this also achieved the distinction of being included, not long ago, in a school textbook as an example of style in a mechanical age.

Physio-topographical imagery is at least as old as *The Song of Songs*, and it is evidently employed in the strange and beautiful *Streams of Lovely Nancy*.

The topographical allusions in *The Furze Field* are also of similar import.

> I have got a furze field, my own dearest jewel,
> Where all my fine pheasants do fly.

The lover is invited first to bring his gun and shoot pheasants, then to bring his fishing-rod and catch fish, and finally to bring his ferret and catch rabbits in a warren. It is perhaps strange that such a song, which appears to have originated in a comparatively sophisticated seventeenth- or eighteenth-century milieu, should have remained in the repertoire of a country singer early in the present century.

The Furze Field is a good example of a large class of songs in which the sexual adventure is described in the language of sport. *The Keeper* (Appendix II) and *The Silly Doe* are hunting songs clearly concerned with sexual pursuit; these and *The Grey Hawk*, which employs the symbolism of falconry, are, I conjecture, of considerable age, almost certainly pre-Elizabethan. *Three Maids a Milking* deals with fowling, and may be more recent. I would place it somewhere in the seventeenth century, but there may well be an earlier form now lost. The metaphorical character of such songs is, of course, always open to question—as it was intended to be. It can only be inferred from the general context of the *lingua franca*. But the effectiveness of the *double entendre* in many rhymes is to be gauged by their acceptability and popularity as a means of amusing the innocent.

> Little Tommy Tittlemouse
> Lived in a little house;
> He caught fishes
> In other men's ditches.

When Halliwell included this in the first systematic collection of English nursery rhymes in 1844, he probably took it for a piece of inoffensive nonsense. It should be remembered that most of such rhymes were not originally intended for the nursery, and that many are fragments of songs and ballads formerly enjoyed by adults. It is not surprising, therefore, that the voice of *Mother Goose* should often betray overtones of the *lingua franca*.

In *Green Besoms*, already referred to, reference is made to the trades of miller, farmer, squire and parson, who are successively invited to enjoy the favours of the broom-gatherer in terms appropriate to their occupations. Traditional song as a rule is concerned with a man's or woman's occupation not for itself but in the context of love-making. The soldier is sung of, not as a fighter, but as a notoriously inconstant lover, since his duties give him opportunities for travel. The sailor is not described at sea, but as a 'brisk' lover, free with his money while it lasts, and anxious to make the most of his all too brief opportunities on shore. To the question *What did your Sailor Leave?* there can only be one answer. A married sailor, however, is a standing invitation to cuckoldry because of his long absences from home; so also is a molecatcher, because he is out at night. A tailor, proverbially a coward, nevertheless has opportunities with women as a perquisite of his trade. The lawyer, unpopular because of his cleverness, is often outwitted in matters of love by a smart girl. Certain occupations are drawn upon repeatedly for their specific contributions to the *lingua franca*; while the agricultural trades are alluded to most frequently, as has already been noted, the metaphorical possibilities of milling (*Mathew the Miller*) and shoemaking (*The Shoemaker's Kiss*) are also exploited. *I am a Coachman* deals metaphorically with the activities of coachman, blacksmith, and fisherman in turn. *Four and Twenty Fiddlers* is a similar catalogue-song dealing cumulatively with fiddlers, tinkers, cobblers, tailors, pensioners (old soldiers), priests, barbers and apostles.

The occurrence of 'fiddlers' in this song is a reminder that many, perhaps most, references to music in traditional songs are directly or indirectly sexual. The 'flute' is a common male sexual symbol; the frequent use of 'fiddling' as a euphemism is probably due to the phallophoric suggestion of the fiddle-bow in action. It is not only by providing such direct sexual imagery, however, that music and musical instruments enrich the popular idiom; they often supply indirectly an atmosphere of erotic suggestion.

> And when I have swimmed and my love I have found
> With all sorts of sweet music my love shall be crowned,
> The drum shall beat aloud and the music shall play
> For to welcome my love home again with ten thousands of joys.
>
> (*Some Rival has Stolen*)

The erotic suggestion of the refrain lines in the fragmentary *Flowers of the Valley* is indirect but unmistakable. Here, evidently, the combination of 'flowers' and musical instruments heightens the atmosphere conveyed by the context.

> There was a woman and she was a widow,
> The flowers that were in the valley,
> A daughter had she . . .
> O the red, the green and the yellow,
> The harp, the lute, the fife, the flute and the cymbal,
> Sweet goes the treble violin,
> The flowers that were in the valley.

Undoubtedly the aesthetic pleasure to be got from both flowers and music was closely associated in the popular mind with sexual pleasure. This applies also to bird-song, especially that of the lark and the nightingale. Whereas the hard, aggressive, male aspect of the fertility theme was most commonly represented by ploughing, mowing and other male occupations, the soft, aesthetic and more passive female aspect was most often represented in the language of flowers. Ploughing and sowing seeds was the function of the man; hay-making was a common occupation in which the man mowed and the woman might help to gather the sheaves; but plucking rushes and flowers was an exclusively female occupation. Flowers in particular were associated with young girls. To gather flowers, as a metaphor for rash or wanton love-making, is one of the oldest and most universal features of the popular idiom, an association which is preserved in the word 'deflower'. Some of the imagery of the *lingua franca* is crude and clumsy; but in its use of the feminine flower symbolism it comes nearest to poetry.

> Handsome men are out of fashion,
> Maidens' beauties soon decay.

You pick a flower of a summer morning,
Before the evening it will fade away.

First comes the oxlip, then the cruel,
Then the pink and then the may,
Then comes a new love, then comes a true love,
And so we pass our time away.

(*Ripest Apples* B)

Feminine beauty is ephemeral and fragile, like that of the flowers; the progression of the human seasons, youth and age, is as inevitable as the seasonal progression of the flowers; in this way human life is seen as linked to the life of nature. There is no sentimentality or mere prettiness in the traditional conception of flowers. While *Died of Love* makes use of the general significance of 'picking flowers' as foolish wantonness, *The Seeds of Love*[1] or *The Sprig of Thyme* indicates a precise relation between specific flowers and human qualities. 'Thyme' is virginity, the 'rose' is wanton passion, the 'violet' modesty, the 'pink' courtesy, the 'lily' purity, 'rue' and 'willow' stand for repentance and a broken heart. The marigold and the primrose are also flowers of wantonness.

In these songs the flower symbolism is integral to the whole theme. In others, no doubt mostly later in date, the allusions are purely incidental; there is a descent, as it were, from symbolism to euphemism. In *Three Maids a Rushing* the rush-gathering is simply a metaphor for wantonness, and has no further connection with the narrative. In *Catch Me if You Can* the 'plants' and 'flowers' are no more than passing references to the pleasures of unwise love-making.

I said, My dear, will you go with me?
I will show you round the count-a-ree,
I will show you plants, I will show you flowers,
I will show you things you never have seen.

In *Queen of the May*, on the other hand, the may-gathering is so much the central theme that the song may be regarded as one in which the literal and the metaphorical meet and are identical. It is

---

[1] This song is an exception to the general rule that the sowing of seeds is a male function. The singer is a young woman, and her action in sowing seeds must be taken not as analogous to the man's action in sowing grain but as the first step in planting a flower garden—that is, preparing to devote herself to love.

at once an account of the traditional presentation of may as a love-token and a celebration of lawful courtship expressed in symbolic terms.

Finally, it should be remembered that not all folk songs are concerned with the theme of fertility; and that not all of those which are concerned with it employ the *lingua franca*, the accepted metaphorical vocabulary used for speaking of matters which were taboo. I have chosen to end my introduction with a somewhat detailed consideration of this aspect of the popular idiom, partly because it is important in the understanding of that idiom, partly because it has been neglected by other writers on folk song. It is essential, however, for the reader of traditional songs to maintain what may be called a sense of context. The incidental use in one song of a word or phrase used metaphorically in another does not necessarily mean that its significance is metaphorical in the former context. To assume that a 'meadow' or a 'ploughman' is intended symbolically in every context is like supposing that the lion in a picture always stands for the British Empire because that is what it means in a *Punch* cartoon. Nevertheless, those words which appear frequently in folk songs in a metaphorical sense may be assumed to have at least metaphorical overtones in appropriate contexts. Is the 'mower' in Marvell's *The Mower to the Glow-worms* simply a familiar rural figure, or is he, metaphorically, a seducer? The answer perhaps is 'both', since both senses would be appropriate in the context, and any seventeenth-century poet would probably be familiar with the *lingua franca*. Is Milton's 'And the mower whets his scythe' metaphorical, then, as it almost certainly would be in an eighteenth-century broadside? Again there is some doubt. Possibly *L'Allegro* is without deliberate *double entendre*, yet the collocation of the 'mower' with the 'ploughman', the 'milkmaid' and the 'shepherd' under the hawthorn must have had metaphorical overtones for many seventeenth- and eighteenth-century readers. It must likewise be assumed that if a Victorian or Georgian poet uses the word 'mower', he means a mower, pure and simple.

While metaphorical language is not to be sought in every traditional poem, nevertheless the *lingua franca* permeates folk song as transmitted from earlier times to the singers of fifty years ago. The reader of unamended texts does not have to look for it; it stares him in the face. Sometimes there is no more than an overtone; some-

32

times it is used with self-conscious ingenuity for the purposes of bawdry; in other instances, and I believe most frequently, it is used from an instinctive sense of delicacy. It satisfied simultaneously the need for artistic expression for the things of greatest importance to people who were not rich in material possessions, and a natural reluctance to sing of such things openly in a way which might give offence. The need was not to ignore the theme, nor to hide it, nor to express it directly. It was rather to adorn and diversify it, and this was done by evolving a language rich in metaphorical reference, drawn from the lives and circumstances of those by whom and for whom folk songs were created.

ENGLISH TRADITIONAL VERSE

from the manuscripts of

S. BARING-GOULD, H. E. D. HAMMOND
AND GEORGE B. GARDINER

ABBREVIATIONS USED IN THE NOTES

B-G Baring-Gould

BM   British Museum

DBFS *A Dorset Book of Folk Songs* (Brocklebank and Kindersley), English Folk Dance and Song Society 1948. Twenty-six songs (text and melodies) from the mss. of H. E. D. Hammond

FSJ   *Journal of the Folk-Song Society*

G   Gardiner

GFH George B. Gardiner: *Folk-Songs from Hampshire*, Novello 1909

Garland S. Baring-Gould and H. Fleetwood Sheppard: *A Garland of Country Song*, Methuen 1895

H   Hammond

HFD H. E. D. Hammond: *Folk-Songs from Dorset*, Novello 1908

IP   James Reeves: *The Idiom of the People*, Heinemann 1958

JEFDSS *Journal of the English Folk Dance and Song Society* (i.e. *FSJ* from 1932 onwards)

ODNR Iona and Peter Opie: *The Oxford Dictionary of Nursery Rhymes*, Oxford 1951

SW   S. Baring-Gould, and others: *Songs of the West*, Methuen. First printed in four parts as *Songs and Ballads of the West*, 1889–91; reprinted in one volume, 1891; third and revised edition, 1905. Unless the edition is specified, '*SW*' refers to all the editions.

NOTE ON THE TEXT

In editing these texts I have followed a slightly different plan from that of *The Idiom of the People*. I have given no composite texts, such as were included in the earlier book, since the nature and number of the variants in **B-G, H** and **G** make this inappropriate. I have transcribed each version exactly as it appears in the mss., minor emendations being indicated in the notes. All the mss. are punctuated, though not consistently, so for the sake of consistency I have adopted a minimal scheme of punctuation.

Each text is followed by the initial of the collector and the name of the singer, with any other details supplied in the ms., including the place and date of collection. Then follow textual notes, and finally any other information which seemed to me relevant.

The songs are arranged alphabetically; the titles have been brought into line with those in *The Idiom of the People* and, so far as possible, with Margaret Dean-Smith's *Guide to English Folk Song Collections*. The titles in the mss. are in many cases arbitrary, and to retain them would be simply to conceal the real identity of the songs and make comparative study even more difficult than it is already. Where changed, however, the ms. titles are recorded in the textual notes.

1 *Abroad as I was Walking*

'Broad as I was a-walking
Down by some green woodside
I heard some young girl singing,
I wish I was a bride.

I thank you, pretty fair maid,
For singing of your song,
It's I myself shall marry you.
Kind sir, I am too young.

The younger the better,
More fitter for my bride,
That all the world may plainly see
I married my wife a maid.

Nine times I kissed her ruby lips,
I viewed her sparkling eye,
I catched her by the lily-white hand,
One night with her to lie.

All the fore part of that night
How we did sport and play,
And all the latter part of that night
I slept in her arms till day.

Till day, till day, till day,
Till daylight did appear.
The young man rose, put on his clothes,
Said, Fare you well, my dear.

What did you promise me last night
As I lay by your side?
You promised me you would marry me,
Make me your lawful bride.

What I did promise you last night
Was in a merry mood.
I vow, I swear, I do declare
I'm not so very good.

Now my parents have brought me up
Like a small bird in a cage
And now I am in child by you,
Not fourteen years of age.

It's all the farmers' daughters
To the market they do go
But it's I poor girl must stay at home
And rock the cradle so,

Rock the cradle, sing and sew,
Sing hushee lullaby.
Was there ever any poor young girl
So crossed in love as I?

G Mrs Goodyear at Axford by Basingstoke, Hants, August 1907

Ms. gives title '*Broad as I was a-walking.*

   6.3   *The young man rose . . .*: cf. Ophelia's song in *Hamlet*, IV.5.51.

GFH gives an emended version of the first four stanzas. *FSJ* 13, 1909, prints stanzas 1, 2, 10 and 11. *FSJ* 17, 1913, prints four stanzas corresponding to stanzas 2, 3, 7 and 10 or 11, contributed by Butterworth. The song is a version of *The Squire and the Fair Maid* (No. 124) but the differences are considerable.

IP No. 28.

2 *All Fours*

As I was a-walking one fine summer's morning,
It happened to be on a sunshiny day
And there I espied a lovely young damsel
As she was a-walking along the highway.

I stepped up to her, I wished her good morning.
Oh where are you a-going so early this morn?
She answered, Kind Sir, I'm going to Croydon,
That sweet pleasant place where I was born.

May I go with you, my fair pretty maiden,
For to bear you sweet company?
She turned herself round and smiling so sweetly,
Kind Sir, you may do just as you please.

Now we had not been walking for scarcely one hour
Before this young couple's affectionates began
I said, My fair maid, come sit down beside me
And then I will show you a sweet pleasant game.

She says, My kind Sir, I'm not given to gamble,
But nevertheless I'm willing to learn.
The game that I will play, it must be all fours
And then I will hold you three to one.

Then I picked up the cards, it being my turn to deal them,
Not knowing she had the deuce in her hand.
Then she led off her ace and stole my jack from me,
Which made her high low jack and the game.

Then I picked up my hat and I wished her good morning,
I left her high low jack and the game.
I said, My fair maid, I will be over this way to-morrow
And then we will play the game over again.

G Mr William Randall at Hursley, Hants, n.d.

Ms. repeats last two lines of each stanza as Chorus.

2.2 *morn*: ms. morning

43

3 All Round My Hat

Yesterday evening I was invited to a wedding
Unto a fair girl that proved so unkind.
As soon as she began for to think on some other
The farmer, her own lovyer, still run in her mind.

When supper was over and all things were ended
They all did conclude to give the bride a song.
The first that begun was the farmer, her own lovyer,
To give the bride a song but it was not very long.

Oh how can you sleep on another man's pillow
Since you pretend that you love me so dear?
Now for your sweet sake I'll wear a mournful willow,
Now and for ever I'll wear it, my dear.

Now I am going for to ask you one favour,
I hope that the same you will grant unto me:
'Tis all this long night for to lie with my mother,
The rest of my life I will lie along with thee.

The favour was granted and all things were ready,
With sighing and crying they all went to bed.
'Twas early next morning the young man arosèd,
He went and he found that his new bride was dead.

All round my hat I will wear the mournful willow,
All round my hat for a twelvemonth and one day,
And if this here willow it should not become me
Then I'll leave it off for ever and evermore.

H   Mrs Crawford at West Milton, May 1906

A version in Cecil Sharp's mss. in four stanzas is printed under the title *Down in my Garden* (with the sub-title *The Nobleman's Wedding*) in *FSJ* 31, 1927.

4 *As I set off to Turkey*

As I set off to Turkey, I travelled like an ox,
And in my breeches' pocket I carried my little box.
My box was four foot high, my box was four foot square,
All for to put my money in when guineas was so rare.

Chorus   To my rite tol lol le riddle riddle lol
             To my rite tol lol li day.

Then I bought me a little dog, his collar was undone,
I learnèd him to sing and dance, to wrestle and to run;
His legs were four feet high and his ears were four feet wide,
And round the world in half a day all on my dog I'd ride.

Then I bought me a flock of sheep, their wool it was so sleek,
And every month at the full of the moon they had six lambs apiece.
Then I bought me a little hen, on her I took much care,
I set her on a mussel-shell and she hatched me out a hare.

That hare it proved to be a milk-white steed about fifteen hands high,
And they as can tell a bigger jest, oh dear, oh dear, what a lie!

G   Mr David Marlow at Basingstoke, October 1906

Ms. repeats Chorus after each stanza and gives two rows of dots after the fourth
stanza. Gardiner adds the note: 'A hyperbolic song like "The Derby Ram".
It was current among young people about 1830–40, when Mr Marlow was
a boy.'

5 Barbara Allen

A

'Twas early in the month of May
When green leaves they were springing
When a young man on his deathbed lay
For the love of Barbara Allen.

He sent to her his servant-man
To the place where she was dwelling,
Saying, Fair maid, you must come to my master
If your name is Barbara Allen.

Slowly, slowly she walked along
And slowly she got to him
And when she got to his bedside,
Young man, said she, you're dying.

Dying, dying? Oh don't say so!
One kiss from you will cure me.
One kiss from me you never shall have
If your poor heart is breaking.

Don't you remember the other day
When in the city dwelling
You gave kind words to other girls
And none to Barbara Allen?

As she was walking through the fields
She heard the bells a-ringing
And as they rang they seemed to say,
Hard-hearted Barbara Allen.

Hard-hearted creature sure was I
To him that loved me dearly.
I wish I had more kinder been
In time of life when he was near me.

As she was walking up the town
She saw the corpse a-coming.
Put him down, put him down, you six young men
And let me gaze upon him.

The more she looked the more she laughed
And the further she got from him
Till all her friends cried out, For shame,
Hard-hearted Barbara Allen!

'Twas he that died on one good day
And she died on the morrow.
'Twas him that only died for love
And she that died for sorrow.

One was buried in the old chancel,
The other in the choir.
Out of him grew a red rose bud
And out of her a sweet briar.

It grew, it grew to the old church top
Where it could not grow any higher,
Tied himself in a true lover's knot
For all false hearts to admire.

B

In Redmore Town where I was born,
The place where she was dwelling,
I choosed her out my bride to be.
Her name was Barbara Allen.

I sent my servant man one day
To the house where she was dwelling.
I says, Fair maid, you must go with me
If your name is Barbara Allen.

So slowly she put on her clothes,
So slowly she came to him,

And when she came to his bedside
She says, Young man, you are dying.

Nothing but death lies on your face
And death is calling on you.
Here's adieu, here's adieu to parents all
And adieu to Barbara Allen.

As she was going up the street
She heard the bells a-ringing,
And as they rang they seemed to say,
Hard-hearted Barbara Allen.

And as she was going back the street
She met his corpse agoing.
She says, Fair maids, pray put him down,
That I may look upon him.

The more she looked the more she laughed,
And the further she got from him,
And all her friends cried out, For shame,
Hard-hearted Barbara Allen.

Mother, mother, make up my bed,
Make it soft and narrow.
If my love die for me to-day,
I'll die for him to-morrow.

So this young man he died one day
And I will die to-morrow.
So this young man he died for love
And I will die for sorrow.

G Version A   Mr Thomas Bowers at Titchfield, Hants, September 1907
   Version B   Mr George Blake at St Denys, Southampton, May 24, 1906

Child (No. 84) has three versions, which contain all the elements in the above two. In a note in *FSJ* 7, 1905, Kidson records that one singer was positive that the song was called *Barbara Ellen*, not Allen, and suggests that *Barbara* is a corruption of 'Barbarous'.

6 *The Barley Rakings*

'Twas in the prime of summertime
When hay it was a making
And harvest time was coming on
And barley was a raking,
A loving couple met one day,
They had a mind to style and play
And did not count it much astray
All in the barley rakings.

When twenty weeks were gone and past
The maiden lay a crying.
When forty weeks were gone and past
The maiden lay a dying.
She sent a letter to her love.
She bade him true and faithful prove,
Conjured him by the powers above,
Remember the barley rakings.

O when this letter to him came
He read it o'er and over.
He put it by—'twas all the same,
Because he was a rover.
A message he sent back again
To let her know 'twas all in vain,
And have no care and have no pain,
And forget the barley rakings.

I have so good a pair of shoes
As e'er were made of leather.
I'll cock my beaver o'er my nose
And face all wind and weather.
O when that I have run my race,
Then if I find no better place
O then again I'll seek your face
And remember the barley rakings.

B-G   Roger Hannaford at Lower Widdecombe, May 1890

1.6   *style*: leap or dance (Anglo-Saxon: stillan—**B-G**).

B-G published in *SW* a re-written version which in his notes he ascribes to his collaborator, H. Fleetwood Sheppard, since none of the authentic versions 'would be tolerable in a drawing-room'. In this 'faithful John' is jilted during his absence by the frivolous 'Betty'.

The following version in **B-G**'s own collection of broadsides (BM L.R. 271 a. 2. Vol. X, p. 2) differs substantially from the oral version given above.

THE BARLEY RAKING

'Twas in the prime of summer time
When barley was a raking
A loving couple they were seen,
Playing and toying on the green,
As they was a barley raking.

When 20 weeks were gone and past,
This maid she was a thinking,
When 40 weeks were gone and past,
This maid was quite down lying.

She sent a letter to her love,
To let him know by the power above,
That he might come to her bed side
And ease her of her aching.

The bastard is none of mine, he cryed,
Then she stamped and swore he lyed,
You rogue, you rascal, she replied,
Remember the barley raking.

Now had I twenty pair of shoes,
Made of the best of leather,
I cock my beaver under my arm
And fear [*sic*] wind or weather

For when you jewel run his race,
And he can't find no better place,
Then he'll return to you sweet face
And we'll live and die together.
          (Pigott, Printer, Old-Street)

7 *Betsy*

A

The gleecher's daughter living near,
A fair young damsel as you shall hear,
Then up to London she did go
To seek for service as you shall know.

Her master having but one son
O she being fair his heart she won.
O Betsy being so very fair
She drawed his heart into a snare.

One Sunday evening he stole her thyme,
Unto young Betsy he told his mind.
By all the swearing powers above
'Tis you fair Betsy, 'tis you I love.

His mother then being standing nigh
Hearing these words that her son did say
Next morning by the break of day
Unto fair Betsy she took her away,

Saying, Rise up, rise up, my fair Bessie,
And dress yourself most gallantlie
For in the country you must go
Along with me for one day or two.

So as we was acrossing over the plain
We saw some ships sailing over the main.
No wit, no wit could this poor woman have
But to sell poor Betsy to be a slave.

In a few days after the mother returned.
O welcome, mother, replied the son.
Come tell me, tell me true, I pray,
Where is young Betsy behind you, say.

O son, O son, I plainly see
What love you bear to poor Betsy.
Your sobbing and sighing are all in vain
For Betsy's sailing across the main.

In a few days after her son lie sick,
No sort of music his heart could take,
But he often did sigh and often cry,
O Betsy, Betsy, I shall die.

In a few days after her son lie dead.
Mother wrung her hands and she tore her head
Saying, If I could fetch but my son again
I'd send for Betsy far over the main.

B

Up to London did Betsy go
To seek some service you soon shall know.
She hadn't been there but a very short time
Before some service did Betsy find.

Her mistress had but one only son.
Miss Betsy's heart he had fairly won.
Her mistress came to her and did say
Pick up your clothes and come with me.

Pick up your clothes and come with me,
Some friends of mine I'm going to see.
And when they came to the seaport town
The ships went sailing both up and down.

And then Miss Betsy she began to say
How she had thrown all her time away.

In a few days after his mother returned.
Your are welcome home, said the son.
But where is Betsy, tell me, pray,
For she does so far behind you stay.

The old man spoke a word most scornfully.
She bring disgrace to her family.
I'd sooner see thee, my son, lie dead
Than a poor servant girl that thou should wed.

In a few days after the son lay dead.
They wrung their hands and they shook their heads
Saying, If my son could but rise again
I'd send for Miss Betsy over the main.

Version A **H** Robert Barrett at Puddletown, Dorset, 1905

Ms. gives title *The Glazier's Daughter*.

Version B **G** Mr Alfred Porter at Basingstoke, Hants, September 1906

A 3.1   *thyme*: Maidenhead, chastity.
B 4   Two rows of dots in ms. indicate that lines 3 and 4 of this stanza
       are missing.
5.1   *his*: ms. her.

I have seen no earlier printed text than that which appears in *JEFDSS*, 1958.
This version, taken down by Mr Peter Kennedy from Mr Harry Cox (born
1885) in Norfolk in 1953, is given below. Among the variations from the
above versions the most interesting is the change from *stole her thyme* (A 3.1)
to *took his time*. In the later version the traditional flower symbol has disappeared, to be replaced by something within the singer's comprehension.

Mr Cox's remarks about his own song, as quoted by Mr Kennedy, are of
great interest as indicating a traditional singer's attitude to a folk song text:
'That song have been in my family over two hundred year ago, my old
grandfa' sang that. That's a good song, it's a long song. Yes I known people
be sent off to America when they'd been a-getting too thick. I know'd things
to happen like that in my time, where they thinks she weren't good enough
for him. Cleared her out—that's almost like in the slave times. Well, she went
to this 'ere Squire's place and they didn't want her there. The old lady see she
was getting too thick along with her son and that didn't suit her. If she had
'a been well up she wouldn't have said nothing. 'Course, 'twas money what
they used to do then, that's what they looked at, you weren't no good 'long
nobody with money. They thought they wouldn't look at such as us.'

BETSY THE SERVANT MAID

(*The Thresher's Daughter*)

A thresher's daughter living near
When shocking news you soon shall hear
When up to London she did go
To seek for service as you shall know.

She went till she came to a squire's hall
And there she did both knock and call
'I hear you want a servant', she said,
'And I am Betsy, the servant maid'.

This squire had only one son
And Betsy's heart so soon he won
And Betsy being so blithe and fair
Soon drew his heart into a snare.

On Sunday evenings he took his time
Unto sweet Betsy he told his mind.
He swore by oaths and powers above
'It is you, sweet Betsy, it is you I love'.

The old woman hearing her son say so
It filled her mind with grief and woe.
'We must contrive to send her away
For to be a slave in Amerikee'.

On Monday morning madam arose
'Betsy, Betsy, pack up your clothes
For I am going some friends to see
And no one but Betsy shall go with me'.

They went till they came to a seaport town
Where ships were sailing up and down.
A boat was hailed and in she went
And the poor girl sail-ed with a discontent.

A few days later the old woman returned.
'Oh, you're welcome home, mother', cried her son,
'You're welcome home, mother, on every side
But where is Betsy the servant maid?'

'O son, O son, O son', said she,
'Your chief delight is on the sea.
I would rather see my son lay dead
Than you should wed with the servant maid'.

A few days later her son fell sick,
So sick in bed, so sad was he
Nothing would cure him that could be tried.
He called for Betsy and then he died.

The old woman seeing her son laid dead
She wrang her hands and tore her head.
'If I could see my son rise again
I would send for Betsy across the Main'.

8 *Bilberry Town*

In Bilberry Town where I was born
And a brewer by my trade O,
I courted a girl called Peggy Brown
And her was a pretty maid O.
   She is a rum un,
   Fal the diddle li tal the dee,
   She is a rum un
   Fal the diddle di do.

Seven long years I courted her
All for to gain her favour
But along came a chap from Bilberry Town
And he swore that he would have her.

Will you go with me, my pretty maid?
Will you go with me, my honey?
O yes, I'll go along with you
Although I'm Johnny's bride O.

I did go to her mammy's house
Enquiring for my honey.
So scornfully the old man reply,
I ain't see'd her since Sunday.

Now her's agone, so let her go,
No more shall her a grieve me.
I'm a young man free, as you shall see,
And a little will relieve me.

H G. Bowditch at Charmouth, March 1906

Ms. gives title *In Milbury Town*. Chorus repeated after each stanza.

9 *Blow Away ye Morning Breezes*

Blow away ye morning breezes,
Blow ye winds, heigh-ho!
Blow away the morning kisses,
Blow, blow, blow!

O thou shalt rue the very hour
That e'er thou knewest the man
For I will bake the wheaten flour
And thou shalt bake the bran.

Thou shalt drink the puddle foul
And I the crystal clear.

For thou shalt wear the sorry clout
And I the purple pall.

B-G Robert Hard at South Brent, n.d.

Described in the ms. as 'song for two female voices'. A row of dots preceding each of stanzas 3 and 4 indicates incompleteness.

SW contains a re-written text incorporating all the above lines. These are evidently a confused fragment from a ballad called *The Knight and Shepherd's Daughter* (Child, No. 110), prefaced by a refrain usually associated with a different ballad, *The Baffled Knight* (*IP* No. 14).

10 *A Bold Dragoon*

In the dragoon's ride from out the north
He came up to a lady,
And then she knew him by his horse
And she loved him very dearly.
O dearly, O dearly.

She took the horse by the bridle rein
To lead him to the stable.
She said, There's hay and corn for the horse
So let him eat whilst able.
O able, O able.

She said, There's cake and wine for you,
There's corn and hay for horses,
There's bread and ale for the king's soldier,
Aye and there's pretty lasses.
O lasses, O lasses.

She stepped upstairs, she made the bed,
She made it plum and easy,
And into bed she nimbly jumped
And said, Dragoon, I'm ready.
O ready, O ready.

O he pulled off his armour bright,
He cast it on the table,
And into bed he nimbly jumps
To kiss whilst he was able.
O able, O able.

They spent the night till break of dawn,
They saw the light full grieving.
O hark! I hear the trumpet sound.
Sweet maid, I must be leaving.
    O leaving, O leaving.

I would the trumpet ne'er might call,
O cruel does it grieve me.
My heart, my very heart will break
Because, dragoon, you leave me.
    O leave me, O leave me.

O when shall we, love, meet again?
O when shall we be married?
When cockle shells turn silver bells
Then you and I shall be married.
    Married, O married.

O what have I for Saturday night
And what have I for Sunday,
And what have I for all the week,
And what have I for Monday?
    Monday, O Monday.

Here's half a crown for Saturday night,
Sheep's head and lung for Sunday.
Here's bread and cheese for all the week
And devil a cat for Monday.
    O Monday, O Monday.

B-G W. Crossing on Dartmoor from an old moorman now dead, in 1878

Stanzas 8 and 9 interpolated from another version, in other respects fragmentary, from Richard Cleave, the Warren Inn, Buckaby Bridge, 1892.

SW contains an original version by **B-G** in which the dragoon, not the lady, is the would-be seducer, and gets his ears boxed. In a note he says: 'The original is too coarse for reproduction and is lengthy. I have condensed the ballad and softened it down.'

11 *The Bold Dragoon*

My father is a knight and a man of high renown.
If I should marry a soldier 'twould pull his honour down
For your birth and my birth it never 'twon't agree,
So take it as an answer, bold dragoon,[1] said she.

Your answer, your answer I do not mean to take.
I'd rather lay my life down all for your sweet sake.
And the hearing of these words made the lady's heart to bleed.
Oh and then she consented, and married was with speed.

After they had been married and returning home again
She saw her honourèd father and seven armèd men.
Oh now, says the lady, we both shall be slain,
For yonder comes my father with seven armèd men.

There is no time to talk, love, there is no time to prattle.
If you will hold my horse, love, then I will fight the battle.
He pulled out his sword and pistol, he made their bones to rattle,
While the lady held the horse and the dragoon fought the battle.

Hold your hand, bold dragoon, hold your hand, said he,
And you shall have my daughter and ten thousand pounds in fee.
Fight on, said the lady, your portion 'tis too small.
Hold your hand, dear dragoon, and you shall have it all.

All you honourable ladies that have got gold in store,
You should never despise a soldier because he's sometimes poor,
And all you lads of honour a-lying on the ground
So send it to Victoria that wears the British crown.

[1] Pronounced with the accent on the first syllable.

H Mrs Poole at Beaminster, June 1906

12 *The Bold Fisherman*

A

As I walked out one May morning down by a river side
'Twas there I spied a fisherman come roving down the tide.

Good morning to you, fisherman, how came you fishing here?
I'm fishing for my lady fair all down the river clear.

'Twas then he rowed his boat to shore and tied it to a stake
And walked up to this fair lady, her lily white hand to take.

Then he pulled off his morning gown and laid it on the ground.
'Twas then she spied three chains of gold all round his neck was
  bound.

Then she fell on her bended knees, Your pardon, sir, she cried,
For calling you a fisherman a-roving on the tide.

Rise up, rise up, my lady fair, and don't downdaunted be,
For not a word that you have said the least offended me.

So take me to your father's house and we will married be
And you shall have your fisherman to row you on the sea.

B

As I walked out one May morning
Down by the river side
There I saw a bold fisherman
Come rolling down the tide.

Good morning to you, bold fisherman,
How come you fishing here?
I come a-fishing for your sweet sake
All on the river clear.

I dare you not come fishing here.
I shall come fishing here,
I come a-fishing for your sweet sake
All on the river clear.

He chained his boat unto a spear
And unto her he went.
He took hold of her lily white hand
Which was his full intent.

Down on her bended knee she fell
And loud for mercy cried
Saying, Not one word as I have said
That has offended you.

They went unto her father's house
And married now they be.
And you shall have a bold fisherman
To roll you on the sea.

They went unto her mammie's house
And married now they be,
And now they have some little boat
To roll them on the sea.

Version A **H** Mr George Roper at Blandford, 1905
Version B **G** Mr Benjamin Arnold at Easton by Winchester, November
1906

Ms. gives title *The Fisherman.*

This song was first published in *English County Songs* (Broadwood and Fuller
Maitland, 1893). Versions were subsequently collected in various counties by
Cecil Sharp, W. P. Merrick, E. J. Moeran and others. All are in substantial
agreement as to the main elements in the narrative. Some versions give 'robes
of gold' instead of 'chains of gold', Lucy Broadwood (*FSJ* 19, 1915) gives
reasons for regarding the song as a medieval allegory symbolizing the mystical
union of Christ (the fisher king) and the soul.

13 *Boney*

Oh Boney was a warrior,
Oh, weigh heigh ya,
A warrior and a terrior,
John Brown's war.

Boney went a-cruising,
Oh, weigh heigh ya,
In the Channel of old England,
John Brown's war.

Nelson went also a-cruising,
Oh, weigh heigh ya,
He fought with noble Boney,
John Brown's war.

Boney got taken prisoner,
Oh, weigh heigh ya,
And Boney got taken prisoner,
John Brown's war.

He got sent to St Helena,
Oh, weigh heigh ya,
There he died a prisoner,
John Brown's war.

G Mr James G. Bounds at Portsmouth Workhouse, August 1907

This variation of the well-known shanty has not been previously printed, so far as I know. The usual form of the fourth line is 'Jean François' or 'John France-wah'.

14 *The Bonny Bunch of Roses*

By the dangers of the ocean one morning in the month of June
The sweet, feathered, warbling songsters their charming notes so
    sweet did tune,
'Twas there I spied a female seemed lying in grief and woe,
And conversing with young Buonaparte concerning the bonny
    bunch of roses, oh.

Oh mother! said young Napoleon, when he pressed his mother by
    the hand,
Do mother, pray, have patience until I'm able to command.
I will raise a terrible army and o'er the frozen realms I'll go,
And in spite of all the universe I will gain the bonny bunch of
    roses, oh.

Oh, son, never speak so venturesome, for in England is the hearts of
    oak,
There's England, Ireland and Scotland, their unity has never been
    broke.
Now, son, look at your father, in St Helena his body lies low,
And you might follow after, so beware of the bonny bunch of
    roses, oh.

So he took his three hundred thousand men, likewise some kings to
    join his throne,
Where he was so well provided, enough to sweep this world along,
But when they came to Moscow they were overpowered by the
    driving snow,
And Moscow was a-blazing, so they lost the bonny bunch of
    roses, oh.

Now it's mother, adieu for ever, for alas I'm on my dying bed.
If I had but lived, I might have been clever, but now I've dropped
    my youthful head,
But whilst my bones do smoulder, weeping willows over me grow,
And the deeds of bold Napoleon shall sting the bonny bunch of
    roses, oh.

G   Mr Charles Windebank at Lyndhurst, Hants, July 16, 1906

Variant texts are to be found in *SW* and in *FSJ* 9, 1906, and on broadsides.
B-G states (notes to *SW*) that it is 'unmistakably an anti-Jacobite production'
later adapted as an anti-Napoleonic song. This would go some way to
explaining the inconsistencies, e.g. in stanza 4. A. G. Gilchrist (*FSJ* 9, 1906)
states that the tune is a dance tune, *The Bonny Bunch of Roses* being a little
girls' dance game. The tune may formerly have been known as 'The Bunch
of Rushes'.

15 *The Broken Token*

As I walked out one summer's morning
A fair young creature I chanced to spy
I steppèd up to her and did salute her
And I said, Young girl can you fancy I?

You appears to be some man of honour,
Some man of honour you seems to be.
How can you 'pose on a poor young woman?
Your servant-maid I'm not fit to be.

If you're not fitting to be my servant
I have a great regard for you.
I'll marry you and make you my lady
And you shall have servants to wait on you.

When he found out his true love was loyal,
It's a pity, said he, true love should be crossed,
For I am thy young and single sailor,
Safe returned for to marry you.

If you are my young and single sailor
Show me the token which I give you,
For seven years makes an alteration
Since my true love have been gone from me.

He put his hand into his pocket,
His fingers being both long and small,
He says, Here's the ring that we broke between us.
Soon as she saw it, down she fell.

He took her up and soon embraced her,
And he gave her kisses, one, two by three,
Saying, I am thy young and single sailor
Safe returned for to marry thee.

G Mr George Blake at St Denys, Southampton, June 6, 1906

Ms. gives title *As I walked out one Summer's Morning*.

Under various titles, most commonly *The Young and Single Sailor*, this song
appears in several collections, e.g. Sharp's *Folk-Songs from Somerset*, and in
FSJ 15, 1910, and 25, 1921, and on broadsides.

Ballads on the theme of the broken ring are common in many European
countries. (See Child, notes to *Hind Horn*, No. 17.)

16 *Bryan-a-Lynn*

Bryan-a-Lynn was a Dutchman born,
His shoes were hemp and his stockings were yarn.
His shoes were hemp, and the water got in.
It's damp to my feet, said Bryan-a-Lynn.
　　All to my tooth, a laugh-a-lum-lee
　　Bryan a ranter and a rover
　　And a bone of my stover
　　Brew, screw, rivet and tin,
　It's damp to my feet, said Bryan-a-Lynn.

Bryan-a-Lynn had no boots to put on,
But two calves' skins with the hair all gone.
They were split at the side and the water ran in.
I must wear wet feet, said Bryan-a-Lynn.

Bryan-a-Lynn has a hunting gone,
A bridle of mouse tails has he put on.
The bridle broke and the horse ran away.
I'm not over well bridled, said Bryan, to-day.

Bryan-a-Lynn has a hunting gone,
A saddle of urchin-skins he put on.
The urchin's prickles were sharp as a pin.
I've got a sore seat, said Bryan-a-Lynn.

Bryan-a-Lynn's daughter sat on the stair.
O father, I fancy I'm wondrous fair!
The stair they broke, and the maid fell in.
You're fair enough now, said Bryan-a-Lynn.

Bryan-a-Lynn, his wife and his mother,
They all fell into the fire together.
Ow-yow! said the uppermost, I've a hot skin.
It's hotter below, said Bryan-a-Lynn.

B-G Thomas Dart at Holcombe Burnell, 1889

Chorus after each stanza as in stanza 1.

B-G gives this song under the title *Tommy a'Lynn* in *SW* 1905 with an additional stanza between 4 and 5, as follows:

> Tommy a'Lynn had no watch to put on,
> So he scooped out a turnip to make himself one;
> He caught a cricket, and put it within.
> It's a rare old ticker, said Tommy a'Lynn.

He traced it back to 1549, since when many versions have been printed, sometimes under other titles, e.g. *Tam o'the Lynn, Tom Boleyn*. A. G. Gilchrist (*FSJ* 33, 1929) gives reasons for concluding that the song was originally an English satire against the wild Irish and Scots with their primitive clothing and rough habits.

17 *The Buffalo*

Come all you gay young fellows that have a mind to range
Into some foreign country, your fortunes to change.
Into some foreign country away from home we'll go
And we'll lie down on the banks on the pleasant Ohio,
And thro' the wild woods we'll wander, and we'll chase the buffalo.

Come all you pretty maidens and spin us up some yarn
To make us some clothing to keep us snug and warm.
You can card and you can spin, maids! and we can reap and mow
And we'll lie down on the banks on the pleasant Ohio,
And thro' the wild woods we'll wander, and we'll chase the buffalo.

There are fishes in the river that are fitting for our use
And high and lofty sugar canes to yield us pleasant juice.
There is all sorts of game, boys, beside the buck and doe
And we'll lie down on the banks on the pleasant Ohio,
And thro' the wild woods we'll wander, and we'll chase the buffalo.

Suppose the wild Indians by chance should come too near,
We would link us heart to heart and have nothing to fear.
We would march through the town, boys, and give the fatal blow
And we'll lie down on the banks on the pleasant Ohio,
And thro' the wild woods we'll wander, and we'll chase the buffalo.

B-G J. Bennoy at Menhenniot, n.d.

B-G adds the note: 'Sung also by James Olver and J. Parsons, all to the same air.'

A very similar text is given by W. A. Barrett in *English Folk-Songs* (Novello, 1891) with a note that 'this is an emigrant's song, and probably belongs to the early part of the eighteenth century'.

18 *Bushes and Briars*

Through bushes and through briars I lately took my way
All for to hear the small birds sing one evening in May.
O I overheard my own true love, O her voice it was so clear,
O long have I been waiting for the coming of my dear.

O I set myself down by my love and she began to moan,
Crying, I'm of this opinion, my heart is not my own.

Sometimes I am uneasy and atroubled in my mind.
Sometimes I think I'll go to my true love and tell to him my mind,
But if I should go unto my love what should my love say then?
It would show to him my boldness, he'd ne'er love me again.

Once upon a time I had colour like a rose
But now I am so pale as the lily that grows.
I am like some other flower, my beauty is agone.
Don't you see what I am come to by the loving of a man?

O I cannot think the reason young women love young men,
For they are so false hearted young women to trepan,
For they are so false hearted young women to trepan.
O the green grave shall seek me if I don't have that man.

H George Dowden at Lackington, Piddlehinton, Dorset, 1905

Ms. gives title *Through Bushes and through Briars.*

This is very similar to the well-known Vaughan Williams version, of which
the words were completed from a broadside. Vaughan Williams (*FSJ* 8,
1906) does not give stanza 5 of the above, but has the following additional
lines after stanza 1:

> I drew myself unto a tree, a tree that did look green.
> Where the leaves shaded over us, we scarcely could be seen.

19 *The Carpenter's Wife*

Well met, well met, my own true love,
Long time am I a seeking of thee.
I'm lately come from the salt, salt sea
And all for the sake, sweet love, of thee.

I might have had a King's daughter,
She fain would have a married me,
But I naught did hold for her crown of gold
And for the sake, sweet love, of thee.

If you might have had a King's daughter
I think you were much to blame.
I would not 'twere found for a hundred pound
That my husband should know the same.

For my husband he is a carpenter,
A carpenter good is he.
By him I have gotten a little son
Or else I would go, sweet love, with thee.

But if I should leave my husband dear,
My fair sweet boy also,
O what have you got far far away
That along with thee I should go?

I have seven ships that sail on the sea,
It was one brought me to land.
I have mariners many to wait on thee
To be, sweet love, at thy command.

A pair of slippers thou shalt have,
They are made of beaten gold.
They're lined within with coney's skin
To keep thy feet from the cold.

A gilded boat thou also shalt have,
The oars be gilded also,
And the mariners shall pipe and sing
As thro' the salt waves we go.

They had not rowed a bowshot off,
A bowshot on the main,
But o'er her shoulder she looked back.
I would I were home again!

They had not rowed a bowshot off,
A bowshot from the land,
But o'er her shoulder she looked and said,
Set me back on the yellow sand.

For I have a child in my little chamber
And I think I hear him cry.
I would not, I would not my babe should wake
And his mother not standing by.

The Captain he smiled and stroked his arms
And said, This may not be.
Behind is the shore and the sea is before
And thou must go, sweet love, with me.

She had not been long upon the sea,
Not long upon the deep,
Before that she was wringing her hands
And loudly did wail and weep.

O why do you wail and wherefore weep
And wring your hands? said he.
Do you weep for the gold that lies in the hold
Or do you weep for my fee?

I do not weep for your gold, she said,
Nor yet do I weep for your fee,
But by the mast-head is my baby dead
And I weep for my dead baby.

She had not abeen upon the seas
The days they were three or four,
And never a word she spoke nor stirred
And she lookèd towards the shore.

She had not abeen upon the seas
But six days of the week
Before that she lay as cold as the clay
And never a word could speak.

They had not a sailed upon the seas
Of weeks but three and four
But down to the bottom the ship did swim
And never was heard of more.

And when the news to England came
The Carpenter's wife was drowned
The Carpenter rent his hair and wept
And then as dead he swound.

A curse be on all sea-captains
That lead such a godless life.
They will ruin a good ship-carpenter,
His little one and his wife.

B-G   J. Paddon at Holcombe Burnell, December 21, 1889

B-G printed in *SW* 1905, under the title *Well Met! Well Met*, stanzas 1, 2, 6, 7 and 8 and a final stanza of his own fabrication. A very fragmentary version was noted by **H** near Weymouth in 1907. In his note **B-G** lists many printed sources of this version of *James Harris or the Daemon Lover*, of which the earliest is a black-letter ballad in Roxburghe and Pepys. This tells of a Plymouth woman, Jane Reynolds, who exchanges vows of eternal faith with a seaman, James Harris. Harris is pressed to sea, and after three years news of his death reaches Jane. She marries a ship's carpenter, by whom she has three children. Four years later Harris's ghost returns and lures Jane on board ship. The carpenter, in distraction, hangs himself.

As **B-G** says, 'the traditional ballad, as compared with the printed ballad, is superior at every point'. Child (No. 243) gives a number of versions, of which none is closely parallel to **B-G**'s version, now printed in its entirety, so far as I know, for the first time.

20 *Catch Me if You Can*

I was walking out one May morning,
There I beheld a fairy queen,
There I beheld a fairy queen,
She was taking of the air, oh.

I said, My dear, will you go with me?
I will show you round the count-a-ree,
I will show you plants, I will show you flowers,
I will show you things you never have seen.

Then this young couple they walked along,
And this young man he sang a song,
And this young man he sang a song,
Thinking to gain a favour.

Since you have gained your will on me
And stole away my liberty,
And stole away my liberty,
Pray grant to me your name, sir.

My name is Catch-me-if-you-can.
I'll marry you when I return,
I'll marry you when I return,
For I'm bound across the oceans.

They sent six men all on horseback
For to fetch this false young soldier back,
For to fetch this false young soldier back,
But the search was all in vain, you know.

72

For his name was Catch-him-if-you-can,
He'll marry you when he return,
He'll marry you when he return
For he's bound to cross the oceans.

When nine long months was over and past
This poor young girl had a child at last,
This poor young girl had a child at last,
But the child it had no father.

For his name was Catch-him-if-you-can,
He'll marry you when he return,
He'll marry you when he return,
For he's bound to cross the oceans.

H Mrs Gulliver, May 1905

21 *The Cobbler*

A

I am a merry cobbler and lately gained my freedom,
I set my affections on her, a fair young damsel pretty.
Chorus
    Must I use my awl for my derry derry down,
    Must I use my awl for my dear, oh?
    Ring ting ting, ring a ting a ting ting,
    Oh you are my dear, oh.

My journeymen and boys are all at home a-mending
While I to the alehouse go and all the time a-spending.
Chorus

Five pounds I have in gold, and that is all my treasure,
Besides an old greatcoat and a jolly bit of leather.
Chorus

Five pounds I'll give you, Patty, if you will but marry.
Oh thank you, sir, she said, but I'd rather longer tarry.
Chorus

B

I am a cobbler brave, just got my freedom.
Oh, I've fixed my mind all on a bonny woman.
Chorus
    With my ring ding, ding a ding a ding
    With my cuckoo and my goo,
    With my ring ding, ding a ding a ding,
    But still she is my dearie.

She's got four hundred pounds besides some leather,
Four pair of high-heeled shoes neatly sewn together.
Chorus

Oh zounds, I've lost my wax, I dunno what's become of it.
It's no use to swear or vex, for here lies some of it.
Chorus

She's neither maid nor wife, nor yet a woman,
She's done something amiss, but still I love her.
Chorus

G Version A Mr Broad at Old Alresford, Hants, October 1907
    Version B Mr George Macklin at Winchester, March 1906

The connection of the 'awl' as a male sexual symbol with the cobbling trade
has been commonplace since at least the middle ages. The meaning of stanza 3
and the chorus in B is anybody's guess.

22 Come all you Lads and Lasses

Come all you lads and lasses, come listen a while,
I'll sing you a song shall cause you to smile.
Now concerning a frolic the truth I must tell,
Misfortunes I had but it's all very well.
  And sing fal the diddle lero, sing fal the diddle lay.

Now I saw two young doxies, they seemed full of glee.
Thinks I to myself one of these is for me.
One of these being well rigged in a new black silk gown,
I tipped her the wink and she came by me and sit down.

Then I called to the waiter to bring me some gin.
She said, My dear jewel, and that's just the thing,
And now, my dear jewel, some lodging provide
For I am the girl that do lie by your side.

So I quickly unrigged and I jumped into bed,
I fetched my right locket right under her head.
So young doxy and I wished each t'other good night,
So I falls fast asleep and I thought myself right.

O but when I awoke I gazed all around.
I saw that young doxy a-searching my room,
When in her all searching and in all her design,
When in her all searching to find out my coin.

Now I had a stick by me the size of my thumb.
I jumped out of bed and I well laid it on.
I stepped round the room after, I followed my blows,
I gave her no time for to slip on her clothes.

O I jumped into bed and I laughed at the fun,
O but when I awoke I found petticoat, stockings and gown,
Nine guineas all in it besides two fi'pun notes,
She left this behind her in her gown and her coats.

H William Bartlett at Wimborne, Dorset, 1905
Chorus line indicated after each stanza.

23 *Creeping Jane*

I'll sing you a song and a very pretty song,
It's concerning of Creeping Jane,
Oh! she never does the work like a horse or a mare
Nor her vally's not the half of a pin, fal the dee,
  Fal the dal the dido,
Nor her vally's not the half of a pin, fal the dee.

When Creeping Jane she came to the first mile post
Creeping Jane she kept lingering behind.
Oh! the rider put the whip into little Jenny's waist
And she passed over the moor like a dart, fal the dee,
  Fal the dal . . .

When Creeping Jane she came to the second mile post
Creeping Jane she looked fresh and gay.
Oh! the rider put the spurs into little Jenny's waist
And he says, My little lady, never mind, fal the dee,
  Fal the dal . . .

When Creeping Jane she came to the third mile post
Creeping Jane she looked fresh and gay.
Oh! the rider put a posy into little Jenny's ear
And he said, My little lady, never mind, fal the dee,
  Fal the dal . . .

Now Creeping Jane she've a-won that race
And she scarcely sweat one drop.
She is able for to gallop over the ground
Where the others are not able for to trot, fal the dee,
  Fal the dal . . .

Now Creeping Jane she's dead and gone,
Another body lies under cold ground.
I will send to her master for to ask one favour,
For to keep her little body from the hound, fal the dee,
    Fal the dal . . .

H S. Dawe at Beaminster, June 1906

  1.4 *vally*: value.
  6.2 *another*: and her (broadside: see below)

A seven-stanza broadside by Such is reprinted in *FSJ* 5, 1904. This makes
sense of 1.3-4, which it gives as follows:

> She never saw a mare or a gelding in her life
> That she e'er valued above half a pin.

24 *The Croppy Boy*

It was early, early, all in the spring,
The birds did whistle and sweetly sing,
Changing their notes from tree to tree
And the song they sung was old Ireland free.

It was early, early, all in the night
This yeoman cavalry gave to me a fright,
This yeoman cavalry was my downfall
And taken I was by the Lord Cornwall.

It was in a guard room where I was laid
And in the parlour where I was tried.
My sentence passed and courage low,
And to a dungeon I was forced to go.

As I was going up Wexford Street
My own first cousin I chanced to meet.
My own first cousin did me betray,
For one fair guinea swore my life away.

As I passed by my father's door
My brother William stood at the door.
My aged father stood there also,
My tender mother her hair she tore.

My sister Mary heard of the express,
She ran upstairs in her morning dress.
Five hundred guineas I will lay down
To see my brother through Wexford town.

As I was going up Wexford Hill
Who could blame me to cry my fill?
I looked behind and I looked before,
My tender mother I shall see no more.

As I was mounted on the scaffold high
My aged father did me deny,
My aged father did me deny
And the name he gave me was the croppy boy.

It was in Dungannon this young man died
And in Dungannon his body lies.
All you good people that do pass by,
Just drop a tear for the croppy boy.

G Mrs Munday at Axford by Basingstoke, October 1907

Croppy: an Irish rebel of 1798, so called because the hair was worn short in sympathy with the French Revolution.

25 The Cuckoo

A

The cuckoo is a pretty bird, she sings as she flies,
Her bringeth good tidings, her telleth no lies.
Her sucketh sweet flowers to keep her voice clear
And when she sings Cuckoo the summer draweth near.

O meeting is a pleasure but parting is grief,
An inconstant lover is worse than a thief.
A thief can but rob me of all that I have
But an inconstant lover will send to the grave.

The grave will receive me and bring me to dust,
An inconstant lover no maiden can trust.
They'll court you and kiss you, poor maids to deceive,
There's not one in twenty that one may believe.

Come all you fair maidens wherever you be,
Don't hang your poor hearts on the sycamore tree.
The leaf it will wither, the roots will decay
And if I'm forsaken I perish away.

B

'Twas walking and talking and a-walking was I
For to meet my true lover, he's coming by-and-by,
For to meet it's a pleasure and to part it's a grief
And a false-hearted young man is worse than a thief.

For a thief he will rob you of all that you have
But a false-hearted young man will bring you to the grave,
For the grave it will rot you and bring you to dust
But a false-hearted young man I'll never more trust.

Oh once I had a colour like a bud of the rose
But now I'm so fair as the lily that grows.
A flower in the morning cut down in full bloom,
What do you think that I'm coming to by the loving of one?

Come all you pretty maidens, whoever you may be,
Don't trust in young soldiers on any degree,
They will kiss you and court you and now all that's true
But the very next moment they'll bid you adieu.

The cuckoo is a fine bird, it sings as it flies,
It brings us good tidings and tells us no lies,
It sucks the sweet flowers for to make its voice clear
And the more it cries Cuckoo the summer draws near.

C

So abroad as I was walking down by some silent grove
By some clear crystal fountain I saw my true love,
When flowers they were springing, young lambs were all
     a-play,
It's down by the banks of violet so carelessly they lay.

So the small birds on the branches so richly did sing
And the dove she is a-mourning for her unhappy time,
The lark all in the morning she rises in the air
And brings me joyful tidings of Nancy my dear.

So the first time I saw my love she quite surprised me
By the blooming of her cheek and the sparkling of her eye.
My love she's tall, she's handsome, most beautiful and fair,
There's not one in the country can with my love compare.

So walking and a-talking and a-walking goes I
And to meet my own sweet William when he'll come by and
     bye,
When meeting is a pleasure and parting is a grief,
An unconstant lover is worse than any thief.

For a thief he can but rob you and take all you have away
But an unconstant lover will bring you to your grave.
Your grave he will rot you and bring you to the dust,
There is not one in twenty, my dear, as you can trust.

D

'Twas down in the valley beside of a grove,
Down by a crystal fountain I saw my true love,
When flowers they were springing, young lambs they were all
    a-playing,
And 'twas down on the banks where sweet violets do blow.

The very first time that I my love did view
By the blooming of her cheeks and the sparkling of her eye
No rest night nor day in my heart could I find
For the thoughts of my Nancy still run in my mind.

The small birds on the branches a-changing of their notes
While the dove she is in mourning for her unhappy love,
My Nancy she is charming, most beautiful and fair,
There is no one in this country can with my love compare.

Go, fetch me pen, ink and paper that I may sit and write,
That I may sit and write to my joy and heart's delight.
The lark all in the morning she rises all in the air
And brings me glad tidings from Nancy my dear.

So fare thee well, dear Nancy, since parted we must be,
Away to yonders mountain where no one shall me see,
Where the rocks and hills shall hide me and bring me to my
    grave,
So fare thee well, dear Nancy, since you I cannot have.

Version A **B-G** Robert Hard, November 8, 1892 and Mary Langworthy
    at Stoke Fleming, January 30, 1892
Version B **H** Mrs Gulliver, May 1905

The **H** ms. gives the word *bis* against the last two lines of each stanza.

Version C **G** Mr William Brown at Cheriton, Hants, n.d.

Ms. gives title *Nancy and William*.

Version D **G** Mr Moses Mills at Preston Candover by Alresford, Hants, July 1907

Ms. gives title *'Twas Down in the Valley*.

IP No. 23.

B-G says (notes in *Garland*) that the sycamore drops its leaves early.

B-G printed a slightly modified text in *Garland*, and **H** a slightly modified text in *HFD*.

This song is of wide provenance and there is no unanimity between various versions as to the elements included or the order in which they appear. It is indeed impossible to determine what elements properly belong to it. Versions C and D, for instance, do not contain the 'cuckoo' stanza at all, but they include elements found in *The Lark in the Morn*. They are, in fact, not so much versions of *The Cuckoo* as hybrids of *The Cuckoo* and *The Lark in the Morn* (see No. 81 B).

The stanzas which appear as 2, 3 and 4 in A are found in another song variously called *Some Rival has stolen my True Love away* and *The Americans that stole my True Love Away*. The latter title is a corruption of *The Merry King*, of which a version collected by Percy Grainger is given in *FSJ* 12, 1908. In a note to this Lucy Broadwood suggests that the 'merry king' refers to Edward IV (see also *Some Rival has Stolen*, No. 122). A version consisting essentially of A together with stanza 1 of B is given under the title *The Forsaken Nymph* in a collection of sea garlands printed by T. & M. Robertson, Saltmarket, 1802 (BM 11621 b. 13 [18]).

26 *Cupid the Ploughboy*

A

As I walked out one May morning
When may was white in bloom
I walked into a tillage field
To breathe the sweet perfume.
I walked into a tillage field
And leaned upon a stile
When there I saw a ploughing boy
Who did my heart beguile.

'Twas Cupid was this ploughing boy
His furrows deep did plough,
He brake the clods that hard he found
The seeds that he might sow.
I wish that pretty ploughing boy
My eyes had never seen.
O Cupid was that ploughing boy
With coulter sharp and keen.

If I should write a letter,
My inmost heart unfold,
Perhaps he would be scornful
And say that I was bold.
I would, I would that ploughing boy
My heart would yield again.
O Cupid was that ploughing boy
Who caused me all my pain.

B

As I walked out one May morning when flowers were all in
  bloom
I went into a flowery field and smelt a sweet perfume.
I turned myself all round and round and listened for a while
And there I saw Cupid the Ploughboy, and he my heart
  beguiled.

As this young man was ploughing his furrows high and low,
Raking his clods together his barley for to sow,
I wished this pretty ploughboy my eyes had never seen.
'Tis Cupid the pretty ploughboy with his arrows sharp and keen.

If I should write a letter to him, my mind to him unfold,
Perhaps he would take it scornful and say I am too bold,
But if he'd take it kinder and write to me again
'Tis Cupid the pretty ploughboy with his arrows sharp and
  keen.

The ploughboy hearing the lady thus sadly to complain,
He said, My honourèd lady, I'll ease you of your pain.
If you will wed a ploughboy, for ever I'll be true.
'Tis you my heart have a-wounded, I can't love none but you.

This lady soon consents for to be his lawful bride.
Unto the church they went and soon the knot was tied.
So now they are united, and gold they have in store.
The lady and the ploughboy each other do adore.

Version A   **B-G**   James Parsons, 1888
Version B   **H**   Mr H. Marsh at Upwey, January 1907

B-G published in the first and second editions of *SW* an altered and confused
text. **H**'s version was printed in *FSJ* 11, 1907 and again in *DBFS*. His
version is substantially the same as an undated broadside in the British Museum
(1875. b. 19).

27 *Dabbling in the Dew*

Where are you going, my pretty fair maid,
With your red and rosy cheeks and your nut brown hair?
Oh 'tis I am going a-milking, kind sir, she answered me,
A-rolling in the dew makes the milkmaid so fair.

Shall I go with you, my pretty fair maid?
Yes 'tis you're kindly welcome, kind sir, she answered me.

Supposing I should lay you down, my pretty fair maid?
Oh then you must help me up again, kind sir, she answered me.

Supposing you should prove with child, my pretty fair maid?
Oh then I must find a father for it, kind sir, she answered me.

Supposing I should run away, my pretty fair maid?
Oh then I must run after you, kind sir, she answered me.

Supposing I should run too fast, my pretty fair maid?
Then the Devil shall run after you, kind sir, she answered me.

H Mrs J. Hann at Beaminster, June 1906

Ms. gives title *The Milkmaid*. Chorus lines in each stanza as in stanza 1.

IP No. 24.

Printed in *DBFS*.

A version noted by Butterworth (*FSJ* 17, 1913) contains two stanzas not in the above:

> What will you do for clothes then, my pretty fair maid?
> My uncle is a linen draper, kind sir, she answered me.
>
> What will you do for boots then, my pretty fair maid?
> My brother is a shoemaker, kind sir, she answered me.

A version noted by **B-G** explains these enquiries. The questioner says to the maid, 'What if I marry you, madam?' (A marginal gloss to the word 'marry'

in the ms. reads: 'Original expressions gross'.) The maid agrees and the dialogue
continues:

> What if a child should then be thine?
> Why then, that child would be also thine.
>
> What should we do for a cradle? he said.
> My brother's a carpenter by his trade.
>
> What should we have to clothe him in?
> Sir, I can weave and also spin.

28 *Death and the Lady*

As I was walking out one day
'Twas in the pleasant month of May,
The birds did sing and young lambs did play
And I met an old man by the way.

His head was bald, his beard was grey
And he was arrayed in crimson array.
I askèd him what countryman
Or what strange place he did come from.

My name is Death: have you heard of me?
Lords, dukes and earls have bowed to me
And you are one of those branches three
So you, fair lady, must go with me.

I'll give you gold, I'll give you store,
I'll give you costly robes to wear
If you will spare me a little time
That I may live to die again.

I value not your gold or store
Nor yet the costly robes you wear.
Your cup is spent and your glass is run,
So you, fair lady, must be gone.

DEATH AND THE LADY
Woodcut from a broadside in the Baring-Gould collection

When I am dead and in my grave
Let on my tombstone be engraved,
Here lies a poor distressèd maid
Who never by man was betrayed.

G   Mr Henry Saville at Portsmouth Workhouse, July 1907

B-G printed in *SW* a text adapted from two versions collected in Devon.
Instead of 3.3 **B-G** has:

For of the branchey tree am I

to which he appends the note: 'What is meant by the "branchey tree" I do
not know, but so the words run in all versions.' In a letter to A. G. Gilchrist
in 1906 he accepted an interpretation which she had given him, namely that
'branchey tree' was a corruption of 'ancestry'. See her article in *FSJ* 1941 for
her ingenious attempt to justify this conjecture by reference to an Italian poem
of the seventeenth century. In *FSJ* 1946 she suggests that 'Branches Three'
(which also occurs in the version in Williams' *Folk Songs of the Upper Thames*)
is merely an emendation, but I see no reason to doubt the authenticity of the
line as taken down by **G**.

29 *The Death of Parker*

Ye gods above, protect the widows and with pity look down on me,
Help me, help me out of trouble and through this sad calamity.
Parker was a wild young sailor, fortune to him did prove unkind,
Although he was hanged up for mutiny, worse than him was left
  behind.
Chorus Saying Farewell Parker, thou bright angel,
          Once thou wast old England's pride
          Although he was hanged up for mutiny
          Worse than him was left behind.

At length I see the yellow flag flying, the signal for my true love
  to die.
The gun was fired which was required to hang him all on the yard
  arm so high.
The boatman did his best endeavour to reach the shore without
  delay
And there we stood waiting just as a marmot to carry the corpse of
  poor Parker away.

In the dead of the night when all was silent thousands of people lay
  fast asleep,
Me and my poor maidens beside me sorrowfully into the burying-
  ground creep,
With trembling hands instead of shovels the mould from his coffin
  we scratched away
Until we came to the corpse of Parker and carried him home without delay.

A mourning-coach stood there a-waiting and off to London we
  drove with speed
And then we had him most decently buried, a funeral to him was
  preached indeed.

G Mr W. Rundle (56) landlord of The Farmers' Inn, St Merryn, near
  Wadebridge, Cornwall, 1905

Chorus after each stanza.

2.2 *u as required*: ms. we inquired. Emendation suggested by **G**.
2.3 *reach*: ms. rouse. Emendation suggested by **G**.
2.4 *marmot*: a version collected by **H** in Dorset (*FSJ* 34, 1930) gives 'mermaid'.
4   Beneath line 2 ms. gives 'Awanting Awanting'.

Versions given by **B-G** in *SW* 1905, and by **H** in *FSJ* 34, 1930. Richard Parker (b. ?1767) married the beautiful daughter of a Braemar farmer, and having spent her money was imprisoned for debt. He joined the navy in 1797 and was elected leader by the mutineers at the Nore. Parker's 'Floating Republic', as it was called, blockaded the Thames, ran up the red flag, and refused to put to sea until their demands for redress of grievances were satisfied. The mutiny was put down by the intervention of warships, and Parker was hung at the yard-arm on June 30, 1797.

In a note in *FSJ* 34, 1930, A. G. Gilchrist says: 'As Parker was buried in the churchyard of St Mary Matfelon, Whitechapel, the story of his widow claiming his body—one version of the ballad says he was buried on the shore and she, with three helpers, dug him up by night—is probably founded on fact.' She adds a reference to a reminiscence by St Loe Strachey in *The Adventure of Living*. The song used to be sung by Strachey's nurse, whose father had been in the mutiny at the Nore. The nurse had added that 'Men have been hung at the yard-arm for singing that song. It was condemned throughout the Fleet.'

30 *Deep in Love*

Must I go bound or must I go free
To love a young man who never loved me?
Why should I act such a childish part
To love a young man with all my heart?

He loves another, he loves not me
And he cares not for my company.
He loves another, I'll tell you why,
Because she's got more gold than I.

Her gold will waste, her beauty blast
And in time she'll come like me at last.

I put my back up against an oak,
Thinking it was some trusty tree,
But first it bent and then it broke
And so did thy false love to me.

I put my hand into a bush,
Thinking some sweeter flower to find.
I pricked my finger to the bone,
Leaving that sweetest flower alone.

Since roses are such prickly flowers
They should be gathered when they're green,
And she did court such an unkind love,
I'm sure she's striving against the stream.

For against the stream I dare not go
For fear that it should overflow,
And not so deep in love am I
I care not whether he live or die.

He gave me honey all mixed with gold,
He gave me words and bows withal,
He gave me a delicate gown to wear
All stitched with sorrow and hemmed with fear.

Now if ever I gain my liberty
And that I trust I soon will be
I'll buy me a delicate gown to wear
Not hemmed with sorrow nor stitched with fear.

Now here's his health I mean to drink
And from his arms I will not slink.
He hath my heart, go where he will,
Although he is false I must love him still.

H   Jacob Baker at Bere Regis, Dorset, 1905

Ms. gives two rows of dots before the two lines of stanza 3.

IP No. 108 (*Waly Waly*).

Published in *DBFS* under the title *Must I be Bound*. For a discussion of this song, see *IP*, p. 38. See also the exhaustive study by J. W. Allen in *JEFDSS* 1954, p. 161. It should be noted, however, that the transcription of *The Effects of Love* (BM 11621.k.4, Vol. I, p. 158) is inaccurate. A correct transcription is given on p. 98 in my notes to *Died of Love*.

Another version is given under the title *Picking Lilies* in a chapbook of *Four Excellent Songs: licensed and entered according to order*, n.d., No. I (BM 11621.b.6 [12]):

> Down in a meadow fresh and gay,
> Picking lilies all the day;
> Picking lilies both red and blue,
> I little thought what love could do.
>
> Where love is planted there it grows,
> It buds and blossoms like any rose,
> It has so sweet and a pleasant smell,
> No flowers on earth can it excel.
>
> There's thousands, thousands in a room,
> My love she carries the brightest bloom;
> Surely she is the chosen one,
> I will have her or I will have none.
>
> I saw a ship sailing on the sea,
> Loaded as deep as she could be;
> But not so deep as in love I am,
> I care not whether I sink or sweem.
>
> I leant my back unto an oak,
> Thinking it was some trusty tree;
> But first it bow'd and then it brake,
> And so did my true love to me.
>
> I put my hand into the bush
> Thinking the sweetest rose to find,
> I prick'd my finger into the bone,
> But left the sweetest rose behind.
>
> If roses be such a prickly flower,
> They ought to be gathered while they are green
> And he that loves an unkind lover,
> I am sure he striveth against the stream.
>
> When my love and I is gone to rest,
> I'll think on her whom I love best,
> I'll wrap her in the linen strong,
> And I'll think on her when she's dead and gone.

31 *The Derby Ram*

As I was going to Derby 'twas on a market day
I met the finest ram, sir, that was ever fed on hay.
  To my ring a ding a Derby, my ring a ding a day,
  Ring a ding a Derby, 'twas on a market day.

Now the wool that's on this ram, sir, it was so thick and long
'Twas almost 'nough to make the blankets in all Yorkshire town.

Now the tail that's on this ram sir, it was so very long
It almost reached from London into the Yorkshire town.

Now the horn upon this ram, sir, it stood so very high
The magpies build their nesties in it for it almost touch the sky.

Now the butcher that killed this ram, sir, he was up to his knees in
    blood
And ninety little butcher boys was washed away in the flood.

It took all the women in Yorkshire for to wheel away his stones
And all the women in Dorset to cover up his bones.

Now the farmer that sold the ram, sir, he must be very rich
And the butcher that bought the ram, sir, he must be a liard.

H T. Gale at Nettlecombe, 1906

Chorus repeated after each stanza.

> 7.2 *liard*: ms. gives this word in quotation-marks. It is possible that the
> obvious change from 'a lying son of a bitch' was made by the singer,
> not the collector.

IP No. 26, text and notes.

A Breton version in *Chansons Populaires de la Basse-Bretagne* (Luzel, Paris,
1890) under the title *An Danvad Penn-Gornic* (*La Brebis à Tête Cornue*) is a
similar catalogue of hyperboles.

32 *Derry Down Fair*

A

As I was awalking down Tavistock Street
With my gay scarlet cloak and my buckles complete,
I was one to entice all the maidens that day
When they set their sweet eyes on young Ramble Away.

As I was awalking through Tavistock Fair
I saw my bright Nancy a combing her hair,
With my cap and my ribbons so bright and so gay
She could not but look at young Ramble Away.

As I was awalking that night in the dark,
I stood at her door and I shone as her spark.
I whistled; she looked from her window to say,
Are you gone, the young lad they call Ramble Away?

When twenty four weeks they were over and past
This fair pretty maiden did sicken at last.
Her gown would not meet nor her apron strings stay,
And 'twas all through the love of young Ramble Away.

My dad and my mammy from home they are gone,
And when they return I will sing them a song.
I'll sing them a song and I'll leave them to say,
Alack! you've been playing with Ramble Away.

So come, pretty maidens, wherever you be,
With courting young fellows don't make yourselves free,
For if you should do so you'll rue the sad day
When you met with the like of young Ramble Away.

B

As I was a going to Derry down Fair
With my scarlet cloak and everything there
In order to entice all buxom and gay
That wished for to go with young Ramble Away.

93

Chorus Ramble Away!
     That wished for to go with young Ramble Away.

Yo! the very first steps I put into the fair
I saw pretty Nancy a combing her hair.
I tipped her the wink and she rolled her black eye.
Thinks I to myself, I'll be with you by and by.
Chorus With you by and by . . .

Yo! as I was awalking at night in the dark
I took pretty Nancy to be my sweet heart.
She smiled in my face, these words she did say,
Are you the young lad that's called Ramble Away?
Chorus Ramble Away . . .

Yo! I said, Pretty Nancy, don't smile in my face,
For I do not intend to stay long in this place,
So I give her three doubles and fair length and share.
I told her I'd ramble but didn't know where.
Chorus Didn't know where . . .

Now come all you pretty maids wherever you be,
From this jolly banquet I'll have you go free.
My hat, cap and feathers, my dear, you shall wear
And a bunch of blue ribbon to tie up your hair.
Chorus Tie up your hair . . .

Version A **B-G** (under the title *Young Ramble Away*) James Parsons, May
    1891
Version B **H** Mr Barrett at Puddletown, Dorset, 1905

A popular broadside of the same type as *Catch Me if You Can* (No. 20). This
is sometimes entitled *Brimbledon Fair* or *Young Rambleaway.*

    The expression 'derry down' in choruses to songs is always associated with
wantonness, and it is probable that Derrydown Fair, like Rosemary Lane and
the modern Shag Alley, is a type-name indicating a specific activity, rather
than a definite locality. (Cf. 'Queer Street'.)

33 Dicky the Miller

As Dicky the Miller was a-riding alone
Who should he meet but his sweetheart Joan
And she was a-dressed in her holiday's clothes
Going a-visiting as you might suppose.
    Sing Fal the lal the lido, diddle dol the day.

Good morning, Joan, will thee be my wife?
I never did see thee so fine in my life.
Then they went down into some grove
All for to taste of the pleasures of love.

Oh if this is the pleasure of being a wife
How well I should like it all the days of my life.
When Joanie went home well pleased of life
Telling of her mother that she must be a wife.

You nasty wench, you brazen face,
I have a good mind your sides to baste.
Since you have lost your very first dane
You never will be a right maid again.

When Dicky the Miller he this understand
He married the pretty girl quite out of hand
For it were he himself who gainerd her love
And fathered the child that was got in the grove.

H   William Miller 1906

After the chorus-line at the end of stanza 1 appears the word 'Repeat'. Otherwise no reference to Chorus. Note singer's name.

4.3   *dane*: as in ms.

34 *Died of Love*

There was three worms on yonder hill,
They neither could not hear nor see.
I wish I'd been but one of them
When first I gained my liberty.

Then a brisk young lad came acourting me,
He stole away my liberty.
He stole it away with a free good will,
He've agot it now and he'll keep it still.

O for once I wore my apron strings low,
My love followed me through frost and snow,
But now they're almost up to my chin
My love passed by and say nothing.

Now there is an alehouse in this town
Where my false love go and sit himself down
And takes strange girls all on his knee
Because they have more gold than me.

So gold will waste and beauty pass
And she will come like me at last.
That mortal man when he served me so
When I was down where the daisies grow.

Now there is a flower I heard them say
Would ease my heart both night and day.
I wish to God that flower I could find
That would ease my heart and my troubled mind.

Then out in the mead the poor girl run
To cull those flowers fast as they spring.
'Twas some she pickèd, some she pulled
Till at length she gained her apron full.

On these sweet flowers she made her bed,
A stony pillow for her head.
Then down she lay and never more spoke,
And now her tender heart is broke.

Now she is dead and her corpse is cold,
I met her false lover and him I told.
Come and walk after your heart's delight,
She will walk with you both day and night.

So dig her a grave long, wide and deep
And strow it over with flowers sweet.
Lay on her breast a turtle dove
That folks may see that she died for love.

H   William Bartlett at Wimborne, Dorset, 1905

Ms. gives title as *The Three Worms*. Last two lines of each stanza repeated as Chorus.

    4.4   Given in ms. as alternative to: And don't you think that's a grief
          to me?
    5.1   *will*: ms. and

IP No. 20 (*A Brisk Young Lover*).

Printed in *FSJ* 19, 1915.

For a discussion of this song, see *IP* pp. 43–45; see also notes by Lucy Broadwood and others in *FSJ* 19, 1915 and 27, 1923.

    It is clear that *Died of Love* and *Deep in Love* are related not only to each other, but also to other songs and ballads of desertion in love, whether by a man or by a woman. Cf. the song *Arthur's Seat Shall be my Bed* quoted by Child in his appendix to *Jamie Douglas* (IV, 105), which concludes with the stanza

> Martinmas wind, when wilt thou blow,
>   And blow the green leafs off the tree
> O gentle Death, when wilt thou come!
>   For of my life I am wearie.

This stanza is incorporated in a version of *Died of Love* given under the title *The Effects of Love: A New Song* on an undated broadside (BM 11621. k. 4, Vol. I, p. 158):

> O! Love it is hot, and Love is cold,
>   And love is dearer than any gold;
> And love is dearer than any thing,
>   Unto my grave it will me bring.

O when my apron it hung low,
He followed me thro' frost and snow;
But now I am with child by him,
He passes by and says nothing.

I wish that I had ne'er been born,
Since love has proved my downfall;
He takes a stranger on his knee,
And is not this a grief to me.

I wish that my dear babe was born,
And dandled on its daddy's knee,
And I in the cold grave did lie,
And the green grass grew over me.

Ye Christmas winds when will ye blow,
And blow the green leaves off the tree?
O, gentle Death, when will you call,
For of my life I am quite weary.

Unloose these chains of love, and set me free,
And let me at liberty;
For was you hear instead of me,
I'd unloose you love, and set you free.

35 *Eggs in her Basket*

Two sailors walked out one morning,
Their pockets were all lined with gold.
As they were walking and kindly talking
A pretty fair maid they did behold.
Chorus. As they were walking . . .

As lovely Nancy sat down a-resting
All with a basket by her side
One of the sailors asked if he should carry it.
Oh yes, kind sir, and if you please.

For, she says, I've eggs all in my basket.
Oh sailors, sailors, I pray take care,
And if you should chance to over-walk me
At the half-way house I'll meet you there.

Then these two sailors walked on quite briskly.
Oh the half-way house they soon passed by,
And lovely Nancy she followed after
And on the sailors she kept her eye.

Then they walked on to the very next alehouse
And called for a quart right of the best,
Saying, Landlord, landlord, bring us some bacon,
For we have eggs and no meat to dress.

The landlord lookèd in the basket
And turned his head all with a smile,
Saying, Sailors, sailors, you are mistaken.
Instead of eggs you've got a child!

One of those sailors sat down a-fretting,
The other turned all with a smile.
Here's fifty guineas for any woman
That will take care of this pretty child.

So lovely Nancy in the next room standing
Heard what those sailors they had to say,
Says, I will take it and kindly use it
If you will see the money paid.

Are you that young and lovely Nancy
That I danced with last Easter day?
Oh yes, kind sir, and I pleased your fancy
And now the fiddler you have to pay.

Oh we'll go down to yonder chapel
And there the knot soon shall be tied
When bells are ringing and sailors singing
And you shall be my lawful bride.

G   Mr Henry Day at Basingstoke, Hants, September 1906

Lines 3 and 4 in each stanza repeated as Chorus.

IP No. 10.

This version is fuller than that given in *The Idiom of the People*, as well as that given in *FSJ* 2, 1900, which lacks the last two stanzas.

36 *The Everlasting Circle*

All in the greenwood there growèd a tree,
So fine a tree as you ever did see
And the green leaves flourished around around around
And the green leaves flourished around,

And all on this tree there growèd a branch,
So fine a branch as you ever did see
And the branch was on the tree
And the tree was in the wood
And the green leaves flourished . . .

And all on this branch there growèd a spray,
So fine a spray as you ever did see
And the spray was on the branch,
And the branch . . .

And all on this spray there was a fine nest,
So fine a nest as you ever did see
And the nest was on the spray
And the spray . . .

And all in this nest there was laid an egg . . .

And all in this egg there was a golden yolk . . .

And all in this yolk there was a gay bird . . .

And all on this bird there was a fine feather . . .

And out of this feather was made a fine bed . . .

And all on this bed a lad did lie . . .

And all with this lad a maiden she did sleep . . .

And all in this maiden a baby was made . . .

And out of this baby a boy he did grow . . .

And the boy he did lay in the ground an acorn . . .

And out of this acorn did grow a great tree

B-G James Parsons, Lew Down, and J. Woodrich, n.d.

As indicated in my note to Sharp's version of *The Tree in the Wood* (*IP* No. 104), the version given above is the only complete one I have seen—that is, the only one in which the 'circle' is completed. Some versions (e.g. *IP* No. 104B) stop short at 'man'; in these, as in the ms. of the version above, the 'maiden' is mentioned before the 'man'. I feel justified in reversing the 'maiden' and 'man' stanzas, as this straightens out the sequence.

The **B-G** mss. contain also:

(1) A version taken down from William Nankivell, aged 62, in 1890 at Marrivale Bridge. This begins:

> O there was a wood and a pretty green wood,
> And all in this green wood grew a fair tree,
> The finest tree that ever you did see,
> And the green grass grew all around,
> And the green leaves flourished thereon.

The enumerations then proceed as above until '*lass*'

(i.e. 'maiden') is reached, after which:

> And out of the lass there came a great lawyer . . .
> And out of the lawyer there came a great parson . . .
> And out of the parson there came a great devil . . .

(2) A transcription of a broadside by Pitts of Seven Dials (n.d.) as follows:

> There was a tree grew in a wood,
> A dainty curious tree.
> For the tree was in the wood
> And the wood was down in the valleys low
>
> And on this tree there was a branch,
> A dainty curious branch,
> For the branch was on the tree,
> And the tree was in the wood,
> And the wood was down. . . .

And so on, with the following items:
A nest. An egg. A bird. A feather. A bed. A maid. A man.

(3) A version taken down from Moses Cleave at Forest Inn, Huckaby Bridge in 1890, as follows:

> All in the hills there came a wood
>   The finest wood that ever you did see.
>   And the wood was in the hills,
>   And the green leaves grew around.

> All in the wood there came a tree,
>   The finest tree that ever you did see
>   And the tree was in the wood . . .

> All on this tree there grew a branch.

> Stood a nest

Stanzas 5 to 7 as in A. Then, as final stanza:

> All on this feather there was a colour
>   The finest colour that ever you did see
>   And the colour was on the feather
>   And the feather was on, etc.

(4) A transcription of the text from Mason's *Nursery Rhymes and Country Songs* (1877), also reprinted in *English County Songs* (Broadwood and Fuller Maitland, 1893).

(5) A similar nursery version heard at Abingdon.

B-G printed the song in *SW*, 1st and 2nd editions, but omitted it from the revised edition of 1905. He altered the words slightly, omitting all reference to the father of the 'babe'; for 'maiden' he substituted 'mother'. In his notes he refers to a Breton version, *Ar Parc Caer* (F.-M. Luzel: *Chansons Populaires de la Basse-Bretagne*, Paris, 1890), of which the modern French rendering is as follows:

LE JOLI CHAMP

J'ai un champ.
  Le joli champ!

Sur le champ est un talus.
  Le joli talus!

Le talus est sur le champ, et le champ m'appartient.

Sur le talus est tombé un gland,
Du bec d'un colombe blanche.
  Le joli gland!

Le gland est sur le talus, le talus est sur le champ, et le champ m'appartient.

Sur le gland s'est élevé un chêne.
Le joli chêne!

Le chêne est sur le gland, etc.

Sur le chêne est une branche.
La jolie branche!

La branche est sur la chêne, etc.

The song accumulates in this manner until the final stanza, as follows:

Le coq est sur la croix, la croix est sur la tour, la tour est sur le couvent, le couvent est sur le moine, la moine est sur la nonne, la nonne est sur la plume, la plume est sur le petit oiseau, le petit oiseau est sur l'œuf, l'œuf est sur le nid, le nid est sur la branche, la branche est sur le chêne, le chêne est sur le gland, le gland est sur le talus, le talus est sur le champ, et le champ m'appartient.

A Welsh version is given in *The Journal of the Welsh Folk Song Society*, Vol. I, 1909. The following is a literal translation of the first and the last stanzas:

On the hill came a tree—O fine tree!
The tree on the hill, and the hill on the earth, and the earth on nothing.
Pleasant and fine was the hill where the tree grew.

From the feathers came a bed—O fine bed!
The bed from the feathers, the feathers from the chicken, the chicken from the egg, the egg from the nest, the nest on the branch, the branch on the tree, the tree on the earth, and the earth on nothing,
Pleasant and fine was the hill where the tree grew.

More recently an Irish version was taken down by Peter Kennedy and Sean O'Boyle from Christy Purcell at Belfast in August 1952. This begins:

O it's a rare bog and a fine bog
And the bog down in the valley O!
For in this bog there grew a tree . . .

In succeeding repetitions the following are added: branch, leaf, nest, egg.
Comic versions were collected, also by Peter Kennedy, at Exeter in 1954, and in Cornwall in 1956, in both of which the order of items is the same as in previous versions, except that after 'feather' the song concludes with 'flea'.
In her notes to the song A. G. Gilchrist (*FSJ* 13, 1909) characterizes it as a 'rigmarole', a description surely very wide of the mark.

37 *A Famous Farmer*

A famous farmer, as you shall hear,
He had two sons, one daughter dear
By a servant man was much admired,
None in the world she loved so dear.

One of these brothers said to the other,
We see our sister means to wed.
Let all such courtship soon be ended,
We'll hoist him to some silent grave.

They asked of him to go a-hunting.
He went without any fear or strife.
These two jewels proved so cruel
They took away this young man's life.

When they returned from the field of hunting
She enquirèd for the servant man.
Come brothers tell me because you whisper,
Come brothers tell me if you can.

Why, sister, we are so much amazed
To see you look so much at we.
We left him in the field of hunting,
No more of him then could we see.

As she laid musing on her pillow
She dreamed she saw her true love stand
By her bedside, he stood lamenting
All covered with some bloody stream.

Pray Nancy dear don't weep for me,
Pray Nancy dear don't weep nor pine.
In that creek where there is no water
Go there you may my body find.

Then she rose early the next morning
With many a sigh and bitter groan.
In that creek where her true love told her
There she found his body thrown.

The blood all on his lips was drying,
His tears were salter than any brine.
Then she kissed him and then she cried
Here lies a bosom friend of mine.

Three nights and days she stood lamenting
Till her poor heart was filled with woe
Until sharp hunger came creeping on her
Then homewards she was forced to go.

Sister we are so much amazèd
To see you look so pale and wan.
Brothers I know you knows the reason
And for the same you shall be hung.

Then these two brothers both were taken
And bound all in some prison strong.
One was tried, found out as guilty,
For the same they both was hung.

G Mr George Digweed at Micheldever, Hants, 1906

I have not discovered any other text of this modern version of the Isabella
story (*Decameron*, Day IV, Story 5).

38 *Fare Thee Well, Cold Winter*

Abroad as I was awalking down by a river side,
I heard two lovers talking, the damsel she replied:
How could you be so cruel, how could you serve me so?
You promised you would marry me about two months ago.

My dear, I was prevented, and could not come till now,
So rest yourself contented I never will break my vow.
Here's neither gold nor silver, nor yet by land or sea,
I take so much delight, love, in your sweet company.

What maiden can believe you, you've said so much before;
The last time that I saw you, you said you'd come no more,
You went and courted Nancy, the girl with a rolling eye,
You went and courted Nancy, you cannot this deny.

I went and courted Nancy, but now I'm come to you.
. . . .
Why should it breed a faction betwixt my love and I?
It's you, my dear, I fancy, with you I'll live and die.

These words they revived her and struck her to the heart
And we will have the wedding before that we do part.
So fare thee well, cold winter, and to the church they passed,
And this couple they got married and th'unlooked for come at last.

G   Mr William Winter at Andover, Hants, n.d.

Ms. gives title *Abroad as I was Walking.*

39 *Fare Thee Well, my own True Love*

Fare thee well, my own true love,
Fare thee well, my darling,
Fare thee well, my own true love,
I'm going over the mountain.

Now my poor girl begins to cry,
With my coat I wiped her eye,
And all the people said she should die
If I went over the mountain.

Now you sees me poverty struck,
I am down upon my luck,
And I am come to see what you've got
To help me over the mountain.

G Mr James Brown at Basingstoke, Hants, September 1906

Ms. gives first two stanzas as one eight-line stanza and four rows of dots after
stanza 3.

40 *Farewell He*

A

Last night I met my love down in yonder shady grove,
I met him with a smile and gave to him the road.
He thought that I should speak to him as I was passing by,
Oh before I'd humble to my love I'd lay me down and die.

He may go or he may stay, he may sink or he may swim,
I do think in my own heart I am quite as good as him.
Aye and if he get another girl we both will agree.
I will defy the lad for ever—let him go, farewell he.

He may go or he may stay, he may sink or he may swim,
I do think in my own heart I am quite as good as him,
For I have got another and both we will agree
I have got the choice of twenty—let them come, farewell he.

B

Here's a quarter a pound of reasons
And a half a pound of sense,
A small sprig of thyme
And as much of prudence.
You can mix it up together
And you will plainly see
He's a false deluding young man,
Let him go, farewell he.

Last night he brought to me
A fine diamond ring.
He thought to have deprived me
Of a far better thing,
But I was most careful
As lovyers ought to be.
He's a false deluding young man,
Let him go, farewell he.

G   Version A   Mr George Smith at Fareham, Hants, July 28, 1906
        Version B   Mrs Ansell at Portsmouth Workhouse, August 1907

Although they have little in common, these are obviously versions or parts of
the same song. (A version collected by **H** and printed in *DBFS* consists
essentially of the first stanza of A and the first of B, together with another
stanza not in either.) Another version is given in *Garland*, but I am unable to
discover the ms. original. **B-G** adds a note to the effect that 'reasons' and
'raisins' were once pronounced alike.

41 *Farewell to Kingsbridge*

On the ninth of November by the dawning of the day
Ere we sailed for New York we did lie in the bay.
O'er the fair fields of Kingsbridge the mist it lay grey,
We were bound against the rebels of North America.

O so sad was the parting 'twixt soldiers and wives
For they knew not if all would return with their lives.
O the women they wept and they cursed the day
That we sailed 'gainst the rebels in North America.

The babes held up their arms with the saddest of cries
And the tears trickled down from their innocent eyes
That their red-coated daddies must hasten away
For to fight with the rebels in North America.

Now God save King George, I will finish my strain.
May his subjects all loyal his honour maintain.
God prosper our voyage and arms across the sea
And pull down the proud rebels in North America.

B-G Roger Huggins, mason, at Lydford, who learnt it in 1860 from a man
named Kelly at Tavistock.

B-G published this song in a modified version in the first two editions of *SW*.
In his notes he says: 'There are old men in Kingsbridge who can recall when
soldiers were stationed there. The song belongs to the year 1778-80. It exists
as a broadside by Such, but without naming Kingsbridge so that probably it
was a song of the time adaptable to other places as well.' This is confirmed by
the Irish version in *FSJ* 7, 1905, which refers to the battle fought against the
American rebels at Kingsbridge near New York in 1776.

42 *Farmyard Song*

I had a cock and he pleasèd me,
I fed my cock under the tree.
The cock went gallicrow,
Join in every neighbour's cock, and well done my cock too.

I had
{
a hen . . .   The hen went chick a chick . . .
a duck . . .   The duck went quek quek . . .
a turkey . . . The turkey went gib a gob . . .
a goose . . . The goose went tess tess . . .
a lamb . . .   The lamb went ma ma . . .
a pig . . .   The pig went gruff gruff . . .
a horse . . . The horse went hurr hurr . . .
a cow . . .   The cow went moo moo . . .
}

Join in &c.

H   S. Gregory at Beaminster, June 1906

H published an altered text in Novello's School Series. This well-known cumulative song is popular in Britain and America.

43 *The Foolish Boy*

My father died, I can't tell 'ee how
And left me six horses to follow the plough.
    Wim-mee—wim-mee—wobble O!
    Jiggee, Jiggee, stobble O!
    Little boys a wobble lived under the gloam.

I sold my six horses and bought me a cow,
I'm a going to get money but I can't tell how.

I sold my cow and I bought me a calf.
By that my bargain I lost just half.

I sold my calf and bought me a cat
And in the chimney corner the pretty creature sat.

I sold my cat and I bought me a mouse
Set fire to her tail and her burnt down the house.

I sold my mouse and I bought me a wife.
Her cut my throat with an old rusty knife.

B-G   Daniel Radford at Mount Tavy, Tavistock, 1888

After the singer's name, ms. adds: ' "I heard this—words and tune forty years ago from an old ploughman." D. R.' Chorus repeated after each stanza. Ms. gives words in West Country dialect spelling: 'My vayther died, I can't tell ee how, And left me six horses to vollow the pleaugh', etc.

For interesting references to other versions of this macabre tale, see *ODNR* No. 156.

44 *The Forsaken Maiden*

A maiden sat a weeping
Down by the sea-shore.
What ails my pretty Sally,
What ails my pretty Sally
And makes her heart sore?

Because I am a-weary
A-weary in my mind.
No comfort and no pleasure,
No comfort and no pleasure
Henceforth can I find.

I'll spread my sail of silver,
I'll loose my rope of silk.
My mast is of the cypress tree,
My mast is of the cypress tree,
My track is white as milk.

I'll spread my sail of silver,
I'll steer toward the sun,
And thou, false love, will weep for me,
And thou, false love, will weep for me,
For me when I'm gone.

B-G   James Parsons, October 1888

B-G published a modified text in *SW*.

45 *Four and Twenty Fiddlers*

Four and twenty fiddlers all of a row,
Four and twenty fiddlers all of a row.
Fiddle fiddle faddle,
Semi semi quaver
Down below.
It is my lady's holiday
So let the lass be merry.

Four and twenty tinkers all of a row,
Four and twenty tinkers all of a row.
Hoo rub-a-dub! hey rub-a-dub!
Fiddle fiddle faddle . . .

Four and twenty cobblers all of a row,
Four and twenty cobblers all of a row.
Cobbler, cobbler stab awl,
Tantarero, tantarero,
Hoo rub-a-dub . . .

Four and twenty tailors all of a row,
Four and twenty tailors all of a row.
One caught a louse, t'other let him loose,
T'other cried 'Knock him down with a goose',
Cobbler, cobbler . . .

Four and twenty pensioners all of a row,
Four and twenty pensioners all of a row.
Push dirk cut a-cross,
One caught a louse . . .

Four and twenty priesties all of a row,
Four and twenty priesties all of a row.
Two ruffles to every shirt,
Push dirk . . .

Four and twenty barbers all of a row,
Four and twenty barbers all of a row.
Devilish hard time,
Shave twice for one penny.
Two ruffles to every shirt . . .

Four and twenty apostles all of a row,
Four and twenty apostles all of a row.
Abram begot Isaac,
Isaac begot Jacob,
Jacob begot the twelve tribes of Israel.
Devilish hard time . . .

H John Hallett at Mosterton, June 1906

4.4 *goose*: tailor's long-handled smoothing-iron.

A ribald cumulative song of whose origin I know nothing—nor can I discover any other text.

46 The Frog and Mouse

There was a frog lived in a well,
  Crock a my daisy, Kitty alone,
And a merry mouse that lived in a mill,
  Kitty alone and I,
  O crock a my daisy, Kitty alone
  Kitty alone and I.

O there has been a gentleman
Who says he will wed you if he can.

O pray is Mistress Mouse within?
O yes, kind sir, I sit and spin.

Then pray, is Master Rat at home?
O no, kind sir, he loves to roam.

Then the cat she seized the rat by the crown,
The young kittens pulled the young mouse down.

And as the frog he went over the brook
He was gobbled up by a lily white duck.

So here's an end to lovers three,
The rat, the mouse and the little frogee.

B-G Samuel Fone, as sung by his mother about 1840.

Chorus lines repeated in each stanza.

B-G gives in the *Garland* an entirely re-written version. This account of a grotesque wedding has been in print in various forms, both in England and in Scotland, from Elizabethan times onwards, and is still current in oral tradition in America. In an article in *FSJ* 1946 A. G. Gilchrist points out that the refrain (which varies very considerably from version to version) has 'the lilt of the dance', while early variants of the refrain indicate that the song was sung as an accompaniment to spinning. For a comprehensive account of the history of the song, see *ODNR* No. 175.

47 *The Furze Field*

I have got a furze field, my own dearest jewel,
Where all my fine pheasants do fly,
And if you comes a-shooting when shooting's in season
I'll tell you, love, how to proceed.
You bring your dog with you, your gun in your hand,
All loaded and primed all at your command.
When the pheasants takes fright, you must take sight,
You shoot the next moment, you're sure to be right.

I have got a fishpond, my own dearest jewel,
Where all my fine fishes do play,
And if you comes a-fishing when fishing's in season
I'll tell you, love, how to proceed.
You bring your rod with you, your nets in your hand,
Your hooks and your angles all at your command.
When you throws in, all the fishes will play,
It's down to the bottom, and that's the right way.

I have got a warren, my own dearest jewel,
Where all my fine rabbits do play,
And if you comes a-ferreting when ferreting's in season
I'll tell you, love, how to proceed
You bring your dog with you, your ferret in your hand,
Your hooks and your angles all at your command,
And the ferret will bolt and the rabbits will play,
For it's down to the bottom, and that's the right way.

G Mr Moses Mills at Preston Candover by Alresford, Hants, July 1907

This comprehensive invitation to a sexual encounter, expressed in sporting
metaphor, must originally have been intended to be sung by a woman. I have
not seen a printed text elsewhere, but such songs are common in late seven-
teenth- and early eighteenth-century garlands and chapbooks.

48 *Gathering Rushes*

As I walked out one morning, thinking to take some sport
Down by a crystal fountain where people did resort,
'Twas there I spied a fair maid and she was all alone
With a bunch of rushes in her hand she'd been gathering all the
    morn.
Chorus She'd been gathering all the morn,
       She'd been gathering all the morn,
   With a bunch of rushes in her hand she'd been gathering all the
    morn.

Good morning to you, fair maid, how came you here so soon?
I have been gathering rushes and now I am returning home.
He said, Fair maid, come along with me down to yon shady grove
And for evermore I will prove true, I'll swear to the powers above.
Chorus I'll swear to the powers above . . .

Then he took her by the lily-white hand and gave her kisses sweet.
She said, Young man be civil, don't me ill entreat.
She says, You're going to delude me because that I am poor and low,
So I pray, young man, don't tease me or break my rushes, oh.
Chorus Or break my rushes, oh . . .

Then this fair maid consented to lay her rushes down,
The morning being dewy she spread her morning gown.
And now if trouble I should gain, the world will on me frown;
I shall remember gathering rushes and spreading my morning gown.
Chorus And spreading my morning gown . . .

G   Mr John Norman at Southampton, June 25, 1906

Ms. gives title *As I Walked out one Morning*

Chorus lines written out in full after each stanza.

Rush-gathering and related occupations such as basket-making were traditionally female (cf. *Green Besoms*, No. 55, and *Three Maids a-Rushing*, No. 132).
'Rushing' is in the *lingua franca* of folk song frequently a metaphor for female
sexual adventure, as ploughing, sowing and reaping are for male. That this

may also be so in the East is suggested by a very beautiful anonymous fourth-century Chinese love-song translated by Arthur Waley in his *170 Chinese Poems* as *Plucking the Rushes*.

49 *Georgie*

A

As I was going over London Bridge
One May morning so early
It was there I spied a fair pretty maid
Lamenting for her Georgie.

Oh have you got a good little boy
As could run an errand so early,
As could run three miles in one half an hour
With a letter to my Georgie?

Come saddle me my milk-white steed,
Come bridle me my pony
That I might ride before King George
To plead for the life of my Georgie.

And when she came before King George
Her Georgie looked as bold as any.
The people cried out, You're come too late
For your Georgie is condemned already.

Then what has my Georgie done to be hung?
Has he robbed or murdered any?
He's only stole six of the King's fat deers
And sold them under vally.

Then your Georgie shall be hung in the chains of gold
Which scarcely you see any
Because he was of a royal, royal blood
And his mother was a royal lady.

B

As I was going over London Bridge
'Twas in the morning early
Oh there I spied a lady gay
Lamenting for her Georgie.

Come saddle me my milk-white steed,
Come saddle me my pony
That I might ride to some fair Lord judge
And beg for the life of Georgie.

George han't stole ox nor han't stole calves,
George han't stole ox nor any,
But he've stole six of the king's fat deer
And sold them in Kilkenny.

The judge looked back over his left shoulder.
Dear lady, do be asy,
For George have confessed and die he must.
May the Lord have mercy on Georgie.

George shall be hanged in golden chains
Where there is sold a-many,
And George is one of the royal blood,
He courted a virgin lady.

I wish I were out on some yonder hill
Where soldiers I've seen many.
With my sword and pistol in my hand
I'd fight for the life of Georgie.

I wish I was back in my father's groves
Where kisses I've had many
With my own true love all by my side.
I'd die for the life of Georgie.

Version A **G** Mrs Barnes at Medstead by Alton, Hants, December 1907
Version B **H** Sergeant Fudge at East Combs, Bishops Lydeard, Somerset,
May 1905

A 5.4 *vally*: value
B 3.3-4 In other versions a variable number of the king's white steeds
are stolen and sold in 'Bohenny' (Bohemia).

Similar versions of this popular ballad were noted by Cecil Sharp (*Folk Songs
from Somerset* I, 1904), by Lucy Broadwood in Sussex (*FSJ* 4, 1902) and by
Ivor Gatty in Norfolk (*FSJ* 15, 1910). These seem to derive from an English
broadside of the seventeenth century, which is in turn derived from one of the
many earlier Scottish versions (see Child No. 209). Earlier editors' attempts
to identify the hero are inconclusive. The English versions taken down by
collectors in the early part of this century are fragmentary.

50 *Go from my Window*

Begone, begone, my Willie, my Billy,
Begone my love and my dear.
O the wind and the rain have sent him back again
And you cannot have a lodging here.

Begone, begone, my Willie, my Billy,
Begone, my love and my dear.
O the weather it is warm, it will never do thee harm
And thou canst not have a lodging here.

Begone, begone, my Willie, my Billy,
Begone, my love and my dear.
For the wind is in the west and the cuckoo's in his nest
And thou canst not have a lodging here.

Begone, begone, my Willie, thou silly,
Begone, my fool and my fear.
O the devil's in the man that he cannot understan'
That tonight he cannot lodge in here.

B-G This song was part of a prose tale in which a girl is made to marry a rich old man but takes a poor man as lover; a year later she has a baby. Her lover visits her when her husband is at home, and she sings the song ostensibly as a lullaby but in reality as a warning to her lover to go away. A. J. Woodrich heard this sung and recited by an old man in an alehouse near Bideford in 1874. James Parsons knew the song but not the tale.

B-G printed a re-written text in *SW*, 3rd edition, and some valuable notes on the popularity of the song from the sixteenth to the eighteenth centuries, as evidenced by quotations from Elizabethan plays and D'Urfey's *Pills*. A version very similar to the above is given in W. A. Barrett, *English Folk Songs*, 1891.

51 *The Golden Vanity*

Now Jack he had a ship in the North Counterie,
She goes by the name of the Golden Vanity.
I'm afraid she'll be taken by some Turkish galléy
As she sails on the Lowlands, Lowlands Low,
As she sails on the Lowlands Low.

Then up spoke the little saucy cabin-boy
Saying, Master, what will you give me if I will her destroy?
It's I will give thee gold and I will give thee store
And you shall have my daughter when I returns on shore
If you sink her in the Lowlands, Lowlands Low,
If you sink her in the Lowlands Low.

This boy bent his breast and he jumped in,
This boy bent his breast and away he did swim.
He swum till he came to some Turkish galléy
As she sails on the Lowlands, Lowlands Low,
As she sails on the Lowlands Low.

This boy had an auger bored nine holes at once,
He bored a hole at the bottom of the slew,
Where some was playing cards and some was playing dice
And he let the water in and dazzled all their eyes,
And he sank them in the Lowlands, Lowlands Low,
And he sunk them in the Lowlands Low.

This boy bent his breast and he jumped in,
This boy bent his breast and away back he swum,
He swum till he came to some starboard side
Saying, Master, take me up, or else I shall die,
As he sunk them in the Lowlands, Lowlands Low,
As he sunk them in the Lowlands Low.

Then they took him up and laid him on the starboard side,
They laid him on the deck and then he did die.
They wrappéd him up in an old cow's hide
And they sunk him in the Lowlands, Lowlands Low,
And they sunk him in the Lowlands Low.

G   Mr Moses Blake at Emery Down, Lyndhurst, Hants, June 1906

4.1   *nine*: other versions have *two* and *fifteen*.
4.2   *slew*: sluice

Versions of this ballad were also collected by Lucy Broadwood, **B-G**, Cecil Sharp and W. P. Merrick. **B-G** traces it back to a seventeenth-century broadside entitled *Sir Walter Raleigh sailing in the Lowlands, showing how the famous ship called the* Sweet Trinity *was taken by a false galley; and how it was recovered by the craft of a little sea-boy, who sunk the galley.* Child (No. 286) prints three versions which differ substantially in detail but agree as to the main lines of the story. Although the incident may be fictitious, there seems reason to believe, with **B-G**, that the song was an attack on Raleigh, who was unpopular because of his arrogance and heartlessness. It is possible that an earlier ballad was adapted for this purpose.

A. G. Gilchrist noted a fragmentary version (*FSJ* 9, 1906) in which the ship's boy asks to be wrapped up in 'my black bearskin' ('bull's-skin': Child B) and heaved overboard to attack the enemy galley. The singer explained that this was the boy's covering at night, which he would wear as a disguise while in the water.

A late broadside version in the **B-G** collection (BM L.R. 271 a. 2, Vol. VI, p. 18) contains the following stanza, a delightful example of the kind of incongruity which is allowed to creep in. One wonders how the cabin-boy acquired his familiarity with the style of a modern Admiralty communiqué.

> The boy he bent his breast and away he swam,
> Saying, Master take me up or I shall be slain,
> For I have effected their total overthrow,
> And I have sunk them in the Lowlands Low.

52 Good Old Man

She What will you have for supper, my good old man?
What will you have for supper? She called him her lamb.
What will you have for supper, my loving husband?
You're the sweetest old man that's alive, alive, alive,
You're the sweetest old man that's alive.

He Three score eggs, my dear, and fol de dol de de
Fol dol diddle dol de de,
Three score eggs, my dear, and fol de dol de de
Fol dol diddle dol de de.

She That will make you sick, my good old man,
That will make you sick . . .

He Then I shall be dead, my dear, and fol de dol . . .

She And where will you be buried to, my good old man?
And where will you be buried . . .

He In the chimney corner, my dear, and fol de dol . . .

She What will you be buried there for, my good old man?
What will you be buried . . .

He To see you play the flirt, my dear, and fol de dol . . .

She I never did but once, my good old man.
I never did but twice. She called him her lamb.
I never did but three times, my loving husband . . .

He Then who was it with, my dear, and fol de dol . . .

She Once with the possun, my good old man,
Twice with the clerk. She called him her lamb.
Three times with the sexton, my loving husband . . .

G Miss Fanny Stephens at Talstaddy, St Columb, died 1885, aged 93

11.1 *possun*: parson

IP No. 36.

53 *Gosport Beach*

On Gosport beach we landed, a place of noted fame,
When I called for a bottle of brandy to treat my flashy dame.
Her outside rig was all of silk, her spencer scarlet red.
We spent the day in sweet content, and then we went to bed.

'Twas early the next morning just at the break of day,
I said, My handsome fair girl, what brought you down this way?
I'm a rich merchant's daughter, from London I came down.
My parents turned me out of doors, that cast me on the town.

I said, My handsome fair girl, I'm sorry for to see
That you should ramble far from home and throw yourself away.
There's no affliction but will turn, for ever I'll prove true
And when from Chatham I return, sweet love, I'll marry you.

So we kissed, shaked hands, did part, tears from her eyes did flow.
I left her broken-hearted, on board she might not go.
As pledge and token of our love her gold she broke in two,
One half she gave to her true love with, Adieu, sweetheart, adieu.

When six long months were ever gone, from Chatham down came
    he
He said, My handsome fair girl, I'm come to marry thee.
Then to the church they took their way, a married life to try,
And I hope they will live happy both until the day they die.

B-G Roger Luxton (aged 76) at Halwell, 1889

B-G did not publish this song. **G** noted a version, very similar but lacking the last stanza. **H** noted a very incomplete version at Cuckold's Corner in Dorset. A text printed by Kidson (*FSJ* 9, 1906) under the title *Plymouth Town* is an inferior broadside version.

54 *Gossip Joan*

Good morrow Gossip Joan,
Where have you been a walking?
I have for you at home
A budget-full of talking,
   Gossip Joan.

My sparrow's flown away
And will no more come to me.
I've broke a glass to-day,
The price it will undo me,
   Gossip Joan.

I've lost a Harry groat
Was left me by my granny,
I can not find it out,
Though I've searched every cranny,
   Gossip Joan.

My goose has laid away,
I know not what's the reason.
My hen has hatched to-day
A month before the season,
   Gossip Joan.

I've lost my wedding ring
Was made of silver gilded
And drink would please a King,
The tabby cat has spilled it,
   Gossip Joan.

My duck has eat a snail,
And is it not a wonder?
The horns bud out at the tail
And split my duck asunder,
   Gossip Joan.

GOSSIP JOAN

My husband he was drunk
And all the night lay snoring.
I whacked him till in a funk
He began screaming and roaring,
　　Gossip Joan.

O I am sick at heart,
I may give me some ginger.
I am all ache and smart
So pray hold out your finger,
　　Gossip Joan.

Let's to the tavern go
And wash down all our sorrow,
My grief in part you know,
The rest I'll tell to-morrow,
　　Gossip Joan.

B-G Sung every Christmas Choir Supper up to 1899 by Henry Davy, carpenter and parish clerk

3.1 *Harry groat*: a coin of the time of one of the King Henrys.
4.1 *laid away*: this expression for laying eggs out of sight is still current.

IP No. 37.

B-G did not publish this song. A version called *Gossip Jones* in *FSJ* 34, 1930, is intended to be sung by a man.

55 Green Besoms

I am a besom maker,
Come listen to my song.
With a bundle of green besoms
I trudge the land along.
Sweet pleasures that I do enjoy
Both morning, night and noon
As I walk o'er the hills so high
A gathering of green broom.
    O come and buy my besoms,
    Bonny green, green besoms,
        Besoms fine and new,
    Bonny green-broom besoms,
        Better never grew.

One day as I was trudging
Down by my native cot
I saw a jolly farmer,
O happy is his lot.
He ploughs his furrows deep,
The seed he layeth low,
And there it bides asleep
Until the green broom blow.

One day as I was walking
'Twas down in yonder vale
I met Jack Spratt the miller
That taketh toll and tale.
His mill, O how it rattles,
The grist it grindeth clean.
I ease him of his jingling
By selling besoms green.

One day as I was walking
Across the hills so high
I saw the wealthy squire
Who hath a rolling eye.

I sing my song, he tips a wink,
And glad the squire did seem.
I ease him of his jingling chink
By selling besoms green.

One day as I was walking
Along the King's high-way
I met the parson riding
And ventured him to stay.
The parish tythe that is your due
Collecting you have been,
But tythe I'll also take of you
By selling besoms green.

O when the yellow broom is ripe
Upon its native soil
It's like a pretty baby bright
With sweet and wavily smile.
My cuts that make the besom
I bundle tight and spare
All honest folks to please 'em
I'm the darling of the fair.

B-G   Will Huggins (mason) at Lydford, November 1888

Chorus (*O come and buy* . . .) after each stanza.

　　2.8   *broom*: ms. *bloom*

　　A fragmentary version recovered by Sharp is as follows:

> One day when I was roving
> Over the hills so high
> I met a buxom farmer
> He had a rolling eye
> He tipped to me the wink
> And wrote to me the tune
> I'll ease him of his jingling
> In gathering of green brooms
>
> And who will buy my besoms
> It's besoms fine and new
> It's bonny green broom besoms
> Better never grew

I bundled up my besoms and I carried 'em to the fair
I sold them three a penny and I got money there
Now it's plough your furrow so deep and sow your corn so low
And there I leave him for to weep and the green besoms for to grow
And who will buy, etc.

(Mss. p. 617)

Another very confused version was noted by **H** at Hazelbury Bryan, Dorset, in 1906:

I am a besom maker, live down in yonder fields
I am a besom maker, live down in yonder hills
I ploughed my furrow deep, I laid my corn to keep
All over the hills so high a-gathering my green broom
   Who'll buy my besoms, besoms fine and new⎤
   Bonny old green besoms better never grew ⎦repeat

B-G prints in the *Garland* a version almost unaltered except for the total omission of stanza 5. The fact that he published it almost unaltered implies complete innocence as to its symbolic character: the same may be said of Heywood Sumner's *The Besom Maker and other Country Folk Songs*, London 1888, where the illustrations depict a *male* besom maker throughout. The besom maker is of course a female figure, and her activities, as indicated in the version above, are strictly immoral. Cf. note to *Gathering Rushes* (No. 48).

56 *Green Broom*

There was an old farmer lived down in the west,
His money and trade was all gone, all gone.
He had a lazy boy, Jack, for his son
And he lay in bed till noon, till noon,
And he lay in bed till noon.

The old man arose, in a passion he goes,
He swore he'd set fire to the room, the room,
If Jack didn't arise and sharp up his knife
And away to the woods to cut broom, green broom,
And away to the woods to cut broom.

And as Jack was a-walking along the highway
He came to the town of Perfume, Perfume,
And a lady looked out of her window so high,
A-bidding her servants to come, to come,
A-bidding her servants to come.

Go down, says she, and let the lad in,
For I fancy both him and his broom, green broom,
For I fancy both him and his broom.

Oh a lady I am and a lady by name,
I lives in this town of Perfume, Perfume,
And if you'll be married I'll be your offer
For I fancy both you and your broom, green broom,
For I fancy both you and your broom.

So Jack gave consent, to the parson he went,
He married the lady in bloom, in bloom.
Here is victuals and drink, boys, now what do you think?
I got it by selling of broom, green broom,
I got it by selling of broom.

G   Mr Richard Read at Bishop's Sutton by Alresford, Hants, n.d.

Ms. gives two rows of dots before the incomplete stanza 4.

Versions recovered in the north, east, south and west of England were published in various collections, all substantially the same as the above. **B-G** in *SW* printed a text emended in such a way as to give broom-cutting a literal, rather than a metaphorical, significance.   D'Urfey's *Pills to Purge Melancholy*, Vol. VI (1720) contains a long and discreetly suggestive version under the title *The Jolly Broom-man*.

57 *The Green Bushes*

'Twas early one morning in the month of May
To hear the birds whistle and see the lambs for to play.
I heard a young damsel, so sweetly sang she,
Down by the green bushes he thinks to meet me.

I'll bring you fine beavers, a gay silken gown,
And fine silken petticoats flounced to the ground
If you'll forsake him and come on with me
Down by the green bushes where he thinks to meet thee.

O none of your beavers, nor gay silken hose.
Dost thou think me so mean as to marry for clothes?
But if you'll prove constant and loyal to me
I'll forsake the green bushes and follow with thee.

Come let us be going, kind sir, if you please,
Come let us be hasting from under the trees,
For yonder he cometh, so cheerful, so free
For by the green bushes he thinks to meet me.

O when he came there and found she was gone
He looked so distressed and he stood all forlorn.
She is off with another and quite forsook me
So adieu ye green bushes for ever, said he.

I will be as a schoolboy, my time pass in play,
No false hearted maiden shall while me away.
No false hearted maiden shall trick me no more,
So adieu ye green bushes, 'tis time to give o'er.

B-G Robert Hards, South Brent, ?1888

B-G published an emended text in *SW*. Similar versions are given in *English County Songs* (Broadwood and Fuller Maitland, 1893), in *FSJ* 19, 1915, and elsewhere.

58 The Greenland Whale Fishery

We may no longer stay on shore
Since deep we are in debt
So off to Greenland let us steer
Some money, boys, to get, brave boys,
So to Greenland bear away.

In eighteen hundred and twenty four
On March the twenty-third
We hoist our colours to the mast head
And for Greenland bore away, brave boys,
And for Greenland bore away.

John Paigent was our captain's name,
Our ship the Lion bold.
We weighèd anchor at the bow
To face the storm and cold, brave boys,
And to Greenland bore away.

We were twelve gallant men on board
And to the north did steer,
Old England left we in our wake,
We sailors know not fear, brave boys,
And to Greenland bore away.

Our boatswain to the mast head went
With a spy-glass in his hand.
He cries, A whale! a whale-fish blows,
She blows at every span, brave boys,
And to Greenland bear away.

Our captain on the quarter-deck
A violent man was he,
He swore the devil should take us all
If that fish were lost to we, brave boys,
And to Greenland bear away.

Our captain on the quarter-deck
A violent man was he,
O'erhaul! o'erhaul! he loudly cried,
And launch our boat to sea, brave boys,
And to Greenland bear away.

Our boat being launched and all hands in
The whale was full in view,
Resolved was every sea-man bold
To steer where the whale-fish blew, brave boys,
And to Greenland bear away.

The whale was struck, the line paid out,
She gave a flash with the tail.
The boat capsized, we lost five men
And never caught the whale, brave boys,
And to Greenland bear away.

Bad news we to the captain brought,
We'd lost five prentice boys,
Then down his colours he did haul
At hearing the sad news, brave boys,
And from Greenland bore away.

The losing of the whale, said he,
Doth grieve my heart full sore,
But the losing of my five brave men
Doth grieve me ten times more, brave boys,
And from Greenland bore away.

The winter star doth now appear
So, boys, the anchor weigh,
'Tis time to leave the cold country
And for England bear away, brave boys,
And from Greenland bear away.

For Greenland is a barren place,
A land where grows no green
But ice and snow where the whale-fish blow
And the daylight's seldom seen, brave boys,
So for England bear away.

B-G R. Gregory at Two Bridges, January 1890

In his *Garland* **B-G** prints an emended and abridged text. At least two quite
different songs with this title appeared on broadsides. No conclusions can be
drawn from the date given in stanza 2, which appears to be entirely arbitrary.
B-G's printed text, for example, gives 'March 20, 1794'. A version given by
Sharp in *Folk Songs from Somerset*, III, 1906, gives 'March 18, 1861'.

59 *The Grey Cock*

A

Once I loved a lass and she lovèd not me
Because I was grown poor, poor a little, poor a little, poor,
But she all in good part hath stole away my heart
And she'll keep it for evermore.

When I came to my true love's door
I knocked both loud and sure, sure a little, sure a little, sure.
My love she arose and slippèd on her clothes
And came down and let me in.

When I behold my true love's arms
My heart grew cold and faint, faint a little, faint a little, faint.
I took her round her middle so small
And carried her to bed.

All the fore-part of the night
We did both sport and play, play so pretty, play so pretty, play,
And all the last part of the night
She sleeped in my arms till day.

My love she kept a cock and a pretty crowing cock
And it crowed in the morning so soon, soon so very, soon so
    very, soon.
My love she thought 'twas day and she hastened me away
But it proved to be the light of the moon.

The wind it did blow and the cocks they did crow
As I tripped over the plain, plain so very, plain so very, plain,
So I wished myself back in my true love's arms
And she in her bed again.

Now I'll prove so true to my own true love
As the stars all in the sky,
And if she should not prove the same by me
She's far better lost than won.

B

Oh once I loved a lass and she lovèd not me
Because I lookèd so poor
But she all in good part has stole away my heart
And will keep it for ever more.

It was under my true love's window one night,
Yo! there die I, hallo so shillo little shillo, little shillo.
My true love she arose and she slipped on her clothes
And so softaly she let me in.

Oh 'twas all the forepart of the night
We did both sport and play, play so pretty, play so pretty, play,
And all the last part of the night
She sleeped in my arms till day.

Now my father keeps a cock, and a wonderful cock
And he crows in the morning so soon.
I thought it had been day when I sent my love away
But it proved to be the light of the moon.

Now I'll prove so true to my love as the sun that do shine
Over the fallow, the fallow, fallow ground,
And if she's not true to me as I am true to she
I would rather she was losed than found.

H Version A   Farmer Mills at Knowle Farm, Beaminster, n.d.
Ms. gives title *Once I loved a Lass.*
Version B   Mr Barrett at Puddletown, Dorset, 1905
Ms. gives title *Oh! Once I loved a Lass.*

A 4 Ms. gives 'etc.' and nothing further after line 1. I have supplied the remainder of the stanza from B.

Version B is given in *DBFS* under the title *O once I loved a lass.* I have adopted the title of the ballad in Child (No. 248) because, although the connection is tenuous, it may well be that the first stanza ('Oh once I loved a lass', etc.) does not properly belong to the song at all. Both versions given above seem confused and corrupt, though certainly of medieval origin, as is indicated by the connection of A 6.3-4 with the famous 'Western wind' quatrain (Chambers and Sidgwick, *Early English Lyrics*). Child assumes the ballad to be an *aubade*, but in an article in the *Journal of American Folklore* (Vol. 67, No. 265, 1954) Dr Albert B. Friedman gives reasons for thinking that it concerns a *revenant* or lover's ghost, due to return to the world of the dead at cock-crow.

60 *The Grey Hawk*

A

I once loved a boy and a bonny sweet boy,
I loved him I vow and protest.
I loved him so well and so truly and well
That I built him a berth in my breast.

Then up the green forest and down the green grove
Like one is distracted in mind
I whooped and hallooed and I played on my pipe
But my bonny boy I could not find.

I lookèd East and I lookèd West,
The weather was pleasant and warm.
Then whom should I spy but my own bonny boy
So close in another maid's arm.

I passed him by and I ne'er cast an eye
Tho' he stretched forth his lily white hand.
I thought he'd been bound to love only I
So I would not attend his command.

The false one he once took me up on his knee
And he lookèd up right in my face,
And he gave a many dissembling kiss
But his heart was not in its right place.

The maid that is loved by my own bonny boy
For certain is greatly to blame,
For many's the night she hath robbèd my rest
But never shall do it again.

O since he is gone, why then let him go
Altho' that my heart ache and burn.
If he loveth another maid better than me
I hope he will never return.

B

Once I had a grey hawk and a pretty grey hawk,
A sweet pretty bird of my own,
And I got a little bell and tied it to her toe
Thinking she would fly not away,
But she took a flight, she flew away quite
And there's nobody knows where she's gone, my brave boys,
And there's nobody knows where she's gone.

It's over the wide forest I rambled away
And through the green fields I did stray.
I hollo'd, I hooped, I played on my flute,
Not my sweet pretty bird could I find, my brave boys,
Not my sweet pretty bird could I find.

Then it's over the greenhills I rambled away
And through the green paths I did stray.
Yo! there did I spy my sweet pretty bird,
She was close by the side of a man, my brave boys,
She was close by the side of a man.

Now he that has got her is welcome to keep her
And do the best with her he can,
But whiles he have her and I have her not
I will hawk with her once now and then, my brave boys,
I will hawk with her once now and then.

How happy's that man that hath a good wife,
Much better is he that's got none,
But cursèd is he that courteth another's
When he has a good wife of his own, my brave boys,
When he has a good wife of his own.

Version A **B-G** Sam Foxe, July 1897
Version B **H** Barrett at Puddletown, n.d.

In Version A the last line of each stanza is repeated as Chorus, and a line space is left blank after 2.2.

IP No. 65.

B-G published a somewhat different version of A in the revised edition of
SW, 1905, under the title *The Bonny Bird*. Version B was printed in *DBFS*.
I have adopted **H**'s title because I believe that his version, supposed to be sung
by a man, is the more authentic. The grey hawk, or goshawk, is a common
symbol of a faithless girl (cf. *The Jolly Goss-hawk*, in *SW*). Most printed texts
conform to the A version above, except that 'boy' is often replaced by 'bird'.
Some editors (e.g. Lucy Broadwood in *FSJ* 11, 1907, p. 85) have conjectured
that this 'bird' is a corruption of the medieval 'burd', i.e. maiden. But I
believe it refers to the 'grey hawk' of **H**'s version, and that its easy confusion
with 'boy' resulted in the composition by broadside writers in the late seventeenth century (e.g. BM 11621. k. 4, p. 45) of the 'female' version given above
as A, which gained wide currency.

61 *The Gypsy Countess*

A

There came an earl a riding by,
A gypsy maid espied he.
O nut brown maid, to her he said,
I prithee come away with me.

I'll take you up, I'll carry you home,
I'll put a safe-guard over you,
Your shoes shall be of the Spanish leather,
And silken stockings all of blue.

My brothers three no more I'll see
If that I went along with you.
I'd rather be torn by thistle and thorn
With my bare feet all in the dew.

I'll lock you up in a castle tall,
I'll bar you up in a room so high,
Thou gypsy maid from greenwood glade,
That ne'er a gypsy shall come by.

Thou shalt no more be set in stocks
And trudge about from town to town,
But thou shalt ride in pomp and pride
In velvet red and broidered gown.

I'll pawn my hat, I'll pawn my gown,
I'll pawn my ribbons, stockings blue.
I'll pawn my petticoat next my shift
To follow along with the gypsies O!

All night you lie 'neath the starry sky,
In rain and snow you walk all day,
But ne'er thy head shall have feather bed
And in thy arms no husband lay.

I love to lie 'neath a starry sky,
I do not heed the rain and snow,
And I will away, come night come day,
To follow along with my gypsies O!

I will thee wed, sweet maid, he said,
I will thee wed with a golden ring,
Then you shalt dance and merry, merry be
And I'll make thee a gay wedding.

I will not wed, kind sir, she said,
I will not wed with a golden ring,
For fickle as wind I fear I'll find
The man that would make my wedding.

Three gypsies stood at the castle gate,
They sang so high, they sang so low.
The lady sat in her chamber late,
Her heart it melted away as snow.

They sang so sweet, they sang so shrill
That fast her tears began to flow
And she laid down her golden gown,
Her golden rings and all her show.

And she put off her silken shoes
That were of Spanish leather O
All forth for to go in the rain and snow,
All forth in the stormy weather,
And down the stair came the lady fair
To go away with the gypsies O.

At past midnight her lord came home
And where his lady was would know.
All servants replied on every side,
She's gone away with the gypsies O.

Come saddle my horse, come saddle my mare
And hang my sword to my saddle bow.
That I may ride for to seek my bride
That is gone away with the gypsies O.

They saddled his horse, they saddled his mare
And hung his sword on his saddle bow
That he might ride for to seek his bride
That was gone away with the gypsies O.

Then he rode high, then he rode low,
He rode through hills and valleys O,
He rode till he spied his own fair bride
Following along with the gypsies O.

What makes you leave both house and lands,
What makes you leave your money O,
What takes you abroad from your wedded lord
To follow along with the gypsies O?

O I want none of your house and lands
And I want none of your money O,
Neither care I for my wedded lord,
I will follow along with the gypsies O.

Last night you slept in a feather bed
Rolled in the arms of your husband O
And now you must sleep on the cold, cold ground
And walk along in the rain and snow.

I care not to sleep in a feather bed
Rolled in the arms of a husband O,
Far rather I'd sleep on the cold, cold ground
And walk along in the rain and snow.

Nay, that shall not be, I swear, said he.
He drew his sword from his saddle bow,
And once he smote on her lily-white throat
And then her red blood down did flow.

B

There was seven gypsies all in a row
And they were brisk and bonny, oh.
They rode till they came to the Yellow Castle gates
And there they sang so sweetly, oh.

The Yellow Castle lady she came down
With a waiting-maid beside her, oh.
They gave to her a nut-brown bowl,
It was made the best of any, oh.

She gave to them a far better thing,
The ring from off her finger, oh.

And she pulled off her Highland boots,
They was made of Spanish leather, oh,
And she put on her Highland brogues
To follow the gypsy laddie, oh.

Now when the lord came home that night
Inquiring for his lady, oh,
The waiting-maid made this reply,
She's following the gypsy laddie, oh.

Then saddle me my milk-white steed
And bridle him so sweetly, oh.
That I might find my own wedded wife
That's following the gypsy laddie, oh.

Then he rode all that summer's night
And part of the next morning,
And then he spied his own wedded wife
Both cold and wet and weary.

Oh why did you leave your houses and lands,
Oh why did you leave your money, oh.
Why did you leave your own wedded lord
To follow the gypsy laddie, oh?

It's what care I for my houses and lands
Or what care I for my money, oh,
Or what care I for my own wedded lord?
I'll follow the gypsy laddie, oh.

There was seven gypsies all in a gang
And they were brisk and bonny, oh,
And they all had to be hanged all in a row
For stealing of the Yellow Castle lady, oh.

Version A **B-G** James Parsons, n.d.
Ms. gives no stanza divisions. Before 13.5 there are three dashes.
Version B **G** Mr James Watson, Portsmouth Workhouse, August 1907
Ms. gives title *The Gypsy Laddie*. Before 3.1 there are two rows of dots.

A 15.1 and 16.1 *mare*: ms. man

B-G printed in *SW* a considerably altered text. He gave the song in two parts, of which Part I corresponds to stanzas 1–10 above, and Part II to stanzas 11–22. In his notes he says that James Parsons sang the song straight through without a break. He also gives reasons for believing that Child was wrong to maintain that the song was originally Scottish. 'The Scotch are wont', he says, 'to take an old ballad, give it local habitation and name, and so make it out to be purely Scottish.'

The song appears in many collections as *The Gypsy Laddie, The Wraggle-Taggle Gypsies*, etc. Version B, above, corresponds closely to Child's G version (a transcription of Roxburghe III, 685). 'Yellow castle' in B is evidently a corruption of 'Earl of Castle's' in Child G, and 'Highland boots' in stanza 4 a corruption of 'high-heeled shoes'.

Child (No. 200) gives ten versions. **B-G** sent the above to Child, who comments as follows: 'The Rev. S. Baring-Gould has most obligingly sent me a ballad, taken down by him from the singing of an illiterate hedger in North Devon, in which "The Gypsy Laddie", recomposed, . . . forms the sequel to a story of an earl marrying a very reluctant gypsy maid . . . This little romance, retouched and repaired, is printed as No. 50 of Songs and Ballads of the West.' This is typical of Child's disdain for oral tradition.

Child gives an account of the supposed origin of the 'Gypsy Laddie' story in Scottish history, an account which **B-G** dismisses as apocryphal.

The first part of **B-G**'s 'little romance' (A 1–10) has not, so far as I know, been recovered by any other collector, or printed anywhere but in *SW*; but despite Child's scepticism and its own somewhat literary phraseology, it may well be authentic, and it gives a most satisfactory reason for the gypsy girl's behaviour, which in the standard versions has always seemed to me abrupt and unexplained. **B-G**'s 'illiterate hedger', James Parsons, could not have got his words from any written source, and we are told that he inherited his songs by oral tradition from his grandfather (*SW*, 1905, Introduction).

Two broadside texts, one by Such, in **B-G**'s collection (BM L.R. 271 a. 2, Vol. VI, p. 26 and Vol. I, p. 99) are similar to several of Child's, and show traces of Scottish influence.

62 *The Hal-an-Tow*

HELSTON FURRY DANCE

Robin Hood and Little John
They are both gone to the fair, O,
And we will go to the merry green wood
To see what they do there, O,
And for to chase O, then chase the buck and doe.
  With Hal-an-tow, jolly rumble-O!
  And we were up as soon as the day O,
  For to fetch the summer home,
  The summer and the may O,
  Now the winter is gone O.

Where are the Spaniards
That make so great a boast O?
Why they shall eat the grey goose feathers,
We will eat the roast O
In every land O, the land wherever we go.

As for the good knight St George,
St George he was a knight O,
Of all the knights in Christendom
St George he is the right O,
In every land O, the land wherever we go.

God bless Aunt Mary Moses
And all her power and might O
And send us peace in Merry England,
Send peace by day and night O,
To Merry England O, both now and ever mo'.

B-G No source given

Chorus repeated after each stanza.

No satisfactory explanation of the title has been given. It is thought to be a
corrupted Cornish word; support is lent to this by the derivation of 'Furry'
from a Celtic word used in Ireland for a long dance. 'Furry', perhaps more

properly 'Faddy', gained currency from its having been derived by classical antiquaries from the Latin 'feria'.

4.1 *Aunt Mary Moses*: the significance is obscure. There may be a reference either to the Virgin Mary or to a reigning sovereign, presumably the wife of William of Orange; or there may be a forgotten allusion to a local personage. Editors normally point out that in Cornwall 'aunt' is merely a term of affection or respect. On the other hand, the seventeenth-century meaning, 'prostitute' or 'procuress', may be appropriate. (See Autolycus' song, *A Winter's Tale*, IV. 2, 11.) This meaning may well apply to 'Aunt Ursula Birdwood' in *The Padstow May Song* B (p. 207).

Cecil Sharp (*The Morris Book*, Part V, Novello 1913) gives an account of the Furry Dance as recollected by a performer who took part in it in the late nineteenth century. As well as the dancers, there was a mock-mayoral procession in which one of the figures was 'an old woman, known as Aunt Mary Moses, covered from head to foot with flowers, riding a donkey and followed by a man beating a large drum with great ardour'. Presumably this female figure was a man dressed as a woman.

This song is part of the May celebrations at Helston in Cornwall, where the famous dance is performed on Furry Day, May 8. **B-G**'s note in *SW* reads, 'The "Helston Furry Dance" is a relic of part of the Old English May Games. These originally comprised four entirely distinct parts. 1st. The election and procession of the King and Queen of the May, who were called the Summer King and Queen. 2nd. The Morris Dance, performed by men disguised, with swords in their hands. 3rd. The "Hobby Horse". 4th. The "Rob Hood".

'In the Helston performance we have a fragment only of the original series of pageants; at Padstow the Hobby-horse still figures.' (See No. 104.)

A description of the Helston festivities was given by a writer in *The Gentleman's Magazine* for June 1790 (quoted in Brand's *Popular Antiquities*, revised Ellis, London 1849):

'At Helston, a genteel and populous borough-town in Cornwall, it is customary to dedicate the eighth of May to revelry (festive mirth, not loose jollity). It is called the Furry Day, supposed Flora's Day; not, I imagine, as many have thought, in remembrance of some festival instituted in honour of that goddess, but rather from the garlands commonly worn on that day. In the morning, very early, some troublesome rogues go round the streets with drums, or other noisy instruments, disturbing their sober neighbours, and singing parts of a song, the whole of which nobody now recollects, and of which I know no more than that there is mention in it of "the grey goose quill", and of going to the green wood to bring home "the Summer and the May-o". And, accordingly, hawthorn flowering branches are worn in hats. The commonalty make it a general holiday; and if they find any person at work, make him ride on a pole, carried on men's shoulders, to the river, over which he is to leap in a wide place, if he can; if he cannot, he must leap in, for leap he must, or pay money. About nine o'clock they appear before the school, and demand holiday for the Latin boys, which is invariably granted;

after which they collect money from house to house. About the middle of the day they collect together, to dance hand-in-hand round the streets, to the sound of the fiddle, playing a particular tune, which they continue to do till it is dark. This they call a "Faddy". In the afternoon the gentility go to some farmhouse in the neighbourhood, to drink tea, syllabub, &c., and return in a morris-dance to the town, where they form a Faddy, and dance through the streets till it is dark, claiming a right of going through any person's house, in at one door, and out at the other. And here it formerly used to end, and the company of all kinds to disperse quietly to their several habitations; but latterly corruptions have in this, as in other matters, crept in by degrees. The ladies, all elegantly dressed in white muslins, are now conducted by their partners to the ballroom, where they continue their dance till supper-time; after which they all faddy it out of the house, breaking off by degrees to their respective houses. The mobility imitate their superiors, and also adjourn to the several public-houses, where they continue their dance till midnight. It is, upon the whole, a very festive, jovial, and withal so sober, and, I believe, singular custom.'

63 *Hares on the Mountains*

Oh Kitty walked out all in her best order
With her pink petticoat calico border.
    Shepherd so bold, shepherd so bold,
    Singing right fal the lal lal, right fal the lal li do,
    Shepherd so bold.

When I was young I sat in my palour.
Now I'm growed old I'm rambling in the corner.

If young women were ducks, they'd swim on the water.
All the young men would strip and swim after.

If young women were hares, they'd run on the mountain.
All the young men would soon ride a-hunting.

If young women were lambs, they'd lie on the common.
All the young men would lie alongside on 'em.

H John Seaward at Charmouth, April 1906

Chorus repeated after each stanza.

   2.1 *palour*: pronounced paylor (note in ms.)

IP No. 38.

   It is not certain whether this is, properly speaking, a version of *Hares on the Mountains* or a different song employing part of it.

64 *High Germany*

Abroad as I was walking and a-talking all alone
I heard two lovyers talking and singing a fine song.
Said the younger one unto the fair one, Bonnie lass, I'll away,
For the king he have needed us and his orders we must obey.

That's not what you promised me when you did me beguile.
You promised that you would marry me when you got me with
    child,
So it's do not forsake but pity on me take, for great is my woe,
Through France, Spain and even Ireland along with you I will go.

Those long weary travellings they will cause you to weep,
Those hills and lofty mountains they will blister your tender feet,
And besides you will not yield to lying in an open field with me all
    night long,
Your parents they will be angry if along with me you will gang.

My friends I do not value, nor my foes I do not fear,
But along with my jolly soldier boy I will ramble far and near.
It's gold shall never deceive me nor any other man, but along with
    you I will go
For to fight the French or the Spaniards or any other daring foe.

For since you've been so venturesome as to venture your sweet life
First of all I will marry you and make you my lawful wife,
And if anyone offend you I will attend you, that you shall see,
You shall hear the drums and the trumpets sound in the wars of
    High Germany.

G Mrs King at Lyndhurst, Hants, June 1906

   5.3 *attend*: ms. suggests defend.

This is not the *High Germany* of IP No. 43 but a different treatment of the
same theme. Decorous versions are given by **B-G** in the *Garland*, by **H** in
HFD, and by E. J. Moeran in *FSJ* 26, 1922. The above version has appeared
on broadsides. **B-G** in his note in the *Garland* says: 'This song, in hopelessly
bad metre and of no poetic merit, is given with only some slight modifications
to suit *les convenances*.'

65 The Highwayman

A

I went to London both blithe and gay,
My time I wasted in bowls and play
Until my cash it did get low
And then on the highway I was forced to go.

O next I took me a pretty wife,
I loved her dear as I loved my life,
But for to maintain her both fine and gay
Resolved I was that the world should pay.

I robbed Lord Edgcumbe I do declare
And Lady Templar of Melbourne Square.
I bade them good night, sat in my chair,
With laughter and song went to my dear.

I robbed them of five hundred pounds so brigh
But all of it squandered one jovial night,
Till taken by such as I never knew,
But I was informed they were Fielding's crew.

The judge his mercy he did extend,
He pardoned my crime, bade me amend,
But still I pursued a thriving trade.
I always was reckoned a roving blade.

O now I'm judged and doomed to die
And many a maid for me will cry,
For all their sighs and for all salt tear
Where I shall go the Lord knows where.

My father he sighs and he makes his moan,
My mother she weeps for her darling son,
But sighs and tears will never save
Nor keep me from an untimely grave.

B

I am a wild and wicked youth,
I love young women and that's the truth,
I love them dearly, I love them well,
I love them better than tongue can tell.

I never robbed not a poor man yet,
I never caused any tradesman to fret.
I robbed Lord Golding, I do declare,
I left him bleeding in Grosvenor Square.

'Twas about seventeen I took a wife,
I loved her dearly as I loved my life,
And to maintain her both fine and gay
I went a robbing on the highway.

Six pretty maidens shall carry you,
Six pretty maidens shall bury you,
Six pretty maidens shall bear your pall,
Give them white gloves and pink ribbons all.

So it's dig me a grave both large, wide and deep
And a marble stone at my head and feet
And in the centre a turtle dove
To show mankind I died for love.

Version A **B-G** James Townsend at Holne, who learned it from his grandfather, William Ford, who died about seventy in 1887
Version B **G** Mr Charles Woodhouse at Micheldever, Hants, May 1906

Ms. gives title *I am a Wild and a Wicked Youth*. Last two lines of each stanza
repeated as Chorus.

A 4.4 *Fielding*: Henry Fielding was appointed chief magistrate of West-
minster in 1748. His work of suppressing crime was carried on
after his death in 1754 by his blind half-brother, Sir John Fielding,
who died in 1780.

IP No. 78.

Printed in several collections under various titles, e.g. *Newlyn Town* and *The
Robber*. It is indexed under the latter title in Margaret Dean-Smith's *Guide to*

English Folk Song Collections, 1954, which gives a succinct account of what is well described as the archetype of the execution ballad. The names in A 3 and B 2 vary considerably from version to version.

66 *Hunting the Hare*

I hunted my merry all into the hay,
The hare was before, the dogs 'Ware away'.
  Hickerly tout, ticklesome trout,
  Hipperly, tipperly eversheen nipperly,
  Eversheen tantivy vandigo van.
  'Twas up the hill, down the fern,
  Here a step, there a turn,
  Turn and sing merrily.
  Hunt hounds, now turn.

I hunted my merry all into the barley
And there the poor hare was pursued by dog Snarley.

I hunted my merry all into the wheat
And there the poor hare began us to cheat.

I hunted my merry all into the rye
And then the poor hare was constrained to die.

I hunted my merry all into the oats
And there the hounds tore out the poor puss's guts.

B-G William Nankivel at Merrivale Bridge, September 29, 1890

Chorus repeated after each stanza.

  1.6 *fern*: reading doubtful, but perhaps 'form', meaning a hare's nest. **B-G** gives 'form' in the printed version.

B-G printed a slightly emended text in the first two editions of *S W*. I can find the song in no other collection. **B-G** describes it as an early seventeenth-century dance, but has no comment to make on the words.

67 *I am a Brisk Young Sailor*

I am a brisk young sailor, all on the seas I'm bound.
For fourteen years and over the ocean I have ploughed
But I value neither storm nor danger by the breaking of the seas
Till at length I was conquered and a captive I must be.

Our ship she is on the ocean and likewise in full sail
From Linstown up to London with a sweet and pleasant gale
And if providence do go with us and fortune do prove kind
I'll be back again to Linstown in fifteen days' fair wind.

And when we gets to Linstown at the Putney we will dine
And there I'll toss a bumper of brandy, ale and wine.
I will free-like spend ten guineas and down it shall be paid
If I could enjoy young Nancy, that handsome chambermaid.

I can't think what's come to me that I should love a child.
I can't think what's come to me that I should be beguiled,
But if I was ten years younger and she as old as me
I would make myself more bolder and speak my mind more free.

Now since I cannot marry the girl that I adore
I'll go and plough the ocean and never come on shore.
I will list unto some country where no one do me know,
Then perhaps my mind may alter, I wish it might be so.

G Mr Richard Hall at Itchen Abbas, Hants, n.d.

68 *I am a Coachman*

I am a coachman out on the high road,
A-kissing and courting is all my mode.
I kiss them, I court them, I lie by their side,
And when I am tired I get up and ride.
 Derry down
 Down down derry down.

I am a blacksmith, the king of good fellows,
I work at the anvil while the man blows the bellows
My iron is good and so are my coals,
And all my delight is in stopping of holes.
 Derry down
 Down down derry down.

I am a fisherman, fisherman Ann
Shall I fish in your fish-pan?
I fished for a roach but I did get a tench,
I tried for a boy but I did get a wench.
 Derry down
 Down down derry down.

H   John Hallett at Mosterton, June 1906

Probably incomplete, since the catalogue of trades, each with its metaphorical sexual significance, may be extended indefinitely. I have not seen this elsewhere, but ribald songs on similar lines are in current circulation.

69 *I'm Going up to London*

I'm going up to London, I'll tell you all how,
On horseback, on horseback, it's on a dun cow.
A white tail, a white mane, a white list on her back,
And there's not a hair on her but what is coal black.
Singing fol le rol liddle oh laddle oh liddle oh,
Fol le rol liddle oh laddle li day.

Oh when I got there, no soul could I see,
But people in clusters stood laughing at me,
Stood laughing and chaffing and making their game
To see my feet off and my shoes going lame.

My horse threw me off, 'twas clean in the dirt,
He damaged my skin and he bruised my shirt.
I hustled and tassled, I mounted again,
And with my ten toes I crept over the plain.

On Saturday night I was going through the park,
One moonshiny morning one night when 'twas dark,
My coat being on, my boots lacèd up,
My hat in my hand to keep my head warm.

G Mr Isaac Hobbes at Micheldever, Hants, May 1906

Chorus repeated after each stanza.

A typical song of 'lies and marvels', this is a version of *In Nottamun Town* (Sharp: *Nursery Songs of the Appalachian Mountains*). Cf. *As I set off to Turkey* (No. 4).

70 *I Live not Where I love*

Come all you maids that live at a distance
Many a mile from off your swain,
Come and assist me this very moment
For to pass away some time,
Singing sweetly and completely
Songs of pleasure and of love.
My heart is with you altogether
Though I lives not where I love.

O when I sleeps I dreams about you,
When I wake I take no rest,
For every instant thinking on you
My heart e'er fixèd in your breast,
O this cold absence seems at a distance
And many a mile from my true love,
But my heart is with her altogether
Though I live not where I love.

So farewell lads and farewell lassies,
Now I think I've got my choice,
I will away to yonder mountains
Where I think I hear his voice.
And if he holloa I will follow
Around the world that is so wide,
For young Thomas he did promise
I shall be his lawful bride.

Now if all the world was of one religion,
Every living thing should die,
Or if I prove false unto my jewel
Or any way my love deny,
The world shall change and be most strange
If ever I my mind remove.
My heart is with her altogether
Though I live not where I love.

H Mr Barrett at Puddletown, n.d.

3.6 *that is*: supplied from broadside BM L.R. 271 a. 2, Vol. IV, p. 454.
4.2 *Every*: sc. And if every.

71 *I Rode my Little Horse*

I rode my little horse, from London town I came.
I went into the country to seek myself a dame,
And if I find a pretty maid, be sure I'll kiss her then,
I'll swear that I will marry her but will not tell her when.

I found a buxom widow with many tons of gold,
I lived upon her fortune as long as it would hold.
I borrowed pounds a hundred, bestrode my horse and then
I swore that I would marry her but would not tell her when.

A vintner had a daughter, the Golden Sun his sign.
I tarried at his tavern and drank up all his wine.
I tapped his richest hogsheads, bestrode my horse and then
I swore the maid I'd marry but would not tell him when.

The guineas are expended, the wine is also spent.
The widow and the maiden, they languish and lament,
And if they come to seek me I'll pack them back again,
I'll promise them I'll marry them but will not tell them when.

B-G Edmund Fry, thatcher, at Lydford, 1889

B-G printed this in *SW*, slightly emended and with a fifth stanza in which the hero finds a maiden whom he consents to marry; this may or may not be of his own composition.

72 *I Sowed some Seeds*

When first to London town I came
I being a stranger I knew not one,
I took my lodging up to some inn.
For full five months I did remain,
I did remain, I did remain.

The landlord had one daughter dear,
She was a beauty, I do declare,
But above her garter I dare not go
For I was a stranger, I fell in danger
For doing so, for doing so.

Her ruby lips, her eyes so blue
Which causèd me to love her true,
The more I kissed her, this girl being young,
The more I kissed, her eyes did glister
Just like the rising of the sun.

In yonder grove I sowed my seed,
In yonder grove I fared away
And for to reap it I could not stay
For being a stranger, I fell in danger,
I ran away, I ran away.

H   Ishmael Cornich, Dorset, 1906

Ms. gives title *When first to London town I came.*

1.5   *I did remain*: phrase given once only in ms.
4.3   *stay*: ms. say

A slightly fuller version than *IP* No. 45. I have not seen the song elsewhere.

73 *I will Give my Love an Apple*

I will give my love an apple without e'er a core,
I will give my love a house without e'er a door.
I will give my love a palace wherein she may be
And she may unlock it without e'er a key.

My head is the apple without e'er a core,
My mind is the house without e'er a door,
My heart is the palace wherein she may be
And she may unlock it without e'er a key.

I will give my love a cherry without e'er a stone,
I will give my love a chick without e'er a bone,
I will give my love a ring, not a rent to be seen,
I will get my love children without any crying.

When the cherry's in blossom there's never no stone,
When the chick's in the womb there's never no bone,
And when they're rinning running not a rent to be seen,
And when they're child-making they're seldom crying.

H Mr J. Burrows at Sherborne, 1906

The first two stanzas appear in Novello's School Series vii; and *FSJ* 11, 1907,
gives all four stanzas slightly emended, the 'child-making' of the final line
being changed to '[love-making]'. *DBFS* gives the words unaltered.

Ballads and folk-tales on the theme of a riddling courtship are common—
e.g. *There was a lady in the west* (*English County Songs*, Broadwood and Fuller
Maitland). The 'cherry' and 'chick' questions in stanzas 3 and 4 above occur
in *Captain Wedderburn's Courtship* (Child No. 46). Child refers to the early
15th-century song (BM, Sloane 2593) which, slightly modernized, is as
follows:

> I have a young sister far beyond the sea.
> Many be the dowries that she sent me.
> She sent me the cherry without any stone
> And so she did dove without any bone.
> She sent me the briar without any rind.
> She bade me love my leman without longing.
> How could any cherry be without stone?
> And how could any dove be without bone?
> How could any briar be without rind?

How could I love my leman without longing?
When the cherry was a flower, then had it no stone.
When the briar was unbred, then had it no rind.
When the dove was an egg, then had it no bone.
When the maiden hast that she love, she is without longing.

Whether the ballad of *Captain Wedderburn* was written round the song, or the song became detached from the ballad, is impossible to say.

See also my note on *Pery Mery Winkle Domine* (*IP* No. 73).

The explanation of the ring without a rent is that, when it is rolled or spun, the join is invisible.

74 *If I Was a Blackbird*

I am a poor girl and my fortune seems sad,
Six months have I courted a young sailor lad,
And truly I loved him by night and by day,
And now in his transport he's sailed far away.

Chorus If I was a blackbird, could whistle and sing,
   I'd follow the vessel my true love sails in,
   And on the top rigging there I'd build my nest
   And lay my head all night on his lily-white breast.

My love's tall and handsome in every degree.
His parents despise him because he loves me.
But let them despise him or say what they will,
While I've breath in my body I'll love my true love still.

He promised he'd meet me at Bonnybrook fair
With a bunch of blue ribbon to tie up my hair,
And if he would meet me I'd crown him with joy
And kiss those fond lips of my dear young sailor boy.

If I was a scholar, could handle my pen,
Just one private letter to him I would send.
I'd write and I'd tell him of my sad grief and woe
And far o'er the water with my true love I would go.

G Mrs Etheridge at Southampton, June 25, 1906 and Mr Alfred Fulford, near Lyndhurst Road Station, Hants, December 1, 1906

Chorus after each stanza.

IP No. 47.

A similar version, omitting stanza 3, is given in *Songs from the Countryside*, Collinson and Dillon, 1946.

75 *Illsdown Fair*

Joe Maybie, Joe Maybie, lend me your old mare,
 All along, all along ay,
That we might ride over to Illsdown Fair,
 Ding along, ding along day,
 When Bill Brewers, Jack Stewers, Harry Hawkins, Dick Josie,
 Harry Olive, Tom Powell, Dick Chapman, Ben Blackman,
 And our uncle, Joe Maybie and all,
 And our uncle, Joe Maybie and all.

When will you return again?
 All along . . .
On Friday noon or Saturday soon,
 Ding along . . .

Friday's gone and Saturday's come,
 All along . . .
Joe Maybie's mare is still standing there,
 Ding along . . .

They throws the reins all over her head,
 All along . . .
When Joe Maybie's old mare she drops down dead there,
 Ding along . . .

G Mr Thomas Cooper at Itchen by Southampton, November 1907

A fragmentary version of the song first given national popularity by **B-G** under the title *Widdecombe Fair*, printed in *SW*.

Sharp also collected two versions in Somerset under the title *Midsummer Fair* with the final chorus line 'To my oore bag boor, bag nigger bag a wallah and bantaballoo'. **B-G** claimed that the song was a Devon one and that all the characters in the chorus were Devon men, including 'Uncle Tom Cobbleigh', whose home he identified. If this is so, when the song was transferred to Hampshire, Cobbleigh was evidently metamorphosed into some local worthy. **G** collected two versions of *Illsdown Fair*, of which the other, taken down from Mr Thomas Hounsome at Alresford, is very nearly the same except for the names in the chorus. Mr Hounsome's list is: 'Bill Brewer, Jack Stewart, Harry Hawkins, Dick Chelsea, Harry Olive, Tom Bowles, Dick Chapman, Ben Blackman and your uncle Joe Maybie, etc.'

76 'Twas Through the Groves

'Twas through the groves the other day
One morning by the break of day,
'Twas there I heard a fair maid say,
The lad I love is gone astray.

O hark, O hark, what voice I hear,
I think it is my dearest dear.
If I had wings I would fly to him
To see what love, true love could bring.

If I had a lock fixed to my breast
I'd keep it locked whilst life shall last,
With a golden lock and a silver key
To keep my heart from going astray.

Over hills and dales and shady rocks
Where shepherds do attend their harmless flocks,
Over hills and dales and valleys low
The hills and dales were covered with snow.

On the banks of lilies I lay my head,
The heavens above shall be my comrade.
There I will lay till the break of day,
The harmless lambs shall around me play.

G Mr Daniel Wigg at Preston Candover by Alresford, Hants, July 1907

77 Jinny Jan

Come to see Jinny, Jan? Jinny, Jan? Jinny, Jan?
Come to see Jinny?
                Can I see her now?
Jinny is washing, washing, washing, Jan,
Jinny is washing, Jan, you can't see her now.
Chorus
   Morning, ladies and gentlemen too,
   Morning, ladies and gentlemen too
   Come to see Jinny, Jan? Jinny, Jan? Jinny, Jan?
   Come to see Jinny and can't see her now.

Come to see Jinny, Jan? Jinny, Jan? Jinny, Jan?
Come to see Jinny?
                Can I see her now?
Jinny is married, married, married, Jan,
Jinny is married, and she's nought to you.
Chorus

Come to see Jinny, Jan? Jinny, Jan? Jinny, Jan?
Come to see Jinny?
                Can I see her now?
Jinny's dead indeed, dead indeed, dead indeed,
Jinny is dead indeed, I swear and vow.
Chorus

Come to see Jinny, Jan? Jinny, Jan? Jinny, Jan?
Come to see Jinny?
                Can I see her now?
Jinny is buried, buried, buried, Jan,
Jinny is buried, to all our woe.
Chorus

Come to see Jinny, Jan? Jinny, Jan? Jinny, Jan?
Come to see Jinny?
                Where lies she now?
Jinny's grave is green, grave is green, grave is green,
Jinny's grave is green with the tears that flow.

B-G   Stanzas 1 to 4 sent by 'a Mr Webber who heard it sung on Christmas Eve at a farmhouse in Bramford Speke in 1864. Known in other parts of Devon; it is enacted by several parties.'

A version of the children's singing game of 'Jenny Jones', of which many variants are given in Lady Gomme's *Traditional Games* (Vol. I, 1894). The game is a dialogue between Jenny's mother and a group of callers, and is in essence a mock funeral. In some versions the dead Jenny comes to life in the form of a ghost and pursues the mourners. I have adopted **B-G**'s punctuation, by which it appears as if there are two persons, 'Jinny' and 'Jan', but in all the other versions these two names are combined, e.g. 'Jenny Jones', 'Janet jo', 'Georgina'.

78 Jolly Old Hawk

I went to my lady the first of May,
O jolly goss-hawk and his wings were grey.
O who will marry my fair lady,
O who will marry her, you or I?

I went to my lady the second of May,
A two twitty bird, a jolly goss-hawk and his wings were grey,
O who will marry . . .

I went to my lady the third of May,
A three drusky cock, a two twitty bird . . .
O who will marry . . .

I went to my lady the fourth of May,
A four legged pig, a three drusky cock . . .
O who will marry . . .

I went to my lady the fifth of May,
Five steers, a four legged pig . . .
O who will marry . . .

I went to my lady the sixth of May,
Six boars, five steers . . .
O who will marry . . .

I went to my lady the seventh of May,
Seven cows, six boars . . .
O who will marry . . .

I went to my lady the eighth of May,
Eight bulls roaring, seven cows . . .
O who will marry . . .

I went to my lady the ninth of May,
Nine cocks crowing, eight bulls roaring . . .
O who will marry . . .

I went to my lady the tenth of May,
Ten carpenters sawing, nine cocks crowing . . .
O who will marry . . .

I went to my lady the eleventh of May,
Eleven shepherds yawing, ten carpenters sawing . . .
O who will marry . . .

I went to my lady the twelfth of May,
Twelve old women scolding, eleven shepherds yawing . . .
O who will marry . . .

B-G   Taken down by I. D. Prickman from Harry Westaway at Prestacott, Belstone, 1889

Ms. gives title *The Jolly Goss-hawk*.

   3.2   *drusky*: as in ms., but **B-G** gives 'dushy' in notes to *Songs of the West*, No. 71. He offers no explanation
   10 and 11   *sawing, yawing*: These two words reversed in ms. *yawing*: ewe-ing

IP No. 51. See notes.

79 *The Keys of Heaven*

A

O will you accept of the mus-el-ine so blue
To wear all in the morning and to dabble in the dew?
No I will not accept of the mus-el-ine so blue
To wear all in the morning and to dabble in the dew,
     Nor I'll walk nor I'll talk with you.

O will you accept of the pretty silver pin
To pin your golden hair with the fine muselin?
No I will not accept . . .

O will you accept a pair of shoes of cork,
The one is made in London and the other's made in York?
No I will not accept . . .

O will you accept of the keys of Canterbury
That all the bells in England may sing and make us merry?
No I will not accept . . .

O will you accept of a kiss from loving heart
That we may be together and never more may part?
Yes I will accept of a kiss from loving heart
That we may be together and never more may part
     And I'll walk and I'll talk with you.

B

My man John, what can the matter be?
I love a lady and she won't love me.
Peace, sir, peace, and do not despair.
The lady you love will be your only care
     And it must be gold that will win her.

Madam will you accept of this golden ball
To walk in the garden or in my lady's hall?
Sir I will accept of no golden ball
To walk in the garden or in my lady's hall
　　　　Neither will I walk nor talk with you.

Madam will you accept of a petticoat of red
With six golden flounces around it outspread?
Sir I will not accept of no . . .

Madam will you accept of the keys of my heart,
To join, to join together and never more to part?
Sir I will accept of no . . .

Madam will you accept of the keys of my chest
To get at my money whenever you think best?
Sir I will accept of the keys of your chest
To get at your money whenever I think best,
　　　　And I will walk and talk with you.
My man John, here's a bag of gold for you,
For that which you have told me has come true,
　　　　And it was gold, it was gold did win her.

B-G　Version A　J. Woodrich, Wollacott Moor, Thriskleton (?), black-
smith, n.d.
　　Version B　Sent by Miss F. Crossing as sung by a Devon nurse at
Teignmouth, 1850

Ms. gives title *Blue Muslin*.

First stanza in Version B repeated as Chorus after stanzas 2, 3 and 4.

For other texts and notes, see *IP* No. 54.

　This song, with a bewildering wealth of variants, has been recovered in
many parts of Britain, as well as in the Appalachian Mountains. It appears to
have originated as part of a singing game, sometimes with dancing. It has been
suggested that the tempter is the devil, and that the coach and six pitch-black
horses which are offered in one of the versions (Broadwood and Fuller Maitland, *English County Songs*) suggest the lady's approaching funeral.

80 *Lamkin*

Says the lord to lady, I'm going out from home.
Beware of false Lankie till I do return.

What cares I for false Lankie or any of his kin
When the doors are all bolted and the shutters all pinned.

False Lankie stepped in the dead hour of the night
When there was no fire burning nor any candle light.

He pinched the poor baby, which made it to cry
While the nurse she sat singing, Lullaby baby by.

Oh come dearest lady and take it in thy lap
For I cannot pacify it with breast milk nor pap.

As she was a-getting from the bed that was warm
False Lankie stood by for to catch her in his arms.

Where is your daughter Betsy? She might be some good
To hold the silver basin to catch your heart's blood.

As Betsy was a-looking from the window so high
She saw her own father come a-riding close by.

Oh father, oh father, don't lay the blame on me.
False Lankie, false Lankie have a-murdered your lady and baby.

False Lankie shall be hung on the gallows so high,
The nurse shall be burned in the fire close by.

The bells shall be muzzled and the dismal knell sound
For the lady and the baby lie asleep in the ground

G   Mrs Goodyear at Axford, Basingstoke, Hants, August 1907

3.1 *stepped in*: **G** suggests stepped in in
5.2 *breast milk*: ms. breast, milk
7.1 *daughter Betsy*: ms. daughter, Betsy
11.1 *knell*: ms. shall. Emendation suggested by **G**
11.2 *ground*: ms. tomb. Emendation suggested by **G**

A corrupt and relatively late version of the ballad in Child (No. 93). In a detailed study (*JEFDSS* 1932) A. G. Gilchrist distinguishes two separate ballads, the earlier one being concerned with a mason who revenges himself upon his noble employer for not paying his wages; the later version concerns a notorious marauder, the motives for whose inhuman conduct are not made clear.

81 *The Lark in the Morn*

A

As I was walking one morning in May
I heard a fair damsel these words for to say.
Of all the callings, whatever they may be,
There's no life like the ploughboy's all in the month of May.

The lark in the morn she rises from her nest
And mounts in the air with the dew upon her breast
And with the pretty ploughboy she'll whistle and she'll sing
And at night she'll return to her nest back again.

When the ploughboy has done all that he has to do
Perhaps to the country wake awalking he'll go,
And there with his lassie he'll dance and he'll sing
And at night they'll return to their home back again.

And as they return from the wake to the town
The meadows being mown and the grass all cut down
If they should chance to tumble all on the new mown hay,
O kiss me now or never, this pretty maid would say.

When twenty long weeks was over and past
Her mammy asks the reason why she's thickened in the waist.
It was the pretty ploughboy, the damsel do say
He caused me to tumble all on the new mown hay.

So good luck to a ploughboy wherever he may be
Who likes to have a lassie to sit upon his knee.
With a jug of strong beer he'll whistle and he'll sing,
And the ploughboy is so happy as a prince or a king.

B

It was down in a valley by the side of a grove
By a clear crystal fountain I saw my true love.
Where the birds they were a-whistling and the lambs they were
    a-playing
On the banks of sweet violets she carelessly did lay.

When first I did view my love she did my heart surprise
With the blooming of her cheeks and the sparkling of her eyes.
Young Cupid he proved cruel, he acted his part.
The loss of young Nancy, this wounded my heart.

All in some dreadful torments we were forced to remain
Like a thief we'd be better bound down in some chain.
No rest night or day could my heart ever find
For the loss of young Nancy that troubled my mind.

Go fetch me pen and paper that I may go and write
To my beautiful Nancy, my joy and heart's delight.
Young Nancy she's charming, she's comely and fair,
No one in this country like Nancy my dear.

The lark all in the morning she fly into the air,
She bring me joyful tidings from Nancy my dear.
My Nancy she's charming, she's comely and fair.
There's no one in this country can whistle like Nancy my dear.

The lark all in the morning she rise from her nest,
She mount into the air with the dew all round her breast.
To those pretty ploughboys she whistle and sing
And at night she return to her own nest back again.

Version A H George Roper at Blandford, Dorset, 1905
Version B G Mr Henry Braxton at Micheldever, Hants, April 1906 (an almost identical text from Mr Samuel Bull at Marchwood by Southampton, June 1907)

A Ms. gives title *The Ploughboy*, B gives title *The Lark in the Morning*.

B 2.3 *acted his part*: as in ms. but **G** adds notes to the effect that 'acted' is an emendation of the singer's 'thragged', which is 'not a word', and that 'dart' is a possible alternative for 'part'.

IP No. 56. See notes.

B-G gives a polite version in his *Garland*, and maintains, as did other collectors of his time, that the 'objectionable' stanzas are extraneous, belonging only to broadside publication and not oral tradition. He states that the broadside version begins 'As I was a-walking one morning in May' and goes on to say, 'But I have never heard any singers begin thus. They have invariably started with "The lark in the morn".' This must be read in the light of version A, above, taken down from a Blandford singer. It is quite unwarrantable to assume that the 'objectionable' stanzas, or any other stanzas, derive from the broadsides. It seems more probable that the latter derive from oral tradition.

Version B is evidently a different song which has become confused with *The Lark in the Morn*.

82 *The Lawyer*

The lawyer he rode out one day
And he rode out for pleasure
And who should he spy but a fair pretty maid,
She was both handsome, tall and clever.

Where are you going, my fair pretty maid,
Where are you going so early?
I'm going, kind sir, down in yonders green grove
For my father's a-mowing of barley.

The lawyer being a nimble young youth
He quickly followed her after,
He takes her round the middle so small
And down on the green grass he laid her.

Hold up your hand, my fair pretty maid,
And hold it up for pleasure.
Here's all for this, here's one sweet kiss,
My two handfuls of gold and silver.

Oh keep thy gold and silver too,
No more will I go a-roaming,
For 'tis all such rogues and rascals as you
That brings all pretty maidens to ruin.

I'd sooner be a poor carter man's wife
Sitting up at my window spinning
Than I would be a lawyer's maid
Dressed up in the finest of linen.

G   Mr Henry Adams at Basingstoke, Hants, September 1906

Last two lines of each stanza repeated as Chorus.

Cf. *IP* No. 64 (*Mowing the Barley*).

   I have not seen the above version elsewhere. The maiden's spirited rejection of the lawyer is a better ending than that given by Sharp. A similar text to the above, collected by **H**, is given in *DBFS* under the title *Lawyer's Wife*, in which the girl prefers the wash-tub (rather than the spinning-wheel) to a seat in the alehouse as the wife of a lawyer.

83 *Let the Hills and Valleys be Covered with Snow*

A

Awake, awake you drowsy sleeper,
Awake, awake, for 'tis almost day.
How can you sleep, love, any longer
Since you have stole my poor heart away?

Awake, awake! How dark thy window,
In shade and silence I exclaim,
It is a youth that loves you dearly,
Come down and ease me of my pain.

Her father heard of their conclusions,
Softel-y he jumps out of bed.
He popped his head out of the window
And there he heard all what they said.

Oh daughter dear, tell me the reason
In your bedroom you can't take no rest.
I will confine you in your chamber
And unto the seas your love I'll press.

You won't confine me in my chamber
Nor my true love you shan't press to sea,
For I will send my love a letter
That he shan't go to Botany Bay.

176

Oh father dear, pay down my fortune,
Pay down my five hundred bright guineas in store,
And with my love I'll cross the ocean,
Let the hills and valleys be covered with snow.

B

Who is that tapping at my window
Or who is that so late at night?
It is I, come to court your Nancy,
And I waited there all for her sake.

Begone, begone, you wake my mother,
My father is so quickly to hear.
Says, I won't be gone for to court no other
But I'll whisper softly in all your ear.

Oh father, father, pay down my fortune,
A thousand pounds in gold, you know.
Then I will cross the wide watery ocean
Where the hills and valleys are covered with snow.

For Jamie's the lad I do admire
And Jamie's the lad I mean to wed,
And if I can't have my own heart's desire
Then singly I'll go unto my grave.

C

Who's there, who's there under my window,
Who is there? she loudly cried.
It's me, it's me, oh you charming creature,
And I long to whisper all in your ear.

Away, away, go and court some other
And whisper softly all in her ear,
For my father he is in the highest chamber
And he will hear you, I greatly fear.

Her father overheard this maiden talking
And to her chamber he then did go
Saying, Daughter, daughter, what is the reason
That in your chamber you take no rest?

Father, father, pay down my fortune,
Five hundred guineas, you well know,
And then I'll cross the briny ocean
With the hills and valleys all covered in snow.

Version A   **H**   Amos Ash, April 1905
Last two lines of each stanza marked *bis*.

Version B   **G**   Mrs King at Lyndhurst, Hants, July 16, 1906
Ms. gives title *Who is that tapping at my window?*
Last two lines of each stanza repeated as chorus.

Version C   **G**   Mrs Etheridge at Southampton, June 25, 1906
Ms. gives title *Who's there, who's there under my window?*

A 1.1   *sleeper*: ms. sleepers. Emendation suggested by **H**.
A 2.1–2   Ms. gives these lines as

> Awake! awake! come dark my window
> That sheds in silence to exclaim:

A note by **H** reads: 'Verse 2 lines 1 and 2 are baffling. To "dark" a window means to darken it by drawing down a blind, without which the window is "bare". Can it be "how dark thy window! In shade and silence I complain"? "Shade" and "shed" have a very similar sound in Somerset, cp. "chember" for "chamber" etc.' I have adopted **H**'s reading, except that I have retained 'exclaim'.

84 *Love it is Pleasing*

When I was young, love, and in full blossom
All young men then came surrounding me.
When I was young, love, and well-behavèd
A false young man came a-courting me.

So love it is pleasing, love it is teasing
And love is a treasure when first it's new
But as it grow older it still grow colder
And fade away like the morning dew.

I left my father, I left my mother,
I left my brothers and sisters too,
I left my home and my kind relations,
Forsaked them all for the love of you.

So girls beware of your false young lovers,
Never mind what a young man say.
He's like a star on a foggy morning,
You think he's near when he's far away.

I never thought my love would leave me
Until one morning when he came in,
He drew a chair and sat down beside me
And then my troubles oh they did begin.

H Mrs Gulliver, May 1905
Ms. gives 'Chorus at will' after each of the last three stanzas.

85 *The Lowlands of Holland*

A

Oh yesterday I was married, last night I went to bed.
Up came a bold sea-captain and stood by my bedside.
Arise, arise, young married man and go along with me
To the Lowlands of Holland to face your enemy.

Holland is a pleasant place which shines as it stands
And there's good accommodation for sailors in that land,
Where sugar there in canes do grow, the tea falls from the tree.
I wish to God my love was nigh, although she's far away.

I'll build my love a galliant ship, a ship of noble fame
Where there's four and twenty stout young men to box her on the
    main,
To box her on the main, my boys, most glorious to behold.
May the God above protect my love, he's a jolly sailor bold.

Nor shall a shoe go on my foot nor a comb go through my hair,
Nor fire bright nor candle-light shall shine my beauty fair,
Neither will I married be until the day I die
For the raging seas and the stormy winds have parted my love and I.

B

As I walked out one May morning down by a riverside
There I beheld my lovely fair, oh then to be my bride,
Oh then to be my bride, my boys, and the chambers to behold.
May the Heavens above protect my love for a jolly sailor bold.

I will build my love a galliant ship, a ship of noble fame
With a hundred and seventy sailor boys to box her about the main,
To box her about the main, my boys, without any fear or doubt
With my true love in the galliant ship I was sadly tossed about.

Said the father to the daughter, What makes you so lament?
There is a lad in our own town can give your heart content.
There is not a lad in our town, neither lord nor duke, said she,
Since the raging sea and stormy winds parted my love and I.

The anchor and the cable went overboard straightway,
The mainmast and the rigging laid buried in the sea.
'Twas tempests and bad weather and the raging of the sea,
I never never had but one true love and he was drowned at sea.

C

Oh the very first night I was married I was laid down on my bed,
The cruel captain he said to me as he stood by my bedside,
Crying, Arise my bride and bonny lad, you must go along with me
To the Lowlands of Germany for to face our enemy.

Then I put my love on shipboard and a lofty ship was she
With four score jolly sailor boys for to bear my love company,
And a score of them was drownded and they kills the other three
And one of them was my true love that was killed in Germany.

Now no scarf then shall go round my neck, no nor comb go through
    my hair,
Nor firelight, no nor candlelight shall ever in my room appear,
Nor never will I get married, no, until the day I die
For I never had but one true love, he was killed in Germany.

Now, says the mother to the daughter, What makes you so lament,
Isn't there lads enough in our town that will give you your heart's
    content?
Yes, mother dear, there's lads enough, but there's nary one for me
Since the stormy winds and raging seas parted my true love and me.

Version A   **G**   Mrs Goodyear at Axford by Basingstoke, Hants, August 1907
Version B   **G**   Mr Stephen Phillimore at Andover, Hants, n.d.
Version C   **H**   Mr William Bartlett at Wimborne, 1905

See *IP*, No. 60, for text and notes.

All the versions of this song are confused, and the clearing up of the confusion presents a problem in scholarship which I have not been able to solve. Neither a broadside in the British Museum referred to by **B-G** nor the two texts in *A Pedlar's Pack of Ballads and Songs* by W. H. Logan (Edinburgh 1869) are any less confused. The sex of the singer changes capriciously; the events in the story are mixed up; and the localities referred to are uncertain. There may have been an earlier original in which a young bridegroom is pressed for service in the Netherlands, but in some of the later versions Holland appears to have become New Holland, the former name for Australia, which has perhaps been confused with the Dutch East Indies.

86 *The Loyal Lover*

I'll make my love a garland,
It shall be dressed so fine.
I'll set it round with roses,
With lilies mixed with thyme,
And I'll present it to my love
When he comes back from sea
For I love my love, and I love my love
Because my love loves me.
    Ri-tol-di-rol, ri-tol-lol,
    Ri-tol-de-tol-dee.

I wish I were an arrow
And sped into the air,
I'd seek him like a sparrow
And if he were not there
Then quickly I'd become a fish
To search the raging sea,
For I love my love, and I love my love
Because my love loves me.
    Ri-tol-di-rol, ri-tol-lol,
    Ri-tol-de-tol-dee.

I wish I were a reaper,
I'd seek him in the corn.
I would I were a keeper,
I'd hunt him with my horn,
I'd blow a blast when found at last
Beneath the greenwood tree,
For I love my love, and I love my love
Because my love loves me.
    Ri-tol-di-rol, ri-tol-lol,
    Ri-tol-de-tol-dee.

B-G James Parsons, November 1891, and Anne Roberts, Scabbe Tor, n.d.

B-G gives in *SW* a slightly different version which he attributes not to James Parsons but to another singer. The Parsons version given above is, however, the only oral version in the ms. He refers to eighteenth-century texts of the song usually known as *Bedlam*, in which the above song, (*The Loyal Lover*) or something like it, occurs as the words of a distracted maid in a madhouse protesting her fidelity to a lover absent at sea. In the end the lover returns and marries her. *The Lover's Magazine* (1740) contains a version of *Bedlam* which begins as follows:

> As through Moorfields I walked one evening in the Spring
> I heard a maid in Bedlam most sweetly for to sing,
> Her chains she rattled with her hands and thus replied she,
> I love my love, because my love loves me.

Whether *The Loyal Lover* is a detached portion of *Bedlam* or an older song incorporated in *Bedlam* by an 18th-century hand is difficult to say. It may well be the latter. It is worth noting that while the symbolism of the first stanza implies a female singer, that of stanzas 2 and 3 is more appropriate to a man. This inconsistency may of course be accounted for by the girl's distracted state.

H collected the following stanza at West Milton in 1906. It is given in *DBFS* under the title *I'll Mount the Air*, and is almost identical with a stanza in a late eighteenth-century garland text:

> I'll mount the air with swallows' wings to find my dearest dear
> And if I lose my labour and cannot find him there
> I quickly will become a fish to search the roaring sea.
> I love my love because I know my lovyer he loves me.

87 *The Maid freed from the Gallows*

A

Hold your hand, hold your hand, oh you cold-hearted judge,
Hold your hand, hold your hand and a while,
For I think I see my own dearest father
Coming over the yonders stile.

Oh father, have you brought any gold for me,
Any money for to set me free
For to keep my body from the cold clay sod
And my neck from the high gallows tree?

No, I haven't a-brought no gold for thee,
No money for to set thee free.
I've come for to see thee hangèd here
And hangèd thou must be.

The song continues with 'mother', 'brother', 'sister' *and* 'true love'
and ends with:

Yes, I have a-brought some gold for thee
And money for to set thee free,
For to keep your body from the cold clay sod
And your neck from the high gallows tree.

B

O dear John, stand here,
Stand here by me for a while
For I think I see my own dear father
Coming over the yonder stile.

O father have you brought any gold
Or have you brought any fee
For to save my body from the cold clay ground
And my neck from the gallows tree?

No, I've not brought any gold
Nor I've not brought any fee
To save your body from the cold clay ground
And your neck from the gallows tree.

O the prickty bush,
It pricks my heart so sore,
If I once get out of the prickty bush
I'll never get in any more.

Version A **G** Hampshire, 1907
Version B **H** G. Wirrall at Marlborough, February 1908

In the Chorus, lines 2/3 are represented by 'It, etc. etc.' I have supplied the lines from standard versions.

For notes, see *IP* No. 61. Child No. 95.

88 *Maria and William*

All through the groves as I were walking
And the meadows they were so green,
There I saw two lovers a-talking,
Which made the small birds whistle and sing.

Although my name it is Maria
I am a girl of high degree.
He courted me both late and early
Until he had gained his will on me.

Oh when he had gained his will and pleasure,
Oh how he did laugh and scorn,
And never again did I see that young man
Until my pretty babe was born.

He saw me dancing with some other,
Jealousy came in his mind,
And therefore to destroy his own true lover
He gave to her a glass of wine.

So soon as she drinked it, soon she felt it.
Oh carry me home, my dear, said she,
For that is strong poison which you have gave me
To take my innocent life away.

If that is strong poison that I gave you
I'll drink the same and you shall see
In each other's arms we'll die together
To warn all young men of jealousy.

Then six long hours she lay a-dying,
Three of them she bitterly cried,
Oh William, William, my sweet William,
It's all for your sweet sake I died.

Oh hark, oh hark, the cocks are crowing,
Daylight now will soon appear,
And into my cold grave I'm going.
It's you, Willy dear, as carried me there.

H Mrs Gulliver, April 1905

Last two lines of each stanza marked *bis*.

89 *Mathew the Miller*

I clapped my hand upon her toe.
What's this, my love, what's this, my dear?
'Tis my toe-a-tap, I go leer,
Toe-a-tap, tit-a-tap in
Where Mathew the Miller the malt grinds in.

I clapped my hand upon her knee.
What's this . . .
'Tis my knee-a-nap, I go leer,
Knee-a-nap, toe-a-tap, tit-a-tap in
Where Mathew . . .

The song accumulates as follows:

I clapped my hand upon her

thigh.	What's this . . .	'Tis my thigh-a-nap, I go leer . . .
rump.	What's this . . .	'Tis my swagger-arse, I go leer . . .
belly.	What's this . . .	'Tis my plimpsack, I go leer . . .
breast.	What's this . . .	'Tis my bumpers, I go leer . . .
neck.	What's this . . .	'Tis my gudgel pipe, I go leer . . .
chin.	What's this . . .	'Tis my chin-a-chop, I go leer . . .
mouth.	What's this . . .	'Tis my grinders, I go leer . . .
nose.	What's this . . .	'Tis my snorters, I go leer . . .
eyes.	What's this . . .	'Tis my lookers, I go leer . . .
head.	What's this . . .	'Tis my raggy locks, I go leer . . .

Where Mathew the Miller the corn grinds in.

H John Hallett at Mosterton, June 1906

A convivial song of the same type as *Gently Johnny my Jingalo* (*IP* No. 34). The metaphorical possibilities of the milling trade are here exploited as in *The Miller and the Lass* (*IP* No. 63). I have not met the word 'plimpsack' elsewhere. The obsolete verb 'plim' means 'to fill or swell'.

90 *May and December*

If you are determined a husband to buy
It shall be no codger who's willing to try.
Her grey hair and wrinkles will not do for me
For May and December can never agree.
   Derry down
   Down hey! derry down.

Give me a young damsel so brisk as a bee
That knows how to please a young fellow like me.
So, Goody, give o'er, don't tease me no more,
You're too old to wed as I've told you before.

I am not so old as you take me to be
So, youth, do not slight me but let us agree.
I'm nimble and active, can caper and prance,
So fast as you pipe, so quick will I dance.

Come, come to my wedding, friends, make no delay,
In eating and drinking we'll spend the whole day.
Young men and old women, 'twill please you, no doubt,
So fill up your glasses and push them about.

H Mrs Young at Long Barton, July 1906

Ms. gives title *If you are Determined*.

Chorus repeated after each stanza.

Evidently the first stanza is confused, but I know no other source for this sprightly dialogue.

91 *Me and Five More*

Me and five more went out one night in Squire Duncan's park
To see if we could get some game, the night it proved dark,
But by our great misfortune traphanded was by speed.
They sent us off to Warwick jail, which made our hearts to bleed.

'Twas at the March assizes, oh then we did appear,
Like Job we stood with patience to hear our sentence there.
There being some old offenders, which made my case go hard,
My sentence was for fourteen years, then I was sent on board.

The ship that bore us from the land—the Speedwell was her name,
For full five months and upwards, boys, we ploughed the raging
    main.
No shoes or stockings had we on, nor hat had we to wear,
But leathern frocks and linsey drawers, our feet and head were bare.

They chained us up by two and two like horses in a team.
The driver he stood over us with his malacca cane.
The fifteenth of September, boys, 'twas then we made the land,
At four o'clock we went on shore all chained hand in hand.

To see our fellow sufferers, I'm sure I can't tell how,
Some chained to the harrow and another to the plough.
They sent me off to Sidney town without any more delay
Where a gentleman he bought me, his book-keeper to be.

I took this occupation, my master liked me well.
My joys were out of measure, boys, I'm sure no tongue can tell.
We had a female servant, Rosanna was her name.
For fourteen years convicted was, all from Northampton came.

We oft-times told our tales of love when we were placed at home,
But now we've crossed the raging seas in foreign lands to roam.

G Mr David Marlow at Basingstoke, Hants, September 1906

Last stanza followed by two rows of dots.

1.3 *traphanded*: trepanned

Cf. *Van Dieman's Land* (*IP* No. 107).

92 *The Miners*

It's of six jolly miners, six miners you shall hear
And they had been a-mining for many a long year
So they travelled old England, Ireland and Scotland all round
And of their delight was a-working underground.

There was one came from Cornwall and two from Derby town,
The other three from Williamsbridge, young lads of high renown,
But of all their delight was to split those rocks in twine
And it's all for the treasure, my boys, as we does undermine.

Sometimes we have money, boys, sometimes we've none at all
But we can have good credit, my boys, when on it we do call.
We call for liquors merrily and drink our healths all round.
Here's a health to all my jolly miners that works all underground.

So 'tis down by the crystal river stream I heard a fair maid sing
Oh haven't you seen my miner or haven't you been this way,
So haven't you seen my miner? so sweetly sang she,
For of all the trades in England it's the miners for me.

G Mr William Brown at Cheriton, Hants, 1905

93 *The Molecatcher*

In Wellington town at the sign of the Plough
There lived a molecatcher—shall I tell how?
He had but one wife, she was buxom and gay
And she and another young farmer would play.

The molecatcher being jealous all of the same thing,
He stepped in the brewhouse to see him come in.
He saw the young farmer get over the stile,
Which made the molecatcher begin for to smile.

He knocked at the door and thus he did say,
Where is your husband, good woman, I pray?
He's a-catching the moles, you need never fear.
She little did think the molecatcher was near.

So he went upstairs to do his design
And the molecatcher followed him quickly behind.
Said he, Little do you think, old chap,
I have caught you in my trap.

I will make you pay dear for tilling my ground
And as for the money, it shall be ten pound.
Ten pound, said the farmer, I never will mind
For it will only cost me about threepence a time.

So now the young farmer must live at the last
For he spent all his money at the sign of the Cross.
He spent all his money, I cannot tell how,
I dare him hang up at the sign of the Plough.

G   Mr George Digweed at Micheldever, Hants, May 1906

6.1   *at the last*: ? a corruption of *at a loss*
6.1   *at the sign of the Cross*: probably a euphemism for 'in the support of
bastard (i.e. cross-bred) children', just as 'the sign of the Plough'
implies fornication.

94 *My own Father Forced Me*

My own father forced me and a soldier to go
To see whether I could forget her or no,
But when I came there with my coat shining bright
I never could forget her by day or by night.

To her own father's house straightway I did go
To see whether I could get her or no,
And when I came there her father replied,
My own daughter broke her heart and for love she has died.

Then I stood amazèd like one that was slain,
With the tears trickling down me like showers of rain,
Crying, oh crying, Oh what sorrows I bear!
My love in her silent grave, I wish I was there.

And down in yon Bedlam they forced me to go
To see whether I could forget her or no,
But the rattling of the chains and the tearing of my hair,
I never could forget her, my own dearest dear.

G Mr George Smith at Fareham, Hants, August 3, 1906

95 *My Valentine*

A

Young Billy Brown was a brisk young lad
When first he raided me away,
He brought me from my parents, he stole me from my home
And now he's left me in this wide world to stray.

He took hold of my lily-white hand
And led me to the garden so green,
But what we done there I will never declare,
The green leaves they were plain to be seen.

He took me by the middle so small
And so gently laid me down,
But what we done there I will never declare
For the winds they came whistling all round.

When six or seven long months were past
This young man he came a-riding by.
She said, Young man, I am in child by you
And the very same thing you can't deny.

Oh my maid, my fair pretty maid,
It need not be any of mine,
Unless that you can tell me both when and where,
The very same hour and the time.

Oh yes, I can tell you both when and where,
The very same hour and the time,
And unless that you consent to marry me, poor girl,
I'll have you in some prison close confined.

Then he gave consent to marry me, poor girl,
And it was to be the very next day,
But instead of getting married to me, poor girl,
He took shipping and so boldly sailed away.

Oh if ever he should return back again
These curly, curly locks I'll unfold.
I never would upbraid him or tell him of his **faults**
But encourage him for being so bold.

B

One Valentine's Day as I have heard 'em say
'Twas early in the morning betime,
A charming pretty lass came at my bed's head,
She fain would have been my Valentine.

I took her all round her middle so small
And gently I laid her down,
But what we did there I never will declare
But this poor girl she losed her 'character'.

When six months being over and seven gone and past
This young man came a-riding by.
She says, Young man, I'm with child by you
And the same thing you never can deny.

Perhaps you may prove with child, pretty maid,
This child it is nothing of mine
Unless you can tell me O where and O when,
The very same hour and the time.

O yes I can tell you O where and O when,
The very same hour and the time:
Down in my father's garden under the red rose bush
Whilst the town clock was striking nine.

Then I will consent all for to marry you,
We'll get married this very next day,
But instead of his marriage he took ship and sailed away
And left this charming girl behind.

So now he's gone, the Lord do know where,
His body might be sailing on the deep.
But how can I blame him for serving me so
And his courage for being so bold.

Version A   **G**   Mr William Messenger at Compton by Winchester, September 1907

Ms. gives title *Young Billy Brown*.

Version B   **H**   J. Greening at Cuckold's Corner, May 1906

A Ms. gives 1.4 as And now he's left me in this wide world to stray, stray, stray, and adds the following line: And now he's left me in this wide world to stray. This repetition, which fits in with the tune, is not indicated in the remaining stanzas. I have accordingly omitted it.

B 2.4   *'Character'*: as in ms.

IP No. 66.

96 *New Garden Fields*

On the eighteenth of August, at the eighth month of the year,
Down by New Garden fields there I first met my dear.
She appeared like some goddess or some one divine
And she came like some torment to trouble my mind.

Oh I am no tormentor, young man, she did say,
I'm a-picking those flowers so fresh and so gay,
I'm a-picking those flowers that nature doth yield
For I takes great delight in the New Garden fields.

And I said, Lovely Nancy, dare I make so bold
Your lily white hand one minute to hold?
It will give me more pleasure than all earthly store,
So grant me this favour and I'll ask you no more.

And she turnèd and said, Young man, I fear you must jest.
If I thought you were earnest I would think myself blest,
But my father is coming there now, did she say,
So fare you well, young man, it's I must away.

So now she's gone and left me all in the bonds of love,
Kind Cupid, protect me, and you powers above.
Kind Cupid, protect me, and pray take my part,
For she's guilty of murder and quite broke my heart.

She turned and said, Young man, I pity your moan.
I'll leave you no longer to sigh alone.
I will go along with you to some foreign part.
You are the first young man that has won my heart.

We'll go to church on Sunday and married we'll be.
We'll join hands in wedlock and sweet unity.
We'll join hands in wedlock and vow to be true,
To father and mother we will bid adieu.

G Mr Alfred Oliver at Axford by Basingstoke, Hants, September 1907

Ms. gives only the first two stanzas. Remainder supplied from a Such ballad sheet quoted in *FSJ* 8, 1906.

97 *O Shepherd, O Shepherd*

O shepherd, O shepherd, will you come home to your breakfast,
To your breakfast, to your breakfast?
O shepherd, O shepherd, will you come home
To your breakfast this morning?

What have you got for breakfast O,
For breakfast O, for breakfast O?
What have you got for breakfast O
If I come home this morning?

Bacon and eggs a bellyful,
A bellyful, a bellyful,
Bacon and eggs a bellyful
If you'll come home this morning.

O no, my sheep are all out in the wide wilderness,
Wilderness, wilderness,
O no, my sheep are all out in the wide wilderness
So I can't come home this morning.

O shepherd, O shepherd, will you come home to your lunch O . . .

What have you got for my lunch O . . .

Bread, cheese and beer a bellyful . . .
If you'll come home to lunch O.

O no, my sheep are all out in the wilderness . . .

O shepherd, O shepherd, will you come home to your dinner . . .
To your dinner to-day?

What have you got for my dinner . . .
If I do come home to-day?

Plum pudding and beef a bellyfull . . .

O no, my sheep . . .

O shepherd, O shepherd, will you come home to your lodging . . .
To your lodging to-night?

What have you got for my lodging . . .
If I do come home to-night?

A clean pair of sheets and a pretty lass . . .

O but I'll go and fetch my sheep out of the wilderness . . .
And I will come home to-night.

H William Bartlett at Wimborne, Dorset, 1905

For a similar comic dialogue, cf. *Good Old Man* (*IP* No. 36).

98 *Oh as I was a Walking*

Oh, as I was walking by myself all alone,
'Twas through those damp meadows I heard a fine song.
'Twas a beautiful fair one and her voice was so clear,
Crying, How happy, happy should I be if my true love was near.

Then she drew herself near to some tree that was green
Where the leaves all did shade her, she scarce could be seen,
But still all her cry was, Will my love come this way?
All for his sweet company, oh here I do stay.

Oh she had not been there long before a young man passed by
With his cherry cheeks like the roses and a rolling black eye.
You may tell by her blushes that her true love was nigh,
He so kindly saluted her and by her sat down.

With one arm all round her neck unto the ruby lips did join
Here is sweet spraddling tales to each other's mind,
See our colours they went away and so fresh come again,
True love he was her Henerey, true love was her pain.

But now this young couple they are joined to the yoke
And they lives like two turtle doves and never do provoke,
But now she is blessed all in the height of her charms
And so constantly she sleeps in her true lovyer's arms.

G Mr Edward Ross at Fareham, Hants, July 25, 1906

Ms. gives stanza 2 as stanza 4.

  4.2 *spraddling*: possibly a form of 'sprawling'.

99 *Old Mother Crawley*

Oh come all you young seamen, I'd have you beware,
Of old Mother Crawley I'd have you take care,
Of old Mother Rogers, so called by name,
She goes a-bumboating, that noted fine game.
   And sing tooral liday,
   Rite tooral lay,
   Rite tooral laddy,
   Rite tooral liday.

Our ship has arrived safe brought up in the Sound,
The tailors and the bumboats they all flock around.
Alongside comes Mother Crawley with her bumboat of store,
You're welcome, my children, to Plymouth once more.

She hands up the soft tack and butter also
And what else is wanted straightforward she'll go.
There's soft tack, there's butter, there's sugar, there's tea,
I know you young lads have been looking for me.

Soft tack is two shillings and butter is four,
Two pounds of sausages five shillings more,
Six eggs fourteen pence—come, boys, be quick, for I'm thronged!
Which makes twelve and twopence, so Jack jog along.

Early next morning on the quarter deck she appears.
Pity, kind gentle folks, both far and near.
Your men owes me money, you see by this paper,
They'll pay the girls first, they all swear by their Maker.

And as for you, boatswain, I'm pretty well sure
You'll settle with me first and pay your score.
For it's this I will promise and that I will do,
They are far better slops than you'll get from the Jew.

Our ship she's got orders for Botany Bay,
The girls and the bumboats must all lose their pay.
Our anchor's apeak, our ship she's wore round,
Farewell, Mother Crawley, likewise Plymouth Sound.

If ever we live to see Plymouth once more
We'll make Mother Crawley's old house for to roar.
We'll sweat her gin bottle as we oft done before,
Maintopsail be with Mr Fore pays the score.

G Mr George Lovett at Winchester, August 1906

Chorus repeated after each stanza.

3.1 *soft tack*: bread.

6.4 *slops*: clothes.

100 *One Man Shall Mow my Meadow*

My one man, my two men shall mow me down my meadows,
My three men, my four men shall carry my grass away,
My four, my three, my two, my one, nay not mo,
For to mow my hay and carry it away
On a beautiful midsummer's day.

My five men, my six men shall mow me down my meadows,
My seven men, my eight men shall carry my grass away,
My eight, my seven, my six, my five, my four, my three, my two,
    my one, nay not mo.
For to mow my hay and carry it away
On a beautiful midsummer's day.

G Mr Charles Woodhouse at Micheldever, Hants, May 1906

Ms. gives title *Haymaking Song*.

A convivial song of the type which, though the 'I' is a girl, is usually sung by
men. It is indefinitely cumulative, the climax of each stanza being the 'Nay
not mo (more)', an ironical protest against the increasing number of mowers.
For further discussion, see Introduction, p. 26.

101 *Open the Window*

One night as I lay on my bed
Some loving thoughts came into my head.
I was sore oppressed, I could take no rest,
Love did torment me so,
And away to my true love I did go.

I went straight to my love's chamber door
And so boldly I did call for her,
I do declare that I am come here
Through bitter frost and snow,
So open the window, my love, do.

My mam and dad are both awake
For I have just heard them speak.
You'll have no excuse, they will you abuse
With many a bitter blow,
So it's go from the window, my love, do.

Your mam and dad are both asleep,
In at the window I did peep,
And they lie so high on their bed so soft
And they draws their breath so slow,
So it's open the window, my love, do.

My love came down all dressed in white,
She appeared like some virgin bright.
Her eyes shone bright as the stars by night.
She had a diamond ring also,
And it's with my true love I did go.

And what we done there I will never declare,
No mortal man shall know
Not whilst I got breath for to draw.

G Mr Charles Bull at Marchwood by Southampton, June 1907
Ms. gives title *One Night as I lay on my Bed*.

102 *Our Ship she lies in Harbour*

There lays a ship in the harbour
Just ready to set sail,
Crying, Heaven shall be my guard, my love,
Till I return again.

Says the old man to the daughter,
What makes you so lament?
Oh the lad that you have sent to sea,
He can give my heart content.

So if that's your inclination,
The old man did reply,
I hope he will continue there
And on the seas may die.

So when nine long weeks was over
And ten long tedious days
I saw the ship come shivering in
With my true love home from sea.

Yonder sits my angel,
She's waiting there for me
And to-morrow to the church we'll go
And married we will be.

So when we got into the church
And turning back again
I met my own rude father
And several gentlemen.

So he says, My dearest daughter,
Five hundred I will give
If you forsake that sailor lad
And go with me to live.

No, it's not your gold that glitters
Nor yet your silver that shines,
I'm married to the lad I love
And I'm happy in my mind.

G Mr William Brown at Cheriton, Hants, n.d.

Last two lines of each stanza repeated as Chorus.

    6.3 *own rude*: a corruption of *honoured* (cf. the otherwise almost identical
        Such broadside, BM L.R. 271 a. 2, Vol. VI, p. 205.)

A slightly different text is given in *GFH*, and a confused version from Surrey
is printed in *FSJ* 4, 1904.

103 *The Owslebury Lads*

The thirtieth of November last eighteen hundred and thirteen
The Owslebury lads they did prepare all for the machinery
And when they did get there, my eye! how they let fly.
The machinery flew to pieces in the twinkling of an eye.
Chorus   The mob, such a mob you never had seen before,
        And if you live for a hundred years you never will no more.

Oh then to Winchester we were sent, our trial for to take
And if we do have nothing said our counsel we shall keep.
When the judges did begin, I'm sorry for to say,
So many there was transported for life and some was cast to die.

Sometimes our parents they comes in for to see us all,
Sometimes they bring some baccy or a loaf that is so small,
Then we goes into the kitchen and sits all round about,
There is so many of us that we are very soon all smoked out.

At six o'clock in the morning our turnkey he comes in
With a bunch of keys all in his hands tied up all in a ring,
And we can't get any further than back and forward the yard,
A pound and a half of bread a day, and don't you think it hard?

At six o'clock in the evening the turnkey he comes round,
The locks and bolts they rattle like the sounding of a drum,
And we are all locked up all in the cells so high
And there we stay till morning whether we lives or dies.

And now it's to conclude and to finish my new song,
I hope you gentlemens round me will think that I'm not wrong,
For all the poor in Hampshire for rising of their wages,
I hope that none of our enemies will know for the want of places.

G   Mr James Stagg at Winchester, 1906

Chorus repeated after each stanza.

No better text has so far come to light of this ballad of the last labourers'
revolts of 1830 (not 1813, as stated in line 1). Widespread dissatisfaction with
low wages caused riots in agricultural districts. Threshing and other farm
machinery was broken, and savage sentences were passed by special judicial
commissions set up in the country towns. The farmers were frequently on the
side of the labourers, but did not often take an open part in their activities. An
exception was John Boys, a small farmer of Owslebury, a village near Winchester, who joined a mob which 'extorted money from Lord Northesk's
steward'. For this he was sentenced to seven years' transportation. (See
Hammond, *The Village Labourer*, 1912.) The special commission began its
hearings at Winchester on December 18, 1830. Of the 245 Hampshire
prisoners the majority received sentences ranging from fines to hanging. Only
two of the capital sentences were carried out. This put an end to the agricultural disturbances in the county. (*Hampshire Review*, Autumn 1953.)

104 *Padstow May Song*

A

THE MORNING SONG

Unite and unite, and it's all how white,
   For summer is a-come in to-day
And whither we are going we all will unite
   In the merry morning of May.

I warn you young men every one
To go to the greenwood and fetch your may home.

Arise, Master . . . and joy you betide,
And bright is your bride that lies by your side.

Arise, Mistress . . . and gold be your ring
And give us a cup of ale that merrier we may sing.

With the merry sing and now joyful spring,
How happy are the birds that merrily do sing.

Arise, Master . . . with your sword by your side,
Your steed is in stable awaiting you to ride.

Arise, Master . . . and reach me your hand
And you shall have a lovely lass with a thousand pounds in hand.

Arise, Master , , , for I know you well and fine,
You've a shilling in your purse, I wish it were in mine.

Arise, Miss . . . and strew all your flowers,
It is but a little while since we strewed ours.

With the merry sing and now joyful spring,
How happy are the birds that merrily do sing.

Arise, Miss . . . from out of your bed,
Your chamber shall be spread with the white rose and red.

Arise, Miss . . . all in your smock of silk,
And all your body under as white as any milk.

Where are the young men that now here should dance?
Some they are in England and some are in France.

Where are the maidens that now here should sing?
They are all in the meadows a flower gathering.

For the merry sing now the joyful spring,
How happy are the birds that merrily do sing.

The young men of Padstow they might if they wold,
They might ha' built a ship and gilded her with gold.

The maidens of Padstow they might if they wold,
They have made a garland and gilded it with gold.

Now fare you well and we wish you good cheer,
We will come no more unto your house until another year.

For the merry sing now the joyful spring,
How happy are the birds that merrily do sing.

B

THE DAY SONG

Awake St George, our English knight O,
  For summer is a come, and winter is a go.
Where is St George and where is he O?
He's down in his long boat upon the salt sea O.
  For to fetch summer home, summer and may O,
  For summer is a come, and winter is a go.

Where are the French dogs that make such boast O?
They shall eat the goose feathers and we'll eat the roast O.

Thou mightst ha' shown a knavish face, or tarried at home O,
But thou shalt be a cuckold and wear the horns O.

Up flies the kite, down falls the lark O,
Aunt Ursula Birdwood, she had an old ewe.
Aunt Ursula Birdwood, she had an old ewe,
And she died in her own park long ago.

B-G Version A 'Taken down from the singing of the man who dances the
Hobby Horse'
Version B 'Taken down from the man who dances before the hobby-
horse', n.d. Chorus ('For to fetch . . .') repeated after each stanza

These two songs, corrupt and confused as they are, are part of the May
celebrations at Padstow in Cornwall. Written and pictorial records do not go
back very far, but students of comparative anthropology have established that
the Padstow celebrations are one manifestation of a fertility ritual which goes
back to pre-Christian times, survivals and revivals of which are found in many
parts of the world. They are perhaps the most purely Dionysian survival to
be found in Britain, incorporating a dance-mime of undisguised sexual
significance. It was these rites which the first Christian missionaries discovered
all over Britain, and which the Roman Church attempted to come to terms
with, either by suppression or by conversion to Christian uses. It was indeed
the success of the pre-Reformation church in adapting pagan practices to the
Christian calendar which later drew down upon these practices the furious
denunciations of reformers who believed them to be of popish origin.

The central figure in the Padstow rites, as in other similar survivals, is the
wild horse, the black, demonic vegetation-spirit and embodiment of male
fertility, known in various parts of Britain as the Hobby Horse. This is not
in origin the same as the hobby horse of the morris dance, but the two became
confused. Tracing the connections between the several British manifestations
of the ritual horse at Padstow and elsewhere, Violet Alford says:

'All these animals are of the magical sort. They represent a wild not a
domestic horse; they snap, they bite, they seize devotees; some die or fall to
pieces; all are closely bound up with fertility of the earth and of humankind,
made of bits of plough, sieves, corn, maize; they pursue women; they visit the
entire town, they undergo rain charms.' (*JEFDSS*, 1939.)

The Padstow rites, like the words of the songs that accompany them, have
become corrupt; bits of them have been curtailed, suppressed, or forgotten;
revived in other forms or replaced by new interpolations. In essence, however,
May Day was a general holiday, a rejoicing for the defeat of winter by summer, a Saturnalia as Baring-Gould called it, to be enjoyed by all classes alike.

At the time when he wrote, the Maypole had disappeared, though it was later revived. This had been supplied on May Eve by the local shipwrights, by whom it was erected in the middle of the town. It was then decorated with gulls' eggs, garlands, and ribbons. At night the eight men (the 'pairs' or 'peers') whose duty it was to attend the hobby would gather at the principal inn and, after a hearty supper, would go round the outlying farms singing what is variously called the 'Night song' and the 'Morning song'. The 'Day song' was sung on the morning of May Day. The horse itself was led from its stable on May morning by the 'pairs', to the music of a drum and fife band and the noise of pistol-shots. The leader of the hobby men was the club-man who danced in front of the horse, sometimes in woman's attire, luring it on to prance and curvet, to snap its jaws and give a mimic display of exultant virility. It was led to a place outside the town known as the Treator Pool, where it was made to drink. This subjection of the creature to a rain charm still further ensured its efficacy as a bringer of fertility. It was then led triumphantly back through the town, accompanied by singing and shouting people, and ran wild among the onlookers, chasing the women and girls. During the day song it was at one point made to lie down as if dead, and was revived by the caresses of the girls, who endeavoured to attract it to them. At times during the long history of the ritual, the hobby was daubed with tar or soot; and the marking of a woman with black was powerful fertility magic.

The significance of the two May songs which belong to the Padstow rites is obvious enough in general, though details are obscure. In the morning song the omitted names of Master and Mistress So-and-so were supplied according to the householder who was being serenaded. In Baring-Gould's time the gathering of flowers and garlands with which houses, and sometimes heads, were bedecked took place during the days preceding May 1st. Flowers were freely 'stolen' from near-by gardens, and such ritual theft was regarded as lucky. In earlier times the gathering of flowers and garlands would no doubt have taken place during the small hours of May morning.

The mention of the ship of gold refers, locally, to the ship-building trade, and traditionally to the ship of plenty associated with Ceres or Demeter, the Earth Goddess in whose honour the May rites were originally performed.

In the day song the reference to the French dogs is doubtless a patriotic interpolation due to local pride in associating Cornishmen with the repulsion of invaders. The enemy, originally winter, was thought by the singers to be the national foe of the time.

Faced with the stanza about 'aunt Ursula Birdwood', the commentator can choose one of three courses: either he can regard it as a nonsensical corruption of something now lost; or he can follow Lucy Broadwood into the intricacies of German mythology and regard it as a reference to St Ursula, whose cult was substituted by the Church for that of the Earth Mother in parts of Europe (see *FSJ* 20, 1916); or he may suspect a more or less ribald allusion to some local personage long forgotten. With respect for Lucy Broadwood's profound scholarship and her knowledge of Teutonic anthropology, I am nevertheless inclined to adopt the third interpretation. See note on 'Aunt Mary Moses' in *The Hal-an-Tow* (p. 147).

105 *Polly Oliver's Rambles*

One night as Polly Oliver was lying in her bed
A project very wondrous came into her head.
She go through the country disguised to rove
And so she would seek for her own dearest love.

So early next morning the fair maid arose.
She dressed herself up in a man's suit of clothes,
Coat, waistcoat and breeches and a sword by her side,
And her father's black gelding fair Polly would ride.

She rode till she came to a place of renown
And there she put up at the sign of the Crown.
She sat herself down with brown ale at the board
And the first that came in was an outlandish lord.

The next that came in was fair Polly's true love.
She looked in his face and resolved him to prove.
O he was a captain, a captain so fine.
He sat at the board and he called for red wine.

A letter, a letter that's come from a friend
Or else 'tis a letter your true love did send,
And under the seal will a guinea be found
For you and your soldiers to drink ale around.

Then what are your tidings, my little foot page?
For you are a boy of the tenderest age
With locks that are curling and smooth is your chin,
A voice as a flute warbles softly and thin.

I am not a foot page, a gelding I ride,
And I am a squire with a sword by my side.
The letter was given me, riding this way,
But who 'twas that gave it I never can say.

The maid being drowsy, she hung down her head,
She called for a candle to light her to bed.
My house it is full, the landlady swore,
My beds are engaged, let him lie on the floor.

The captain he answered, I've a bed at my ease
And you may lie with me, young boy, if you please.
I thank you, sir captain, fair Polly she said,
I'll lie by the fire, on the saddle my head.

To lie with a captain's a dangerous thing.
I'm a new listed soldier to fight for the King.
Before the lark whistles I must ride away
And miles must make many before break of day.

Then early next morning this fair maid arose
And dressed herself up in her own woman's clothes.
Down over the stair she so nimbly did run,
As he had proved constant to his lovèd one.

So now she is married and lives at her ease,
She goes where she wills and comes where she please.
She has left her old parents behind her to mourn
And give hundreds of thousands for their daughter's return.

B-G 'Taken down from the bed-ridden wife of J. Masters of Bradstone by
Rev. W. W. Martyn and sent to me'

106 *Poor Old Horse*

I mind when I was a hobby colt, a hobby colt so gay,
And when my mother weaned me I thought that I should die.
Poor old horse, poor old horse.

I mind when I was a brewer's horse, a brewer's horse so gay.
I jumped right in the mashing-tub and drank up all the beer.
Poor old horse, poor old horse.

I mind when I was a gentleman's horse, a gentleman's horse so gay.
I had the best of all the corn and the primest of all hay.
Poor old horse, poor old horse.

But now I'm old and getting grey and fit for nothing at all.
I have to eat the sour grass that grows upon the wall.
Poor old horse, poor old horse.

My master rode me out one day and tied me to a stile
While he ran away with the miller's maid when he could have rode
     five mile.
Poor old horse, poor old horse.

My flesh shall be the doggies' food, my bones they'll throw away.
My skin shall be my master's pride and so I shall decay.
Poor old horse, poor old horse.

H Beatrice Crawford (13) at West Milton, May 1906

IP No. 77.

The above version is the only one I have seen which explicitly identifies the
'poor old horse' of the well-known song with the 'Old Hob' or hobby horse
of tradition. According to M. H. Mason (*Nursery Rhymes and Country Songs*,
2nd edition, 1909), the song was part of a Christmas observance in which
house-to-house visits were paid by a company whose chief member represented the horse. A horse's skull, painted black and red, was supported by a

man concealed under a cloth. The song itself was preceded by the following introduction:

> By leave, you gentlemen all,
> Your pardon I do crave,
> For making bold to come,
> To see what sport you'll have.

> There's more in company,
> They're following close behind;
> They've sent us on before,
> Admittance for to find.

> These blades they are but young;
> Never acted here before;
> They'll do the best they can,
> And the best can do no more.

It is obvious from evidence gathered in many districts, over several centuries, that what had degenerated in the nineteenth century into a mere begging expedition was a fragment of a ritual connected with the ending of the old year at All Hallows Tide and the beginning of the new year on All Souls' Day. This ritual, which had been adapted to Christian usage, was of pagan origin, and was connected with the completion of the harvest and of the ensuring of fertility for the coming year. These conceptions were symbolized in the mummers' play of St George, of which the principal characters were St (or King) George, his enemy (the Black Prince, Turkish Knight, Slasher, etc.), a female figure (Mary, Martha, Cicely, etc.), and a quack doctor. In this farce of death and resurrection there are numerous subsidiary characters, amongst whom frequently appears the 'poor old horse' of the song, which prances and snaps, as in the performance at Padstow (see note, p. 207). In a Cheshire version of the mummers' play, the Soul-Cakers' Play from Guilden Sutton (*JEFDSS* 1947), the leader of the horse introduces him with these words:

> Once he was alive and now he's dead,
> Nothing but a poor old horse's head . . .
> This poor old horse has but one leg
> And for his money he has to beg . . .
> This poor old horse has an eye like a hawk,
> And a neck like a rainbow and a
> Foot like a paver's jammer
> And as many wimbles and jinkles
> On his forehead as half an acre of ploughed land,
> Wey! whoa! stand up Dick and show yourself.

The horse's head or skull was obtained from a knacker's yard or hunting stables after its flesh had been eaten by the hounds. This gave point to the words of the song.

As I see it, then, the horse is in origin the black stallion of the old fertility rites, now dead for the duration of winter; the alms given to the horse, like the soul-cakes distributed to the poor, guaranteed the ultimate revival of fertility. (For further consideration of the subject of the above notes see the articles by Douglas Kennedy ('Dramatic Elements in the Folk Dance', *JEFDSS* 1949), by Alex Helm ('The Cheshire Soul-Caking Play', *JEFDSS* 1950) and the anonymous article on 'Two Variations of the Folk Play and a Further Account of the "Old Hoss",' *JEFDSS* 1947.)

107 *Queen of the May*

A

As I walked out one midsummer's morn
Through the fields and meadows so gay
'Twas who should I spy but a fair pretty maid
As she gath'rèd her armfuls of may.

Where are you a-going, my fair pretty maid,
Through the fields and meadows so gay?
Oh kind sir, she said, I'm going far away
To gather my armfuls of may.

Shall I go with you, my fair pretty maid,
Through the fields and meadows so gay?
No, kind sir, she said, I will rather refuse
For I'm 'fraid you would lead me astray.

He then caught her hold by her lily-white hand
Through the fields and meadows so gay.
He then placed her down 'pon the green mossy bank
Whilst he gath'rèd his armfuls of may.

She then rosed up and she gave him a smile
And thanked him for what he had done.
He then placed a rose at her lily-white cheek
Saying, My dearest, it is not a thorn.

QUEEN OF THE MAY

Now my dearest, said he, now my bride you shall be
And the people have nothing to say.
For the church bells shall ring, now my bride you shall be
Whilst they crown you the sweet Queen of May.

B

Now the winter is gone, the summer is come
And the meadows they look pleasant and gay.
I espied a fair maid and so sweetly sung she
And her cheeks wore the blossom of May.

I said, My fair maid, oh it's how come you here
In these meadows so soon in the morn?
Oh, the maid she replied, I would rather be excused,
I'm afraid you will lead me astray.

Then I took hold of her lily-white hand,
'Pon the green mossy banks we sat down.
Then I planted a kiss on her sweet and ruby lips
While the small birds were singing all round.

Oh when I returned oh she gave to me a smile
And she thanked me for what I had done.
Then I planted a sprig in her snowy white breast
And believe me there never grows a thorn.

'Twas early next morning I made her my bride
That the people might have nothing to say.
Then the bells they did ring and the bridemaids did sing
And I crowned her the Queen of the May.

H Version A Mrs Gulliver, May 1905

Ms. gives title *The Sweet Queen of May*.

Version B S. Dawe (80) at Beaminster, June 1906

Last two lines of each stanza repeated in both versions.

A fuller version of the song given as *As I walked through the Meadows* in **IP** (No. 6).

108 *The Ragged Beggar man*

It's of a ragged beggar man came tripping o'er the plain,
He came unto a farmer's door, a lodging for to gain.
    Robellow, zangalee, robellow—below.
The farmer he came out to view, he looked the man around.
Says he, For ragged beggar men no shelter here is found.
    Robellow, zangalee, robellow—below.

Then down the stair came the daughter fair, and viewed him cheek
    and chin
And said, He is a handsome man, I pray you take him in.
The maiden bade him to the barn and make a bed with hay,
She made it plum and easy, that the beggar there might lay.

She went into her father's house, she brought him cake and wine,
She gave him of her father's clothes all laced rich and fine.
The father laughed a mocking laugh, Thou art a silly fool
To feed and clothe a beggar man that fasts and lieth cool.

She rose so early in the morn to unbar the linney door
And there she saw the beggar man astanding on the floor.
He caught the maiden in his arms and to the bed he ran,
Now fie! for shame, the maiden said, thou art a forward man.

She lay as still as any mouse, as if she had been dead,
He gave her kisses two and three and stole her maidenhead.
I'm sure thou art no beggar man, of gentlemen art one,
For you have spoiled an honest maid and I am quite undone.

I am no squire, I am no lord, of beggars I be one,
And beggars they be robbers all, by such are you undone.
I took you for a nobleman, I took you for a squire,
In truth thou art the finest lad that runneth in the shire.

My mother she will loudly chide, my father curse and ban
That I have played the fool this day all with a beggar man.
She took the bed all in her hands and dashed it o'er the wall
Saying, Go you with the beggar man, my maidenhead and all.

B-G   William Setter at Two Bridges, J. Gerrard at Chagford, and James
Parsons at Lew Down, n.d.

Chorus line repeated after line 2 and line 4 of each stanza.

109 *The Rambling Sailor*

'Twas early morn that I did rise,
I left my love a sleeping,
I left her for an hour or two,
She'll soon awake to weeping.
O if she lie till I return
She may lie there till day of doom
For I travel the country through and through
And am ever a rambling sailor.

O when I came to London town
I saw of ladies plenty.
I boldly stepped up unto them
To court them for their beauty.
I said, My dear, be of good cheer,
I'll ne'er depart, you need not fear,
But I travel the country through and through
And still am a rambling sailor.

And if you need to know my name,
My name it is Ben Johnson.
A commission I hold from the Queen
To court all girls that are handsome.
I court them all, marry none at all,
My heart is round and rolls as a ball
And I travel the country through and through
And still am a rambling sailor.

216

B-G Roger Hannaford at Lower Widdecombe, May 1890

B-G published in *S W* a version, largely of his own composition, incorporating half-a-dozen lines from the above. Of this published version he says in his notes that he has only 'modified the words where objectionable'. The song was, as he says, originally a broadside, *The Rambling Soldier*, and was adapted as a sailor's song. I append the broadside version from **B-G**'s ms., which was printed by Whiting of Birmingham about 1817, of which **B-G** says, 'This is unquestionably the original from which *The Rambling Sailor* was concocted.'

THE RAMBLING SOLDIER

I am a soldier blythe and gay
That has rambled for promotion.
I've laid the French and Spaniards low,
Some miles I've crossed the ocean.
I've travelled England and Ireland too,
I've travelled bonny Scotland through
I've caused some pretty girls to rue
I am a roving rambling soldier.

When I was young and in my prime,
Twelve years I was recruiting.
Thro' England, Ireland, Scotland too,
Wherever it was suiting.
I led a gay and splendid life,
In every town a different wife,
And seldom was there any strife
With the rambling, roving soldier.

In Woolwich town, I courted Jane,
Her sister and her mother
I mean to say, when I was there,
They were jealous of each other.
Our orders came, I had to start
I left poor Jane with a broken heart
Then I straight to Colchester did depart,
The gay and rambling soldier.

The King's permission granted me
To range the country over,
From Colchester to Liverpool
From Plymouth down to Dover.
And in whatever town I went
To court all damsels I was bent,
And marry none was my intent
But live a rambling soldier.

217

With the blooming lasses in each town
No man was ever bolder,
I thought that I was doing right,
As the King did want new soldiers
I told them tales of fond delight,
I kept recruiting day and night,
And when I had made all things right
Off went the rambling soldier.

And now the wars are at an end
I am not ashamed to mention
The King has given me my discharge
And granted me a pension.
No doubt some lasses me will blame,
But me they never once can shame,
And if you want to know my name,
'Tis Bill the Rambling Soldier.

110 *The Red Herring*

As I was awalking all on the sea sand,
I picked up a herring all in my right hand.
   It was big herrings, little herrings, all a-brought in,
   So I think I made well of my jolly herring.
   Hark, hark! Hudlie.
   Why hast thou not told me so?
   So I did long ago.
   Well, well, well and agin.
   So I think I made well of my jolly herring.

O what do you think I made out of my old herring's head?
I made fine ovens as ever baked bread.

O what do you think I made out of my old herring's eyes?
I made forty men's pasties and fifty women's pies.

O what do you think I made out of my old herring's back?
I made so fine horses as ever carried pack.

O what do you think I made out of my old herring's ribs?
I made fat bullocks and the bravest of cribs.

O what do you think I made out of my old herring's guts?
I made so fine boys as ever trod mucks.

O what do you think I made out of my old herring's fins?
I made so fine fans as ever blowed winds.

O what do you think I made out of my old herring's tail?
I made so fine ships as ever set sail.

O what do you think I made out of my old herring together?
I made so fine cobblers as ever sewed leather.

B-G   Taken down from 'Lucky' Fewins at South Zeal by J. D. Pickman, n.d.

Ms. gives title *The Herring's Head*. Chorus repeated after each stanza.

1.5   *Hudlie*: How y' do lie (note in ms.)
6.2   *mucks*: followed by a ? in ms.

For other versions of this song of lies, see *IP* No. 79 and *FSJ* 20, 1916.

111 *Ripest Apples*

A

Madam, madam, I am come a-courting
If thy favour I can win.
If thou kindly entertain me
Perhaps some day I will call again.

Walk in, kind sir, thou art a-welcome
Though I never saw thee before.
I must and will have a handsome fellow
Whether he be rich or poor.

Handsome men are out of fashion,
Maidens' beauties soon decay.
The finest flower on a Midsummer morning
Will soon fade and die away.

For they will kiss you and they will court you,
They will vow and they will swear.
They tell you more in one half hour
Than you find true in seven long year.

False love is plenty, true love is scanty
Love is well when it is new.
As it grow older so it grow colder
And fades and dies like the morning dew.

B

A pretty maiden walking in her garden
But her name I do not know.
I'll go and court her for her beauty,
Let her answer be yes or no.

Madam, madam, I am come a-courting
That your favour I may gain,
Sit you down, you're kindly welcome,
Then perhaps you may call again.

Madam, I have gold and silver,
Madam, I have house and land,
Madam, I have a world of pleasure,
I leave it all at your command.

Don't tell me of your gold and silver,
Don't tell me of your house and land,
Don't tell me of your world of pleasure,
All I want is a handsome man.

Handsome men are out of fashion,
Maidens' beauties soon decay.
You pick a flower of a summer morning,
Before the evening it will fade away.

First comes the oxlip, then the cruel,
Then the pink and then the may,
Then comes a new love, then comes a true love,
And so we pass our time away.

Once I lay on a young man's pillow,
Which I thought it was my own.
Now I do so lie under the willow
All for the sake of a false young man.

H Version A Mrs Forsey at Wotton, May 1906
   Version B Mrs Sims

Ms. gives title *Madam! Madam!*

B 6.1 *cruel*: 'small form of cowslip', note by **H.**

See *IP* Nos. 68, 69, and Introduction. I have adopted the present title for these two variants, since of the several related songs published variously as *O No John, Twenty Eighteen*, etc. *Ripest Apples* is the closest. Both the above versions are given almost unaltered in *DBFS*.

All the songs in the *O No John* and *Ripest Apples* group appear to be connected with a singing game variously called *Lady on Yonder Hill* and *Lady on the Mountain* (see *Traditional Games*, Gomme, Vol. I, 1894), a courting game somewhat similar to *Kiss in the Ring*, though evidently not originally a children's game. Which came first, the ballad or the game, it is impossible to say. Lady Gomme quotes the following curious dialogue form of the singing-game from Suffolk, which may be part of a forgotten mummery acted by strolling players:

There stands a lady on yonder hill,
Who she is I cannot tell;
I'll go and court her for her beauty,
Whether she answers me yes or no.
Madame I bow vounce to thee.
Sir, have I done thee any harm?
Coxconian!
Coxconian is not my name; 'tis Hers and Kers, and Willis and Cave.
Stab me, ha! ha! little I fear. Over the waters there are but nine, I'll meet you
    a man alive. Over the waters there are but ten, I'll meet you there five
    thousand.
Rise up, rise up, my pretty fair maid,
You're only in a trance;
Rise up, rise up, my pretty fair maid,
And we will have a dance.

In this dialogue between a boy and a girl, at the words 'Stab me' the boy pretends to stab the girl, who falls to the ground and is then raised to her feet.

112 *Rosemary Lane*

I am a bold sailor that sailed on the sea,
I gained the good will of my captain and crew.
I sailed into harbour one night for to lie
And that's the beginning of my true love and I.
Chorus Then it's home, dearest home, in my own counterie,
        Home, dearest home, and it's there let me be,
        Where the oak and the ash and the bonny ellum tree
        They're all growing green in the North Amerikee.

He asked for a candle to light him to bed,
Likewise for a napkin to tie round his head.
She waited on me as a fair maid should do
And I gave her the wink to jump into bed too.

She jumped into bed for to keep herself warm
Not thinking a sailor would do her any harm.
She kissed him, she cuddled him, she bid him draw near,
She wished that long night had been seven long year.

Now when the baby's born you shall put it out to nurse
With silver in his pocket and gold in his purse.
You shall dry off your breasts as a virgin so free
And pass for a virgin in some strange counterie.

But if it be a girl you shall dangle it on your knee
But if it be a boy you shall put him to the sea.
With his long quarter shoes and his jacket so blue
He shall walk the quarter deck as his daddy used to do.

Come all you fair maidens, a warning take by me
And never trust a sailor one inch above your knee
For I have trusted one and he has deceivèd me
And he's left me with a baby to dangle on my knee.

H William Chubb at Beaminster, June 1906

Ms. gives title *Home Dearest Home.*

For other versions, see *IP* No. 81.

113 *The Royal Light Dragoon*

Come all you saucy landladies, what makes you look so gay?
O I do well assure you, the Light Horse comes in to-day,
Well mounted on their short tail nags comes prancing into town
And the very first thing that they will do, they'll pull your hayricks
   down.

The landlord give them diet, the best he can afford,
O for to keep the Light Horse quiet and from drawing of the sword.
In bed they lies like gentlemen with arms all round the room
And 'tis death to those that do oppose the Royal Light Dragoon.

They gets up of a summer morn and goes to exercise
Whiles the pretty girls stand all round the boys with tears all in
   their eyes.
We get up of a summer's morn and do our work by noon
And spend a summer evening with the saucy Light Dragoon.

Now if we should kiss those pretty girls, and that perhaps we may,
They'll speak unto our officers, and they will send us away
Into some foreign countary, where riots will be soon,
And 'tis death to those that do oppose the Royal Light Dragoon.

Now if we should marry those pretty girls and make them our
   lawful brides
They'd tire us of our comfort and weary us of our lives,
For we must rock the cradle, boys, from stable time till noon,
And 'tis death to those that do oppose the Royal Light Dragoon.

So now the riot's come, my boys, and now we must away
Into a place called Holland our orders to obey.
Here's a good success to the pretty girls and I wish them well for me.
They do like to spend a time in a soldier's company.

H W. H. C. Bartlett at Wimborne, Dorset, 1905

3.4 *with*: ms. at
6.1 *riot*: i.e. rout, marching orders

114 *Sailor Cut Down in his Prime*

A

One day as I strolled down the Royal Albion
Dark was the morning, cold was the day,
Then who should I spy but one of my shipmates
Draped in a blanket far colder than clay.

He called for a candle to light him to bed,
Likewise an old flannel to wrap round his head.
His poor head was aching, his poor heart was breaking,
For he was a young sailor cut down in his prime.

We'll beat the drums loudly, play the pipes merrily,
Play the dead march as we bear him along,
Take him to a churchyard and fire three volleys over him.
There goes a young sailor cut down in his prime.

But now he is dead and laid in his coffin
Six jolly sailor boys march on each side
And each of them carries a bunch of white roses
That no-one might smell him as we passed 'em by.

At the corner of the street there's two girls a-standing,
Each to the other does whistle and sing,
Here come a young fellow whose money we squandered,
Here come a young sailor cut down in his prime.

'Pon top of his tombstone you'll see these words written,
All you young fellows take a warning by me
And never go courting these girls of the city
For these girls of the city were the ruin of me.

B

As I was a-walking down by the seaside,
As I was a-walking there one day,
O who should I spy but my own daughter Mary
Wrapped up in some flannel some hot summer's day.

O mother, O mother, come sit you down by me,
Come sit you down by me and pity my case.
It's of a young officer I was lately deserted,
See how he has brought me to shame and disgrace.

O daughter, O daughter, why didn't you tell me,
Why did you not tell me, we'd took it in time.
It's young pill a cosha, the pill o' white margery,
But now I am a young girl cut down in my prime.

O doctor, O doctor, come wash up your bottles,
Come wash up your bottles and wipe them quite dry.
My bones they are aching, my poor heart's a-breaking
And I in a deep solemn fashion must die.

Have six jolly men to bear up my coffin,
Have six pretty fair maids to bear up my pall.
Give to each pretty fair maid a glass of brown ale
Saying, Here lies a maiden, a true-hearted girl.

Come rattle your drums and play your fifes merrily,
Merrily play the dead marches along
And over my coffin throw handfuls of laurel
Cry, Here lies the bones of a true-hearted girl.

Version A   **H**   J. Curtis at Lyme Regis, March 1906

Ms. gives title *The Unfortunate Rake*. The word 'Chorus' appears after stanzas 2, 4 and 6, but it is not indicated which lines are the Chorus.

Version B   **G**   Mr Henry Adams (71) at Basingstoke, Hants, September 1906

Ms. gives title *The Doctor*. Last two lines of each stanza repeated as Chorus.

See *IP* No. 86 for another text and notes.

Version B is the female version of the song known variously as *Sailor Cut Down in his Prime, The Unfortunate Rake, Saint James' Hospital,* etc. It clears up the confusion evidenced by the version in *FSJ* 17, 1913, entitled *The Young Girl Cut Down in her Prime.* It is clear that the cause of death is syphilis.

In the ms., line 3.3 is not, like the remainder, typewritten, but is in **G**'s own hand, and the footnote reads: 'Dr Calvert of Melrose has tried botanical works and books on materia medica for a solution of this corrupt line, but without success. Margery may stand for marjoram.' But against the word 'margery' in 3.3 there is a pencilled note, also apparently by **G**, no doubt at a later date, which reads, 'white mercury'. This is correct, since mercury was formerly used in the treatment of syphilis. (Cf. the aphorism current in medical circles, 'A night with Venus and a lifetime with Mercury.')

Young pill a cosha means 'yon pill o'cochia' (colocynth, the coloquintida of *Othello,* I.3.356), once extensively—now occasionally—used in the treatment of female ailments.

Attached to the ms. is a sheet containing the following notes, evidently in Frank Kidson's hand:

'This is evidently a version of the "Unfortunate Lad" (or Rake) with the sexes reversed. The words are very similar to those on the ballad sheet referred to in FS Journal Vol. I, p. 254. . . . Corresponding lines of ballad

UNFORTUNATE LAD

Had she but told me of it in time
I might have got salts and pills of white mercury
But now I'm cut down in the height of my prime

'I must say I do not like the insertion of this ballad (words) and then on several others in this collection equally objectionable we ought to decide how far "unclean" words should be admitted. . . .' FK.

115 *The Saucy Sailor Boy*

Come, my only one, come, my fond one,
Come, my dearest, unto me.
Won't you wed with this poor sailor boy
Just returnèd from the sea?

No, you're a ragged love, no, a dirty love
And you smells so strong of tar.
You be gone, you saucy sailor boy,
You be gone, you Jack-tar.

If I am a ragged love, if I'm a dirty love,
If I smell so strong of tar,
I have silver in my pocket, love,
And I've gold all in bright store.

So soon as she heard him say it,
On her bended knees she fell
Saying, I'll wed with my dear Henery
For I love my jolly sailor well.

No, I'd rather cross the briny oceans
Where there's no field to be seen.
Since you've refused the offer, love,
Some other shall wear the ring.

H Mrs Gulliver, April 1905

Ms. gives alternative title *Come my Only One.*

  5.2   The Such broadside (BM L.R. 271 a. 2, Vol. VI, p. 76) gives *Where the meadows are so green*

Versions collected in Oxfordshire and Sussex by George Butterworth are given in *FSJ* 17, 1913; and an emended version by **B-G** in *SW*.

116 *The Seeds of Love*

A

Come all you maidens fair
That are just now in your prime,
I would have you to weed your gardens clean,
See that no man steals your thyme.

For it's once I had old thyme enough
To flourish both by night and by day
Till it chanced there came along a false young man
And he stole all my old thyme away.

Now my old thyme it is all gone
And I cannot get any new.
There's the very very place where my thyme it stood
And it's all overrun with rue.

Oh rue, oh rue is a running, running root
And it runs so far underneath.
Then I will pluck that running, running root
And I'll plant in a jolly old tree.

Now here stands the jolly old tree,
He neither will wither nor die,
And I'll prove as true unto my true love
As the stars are unto the sky.

Then our gardener being there standing by,
When I asked him to choose for me,
He chose me the violet, the lily and the pink
And I really overlooked them all three.

For the lily is a flower that will fade so soon

. . . .

The violet and the pink I really overlooked,
I would have them to tarry till June.

In June, in June there a red rosy bud
And that is the flower for me.
Long time I have aimed at the red rosy bud,
Now I've gained the old willow tree.

Green willow I am forced for to wear,
For to drive all sorrows from me,
That all the world might plainly see
I died for a false young man.

B

Oh early in the spring-time of the year
As the sun did begin for to shine
There were three branches for me to choose one
And the first I chose was thyme.

Thyme, thyme is a precious thing,
It flourish night and day,
But who come along but my jolly sailor boy
And he stole all my thyme away.

My gardener he stood by
And I asked him to choose for me.
He chose me the lily, the violet and the pink
But these flowers I refused all three.

The violet I did forsake
Because it fades so soon.
The lily and the pink I did overlook
And I vowed I'd stop till June.

THE SEEDS OF LOVE

In June grows a red rosy bud
And that is the flower for me.
He oftentimes pluckèd at the red rosy bud
Till he gained the will of me

My gardener he stood by
And he told me to take great care
For into the middle of that red rosy bud
There grows a sharp thorn there.

But I did not take great care
Till I had felt the smart
And I oftentimes pluckèd at the red rosy bud
Till it piercèd my tender heart.

Oh begone, you false young man
And leave me here behind
And the grass that is now trodden underfoot
In time 'twill rise again.

Oh the gilly-flowers they smell sweet
And so do the rose in June
And so do I and a pretty fair maid
If she hadn't a-loved too soon.

Stand you up, stand you up, my jolly oak,
Stand you up and do not die,
For I will be so true to the girl I love so dear
As the stars shine so bright in the sky.

C

Once I'd a sprig of thyme
That did flourish both night and day,
Till at length came along a pretty ploughboy
And stole my thyme away.

And now my thyme is gone
And I cannot plant any more,
For the very same place where my thyme did grow
Is all covered over with woe.

The gardener standing by
Choosing the flower for me,
The primrose, the violet and the vine,
And I refused all three.

The primrose I did not like
Because it flowered so soon,
The violet and vine I did o'erlook
And I vowed I'd stop till June.

In June there grows the rose
And that was the flower for me
Till at length came along a pretty ploughboy
And sat upon a willow tree.

Green willow it will twist,
Green willow it will twine.
I wish I were in the young man's arms
Where he gained this heart of mine.

D

Once I had plenty of thyme,
I could flourish by night and by day
Till a saucy lad he returned from sea
And stole my thyme away.

O and I was a damsel so fair
But fairer I wished to appear
So I washed me in milk and dressed me in silk
And put the sweet thyme in my hair.

With June is the red rose in bud
But that's not the flower for me,
So I pluckèd the bud and it pricked me to blood,
And I gazed on the willow tree.

O the willow tree it will twist
And the willow tree it will twine.
I would I were back in my saucy love's arms
For 'tis he that hath stolen my thyme.

O 'tis very good drinking of ale
But it's far better drinking red wine.
I would I were back in my saucy love's arms
For 'tis he that hath stolen my thyme.

E

DEAD MAIDS' LAND

A garden was planted around
With flowers of every kind.
I chose of the best to wear in my breast,
The flower best pleasèd my mind.

A gardener standing by
I askèd to choose for me.
He chose me the lily, the violet, the pink,
But I likèd none of the three.

A violet I don't like,
A lily it fades so soon,
But as for the pink, I cared not a flink,
I said I would stop till June.

The lily it shall be thy smock,
The jonquil shoe thy feet.
Thy gown shall be of the ten-week stock,
Thy gloves the violet sweet.

The gilly shall deck thy head,
Thy way with herbs I'll strew.
Thy stockings shall be the marigold,
Thy gloves of the violet blue.

I will not have the ten-week stock
Nor jonquils to my shoon,
But I will have the red red rose
That flowereth in June.

The rose it doth bear a thorn
That pierceth to the bone.
I little heed what thou dost say,
I will have that or none.

The rose it doth bear a thorn
That pierceth to the heart.
O but I will have the red red rose,
I little heed the smart.

She stoopèd to the ground
To pluck the rose so red.
The thorn it pierced her to the heart
And this fair maid was dead.

A gardener stood at the gate
With cypress in his hand,
And he did say, Let no fair maid
Come into Dead Maids' Land.

Version A   **G**   Mr David Marlow at Basingstoke, Hants, September 1906
Version B   **H**   S. Gregory at Beaminster, June 1906
Last line of each stanza repeated.
Version C   **H**   Miss Brown at Lydlinch, Dorset, 1905
Ms. gives each stanza as two lines only.
Version D   **B-G**   Joseph Dyer, labourer (65), at Mawgan in Pyder, July 6, 1891
Ms. gives title *Flowers and Weeds*.
Version E   **B-G**   Thomas Paddin, labourer, Holcombe Burrell, December 1889

A 7.2   as in ms.
E 3.3   *flink: sic*

IP No. 91. (In my notes I there explain *thyme* as 'hope', but it is clear that it stands more specifically for 'virginity'.)

H printed B in *FSJ* 11, 1907. **B-G** published in *SW*, 1st and 2nd editions, a text consisting of E stanzas 4–10 preceded by a stanza of his own composition. In *SW*, 3rd edition, he prints a deplorable piece of nonsense, but in his notes gives what is substantially the same as D. Child (No. 219) gives three Scottish versions, one fragmentary, of a ballad entitled *The Gardener*. It looks as if this is the stock from which all the versions of *The Seeds of Love* and *The Sprig of Thyme* sprang. The Child ballad is essentially the same as *The New Lover's Garland*, No. II of *Five Excellent New Songs* (BM 11621. b. 6 [8]), as follows:

> The waking all the winter's night,
> And the tippling at the wine,
> And the courting of a bonny Lass
> Will break this heart of mine.

> (Chor.) Brave sailing here my dear,
> And better sailing there,
> Better sailing in my lover's arms,
> O! give I were there.

> I had a bed of thyme
> And it flourished night and day,
> There came by a Squire's Son
> That stole my heart way.
> Brave sailing here, etc.

> And up comes the gardener lad,
> And he gave me profers free,
> He gave to me the jully flowers,
> To clothe my gay bodie.

> The gardener stood in his garden,
> And the prim-rose in his hand,
> And there he spi'd his own true love
> As tight 's a willy wand.

> If he'll be a lover true, she said.
> A lover true indeed
> And buy all the flowers of my garden,
> I'll shape to thee a weed.
> Brave sailing here, etc.

235

The Prim-rose shall be on thy head,
  And the red rose on thy breast,
And the white-rose shall be for a smock,
  To cover thy body next.
  Brave sailing here, etc.

Thy grove shall be of the jully flowers,
  Comes Lockren to thy hand,
Thy stockings shall be of the thyme,
  Fair maid it is a pleasant view.

Put on Fair Maid when ever you please,
  And your shoes shall be of the Rue.
Brave Sailing here my Dear,
  And better Sailing there,
And Brave Sailing in my loves arms,
  O! If I were there.

The young Maid's Answer

You shape to be, a young Man, she says,
  A weed amongst the flowes,
But I will shape to you, young Man,
  A weed amongst the flowers.

The hail-stones shall be on thy head,
  And the Snow upon thy breast,
And the east-wind shall be for a shirt,
  To cover thy body next.
  Brave sailing there, etc.

Thy boots shall be of the stangle,
  That nothing can betide;
Thy steed shall be of the wan-water,
  Loup on young Man and ride,

Brave sailing there my dear,
  And better Sailing here,
And 'tis brave sailing 'twixt my love's arms,
  O! if I were there.

Printed and sold by William Forrest [rest cut off—n.d.]
The most serious corruption in the above is stanza 1 of the maid's answer: according to the Child versions, this should read:

You shape to me, young man, says she,
  A weed among the flowers,
And I will shape another for you,
  Among the winter showers.

Another version appears as *The Maid's Lament for the loss of her Maiden-head*, No. III of *Four Excellent Songs*, printed and sold by William Forrest at the head of the *Cow-gate* 1766 (BM 11621. b. 6 [13]):

All you Maidens Fair,
    That glory in your prime;
Take care and keep your gardens clean,
    Let no man steal your thyme.

When I was a maiden fair
    I flourished night and day,
And there came by a proper youth
    Stealt all my thyme away.

My thyme it is all spent,
    For I can plant no new,
The very place where my thyme grew;
    And 'tis all laid o'er with rue.

Stand up my little hope,
    And do not me deny;
If this young Man come not back again,
    I'm sure undone am I.

The Gardener sent his word
    And he gave his choice of three;
The spink revileth the prim-rose,
    And she denied all three.

The prim-rose she denied,
    It's an herb that grows too soon;
The tulips is over wet,
    And duly wet full June.

Forsaken folk must live,
    Altho' it be in pain;
And the Grass that's trodden under feet,
    Tho' time will rise again.

Here the obvious corruptions in stanzas 5 and 6 are evidently due to the inability of some early collector to make sense of what a rural singer sang. For *The spink revileth* read *The pink, the violet*. I am at a loss to know precisely what is meant by *The tulips is over wet*, but *And duly wet full June* must stand for *And I will wait for/till June*. It is probable that in stanza 4 *hope* is a corruption of *oak*.

THE SEEDS OF LOVE

A broadside version (BM L.R. 271 a. 2, Vol. VIII, p. 221) contains yet another variant which I have not seen elsewhere:

I'll make a posy of hyson no other I can touch
That all the world may plainly see I love one flower too much,
My garden is run wild where I shall plant anew
For my bed that once was covered with thyme is all overrun with rue.

Hyson is presumably not 'green tea from China' but a corruption of *hyssop*, referred to in the Old Testament both as a means of purification and as an emblem of humility.

These examples, and the five versions given above, indicate the multiplicity and variety of a song of wide provenance, whose age it is impossible to determine. They demonstrate also the impossibility of deciding whether we have one song which has developed in several directions or several songs which have coalesced in the popular tradition.

117 *Seventeen Come Sunday*

As I walked out one May morning
One May morning so early
O there I spied a fair pretty maid
All in the dew so pearly.
    With a fa-la-la—with a fa-la-la
    All in the dew so pearly.

O where are you going my fair pretty maid?
O where are you going my lambie?
Then cheerfully she answered me,
An errand for my mammie.

How old are you my fair pretty maid?
How old are you my honey?
Then cheerfully she answered me,
I'm seventeen on Sunday.

Will you take a man my fair pretty maid?
Will you take a man my lambie?
Then cheerfully she answered me,
I dare not for my mammie.

If you will come to my mother's house
When the moon is shining clearly
I'll lift the pin and let you in
And my mammy will not hear me.

O then I went to her mother's house
When the moon was brightly shining,
Then she lifted the pin and she let me in
And we lay with our arms entwining.

Then she said to me, Will you marry me?
As she let me out in the morning,
For by thee I'm one as is quite undone,
O leave me not in scorning.

Then she said to me, Will you marry me?
O say this now or never,
For if that you are not good and true
Then I am undone for ever.

B-G   Edmund Fry at Lydford, 1889

Ms. gives title *As I walked out*.

Chorus repeated after each stanza, but ms. does not make it clear that the second line of the Chorus presumably repeats the fourth line of the preceding stanza.

IP No. 44.
   SW contains a re-written version. The above are the words **B-G** considered unprintable. For full notes see *IP*.
   A broadside version from **B-G**'s collection (BM L.R. 271 a. 2, Vol. VII, p. 65) has the following additional concluding stanza:

> Now I'm with my soldier lad,
>   Where the wars they are alarming,
> A drum and fife is my delight
>   And a pint of rum in the morning.

118 *The Shoemaker's Kiss*

There was an old woman lived down in the West.
Hey ho! her name was Nanny.
She had a fine daughter that never was kissed,
It was all in the morning so early.

One morning she rose and put on her clothes,
And away to the shoemaker's shop she did go.

Shoemaker, shoemaker, have you got any shoes?
Yes, yes, pretty maiden, I think I'll fit you.

Come in, pretty maiden, sit down by my side.
Good Lord, how he caught her and kissed her sweet lips.

When twenty long weeks was all over and past
This little bold wench she got thick in the waist.

When forty long weeks was over and past
This little bold wench had a big bonny lass.

O daughter, O daughter, how came you by this?
O mother, O mother, it was the shoemaker's kiss.

O now that I've got a brave bonny child
. . . I'll put it to nurse,
Good Lord! it will shrink the poor shoemaker's purse.

H   G. Bowditch at Charmouth, March 1906

Ms. gives sub-title *So Green as the Leaves are Green.*

Chorus lines in stanza 1 repeated in each stanza.

4.2   *caught her and kissed*: ms. kissed her and caught
8   Stanza defective in ms.

119 *The Silly Doe*

Give ear unto my mournful song,
Gay huntsmen every one,
And unto you I will relate
My sad and doleful moan.

O here I be, a silly doe,
From Elford town I strayed,
In leaving of my company
Myself to death betrayed.

The master said I should be slain
For leaving of the bounds.
O keeper, shoot her if you can
Or chase her with your hounds.

The Cornish duke of royal blood
And hounds of noble race,
They picked a pack the very next day,
After me did chase.

They roused me out one winter morn,
The frost it cut my feet,
And then my blood came trickling down
And made the scent lie sweet.

For many miles they did me run
Before the sun went down.
O I was brought to give a teen
And fall upon the ground.

The first rode up, it was the Duke,
Said, Now I'll have my will.
A blade from out his pocket drew
And did my red blood spill.

So with good cheer they murdered me
As I lay on the ground,
The Duke of Cornwall and the pack
Of huntsmen standing round.

B-G   George Cole (76) at Rundlestone, Dartmoor, June 1892

B-G published an emended text in the *Garland*, and I know of no other published version. In his note he says that 'Dartmoor is a forest under the Prince of Wales, as Duke of Cornwall', and that 'Elford town' is Yelverton. Chasing the doe is a common metaphor for sexual pursuit, and may have been used as a disguise for a local scandal involving an important personage. Cf. the sonnet by Sir Thomas Wyatt, *Who so list to hount, I knowe where is an hynde'*, which may refer to Henry VIII and Anne Boleyn. Cf. also *The Keeper* (*IP* No. 52), which has also been said, without authority, to refer to Henry VIII.

120 *Sing Ovy, Sing Ivy*

My father gave me an acre of land,
Sing ovy, sing ivy.
My father gave me an acre of land,
A bunch of green holly and ivy.

I harrowed it with a bramble bush.

I sowed it with two peppercorns.

I rolled it with a rolling pin.

I reaped it with my little penknife.

I housed it into mouse's hole.

I threshed it out with two beanstalks.

I sent my rats to market with that.

My team o'rats came rattling back,
Sing ovy, sing ivy,
With fifty bright guineas and an empty sack,
A bunch of green holly and ivy.

G Mrs Goodyear at Axford by Basingstoke, Hants, July 1907

Stanzas 2–8 constructed on the same pattern as 1.

This was printed, with one emendation, in *GFH*. Halliwell gives a very similar version, and others were collected in Sussex by W. P. Merrick (*FSJ* 3, 1901), in Wiltshire by R. Vaughan Williams (*FSJ* 8, 1906), and in Hampshire by H. Balfour Gardiner (*FSJ* 13, 1909).

It is a riddle song (cf. *I will give my love an apple*, No. 73) apparently derived ultimately from the ballad of *The Elfin Knight* (Child No. 2), in which similar tasks are set. The Elfin Knight undertakes to be a young girl's lover if she will make him a seamless shirt; to which she replies by setting him the ploughing task. The chorus lines incorporating the male and female symbols, holly and ivy, belong to the song but not to the ballad.

121 *Sir Hugh*

Oh rain, oh rain so very fast,
The wind doth wither and blow.
There was three little boys went out to play,
To play with their sweet silver ball.

They tossed him high, they tossed him low,
They tossed him over into the Jew's garden.
The very first of them that did come out,
The Jewess was dressed in green.

Come in, come in, you little Sir Hugh,
Come in and fetch your ball.
I can't come in nor I won't come in
Without my playmates all.

At first she showed me an apple so red
And next was a diamond ring,
Next was the cherry so red as blood
And so she got me in.

She set me into a silver chair
And fed me with sugar so sweet.
She laid me on the dressing-board
And stuck me like a sheep.

She throwed me into a new-dug well,
It was forty cubits deep.
She wropped me up in red mantel
Instead of a milk-white sheet.

'Twas up and down the garden there
This little boy's mammie did run.
She had a little rod all under her apron
To beat her little son home.

Oh here I am, dear mother, he cries,
My grave is dug so deep.
The penknife sticks so close to my heart,
So 'long with you I can't sleep.

G   Mr James Pikset at Portsmouth Workhouse, August 1907
4.4.   *she*: ms. he

This follows the general lines of most English versions, but is not exactly
similar to any of those given by Child (No. 155). For a full discussion of the
historical background to the legend of St Hugh of Lincoln, see Child's notes.

122 *Some Rival has Stolen*

Come all you damsels, I pray you draw near
For to hear the sad tidings which I bring you here.
It's of a young man who lays now confined
For to sing you this ditty I am now inclined.

A rifle hath stolen my dear jewel away
And I in old England no longer can stay,
So I'll swim the wide ocean all on my bare breast
For to find out my true love, the one whom I love best.

And when I have found out my joy and heart's delight
I will cherish her most dearly by day and by night,
I will prove to her more constant than the true turtle-dove
For ever and for ever I'll be true to my love.

And when I have swimmed and my love I have found
With all sorts of sweet music my love shall be crowned,
The drum shall beat aloud and the music shall play
For to welcome my love home again with ten thousands of
     joys.

G   Mr Richard Read (67) at Bishop's Sutton, Hants, n.d.
Last two lines of each stanza repeated as Chorus.

Ms. gives title *Come all you Young Damsels*.

   2.1   *rifle*: a corruption of rival

This is a version of *The Merry King* (see notes to *The Cuckoo*, No. 25).

   Most of the variants of this song agree in emphasizing the splendour of the music with which the lovers' reunion is to be celebrated. Stanza 4 of a version printed by W. P. Merrick in *FSJ* 3, 1901, is as follows:

> We'll make the bugle speak, and the serpent shall sing,
> Here's instruments of music for to make those valleys ring;
> The huntsman he shall holloa, and the hounds shall make a noise,
> For to fill my love's heart with ten thousand of bright joys.

123 *The Sprig of May*

As I walked out one May morning
Across the dreary moor
I met a maid, she lamenting said
And all her pleasure was to marry me.

I asked her fair whether I should go
Across one flowery field.
She appears like a maid, she answers no,
But her full intent was that I should go.

In crossing of one flowery field
My finger I chanced to break.
She says, Young man, I should like to see
You break your finger to pleasure me.

So May is over and so is June,
July and August too.
It's by experience I know full well
One sprig of May made her belly swell.

G   Mr Rickart Fernhill at Broomhead by Launceston, Cornwall, n.d.

I have not seen this elsewhere. Just as the 'sprig of thyme' is a metaphorical representation of chastity, so 'sprig of may' represents wantonness. The metaphorical character of the 'dreary moor', the 'flowery field' and the finger-breaking is obvious enough.

The Squire and the Fair Maid

As I was walking out one day
Down by a river's side
I heard two lovers in discourse,
A squire and his fair bride.
You are so comely, sir, she said,
And have a ready tongue.
I would you were my bride, fair maid.
Nay sir, I am too young.

The younger you are the better you are,
The better you are for me.
I vow and swear and do declare
I'll marry none save thee.
He took her by the lily-white hand
To talk with her awhile,
He took her by the lily-white hand
And led her o'er the stile.

He led her to some wedding room,
She kissed his ruddy cheek,
She stroked his flowing, flaxen hair.
No word then might he speak.
And in the beginning of the night
They had both jest and play
And the remainder of the night
Close to his breast she lay.

The night being gone, the day came on,
The morning shined clear.
The youth arose, put on his clothes
And said, Farewell my dear.
Is this the promise that you made
All by the river side?
You promised me you'd marry me,
Make me your lawful bride.

If I to you a promise made
That's more than I can do.
Man loveth none so easy won,
So ever fond as you.
Go get you where are gardens fair,
There sit and cry your fill,
And when you think on what you've done
Then blame your forward will.

There is a herb in your garden,
Some people call it rue.
When fishes fly as swallows high
Then young men will prove true.
She went all then to her garden,
She sat her down to cry,
Was ever found on God's good ground
One crossed in love as I?

Was ever girl in city or town
So used as I have been?
Was ever girl so used as I
For wearing a gown of green.
Sing lullaby, sing lullaby!
For that alone I'm able O.
Whilst others roam I stay at home,
At home and rock the cradle O!

B-G J. Hoskins at South Brent and James Parsons at Lew Down, n.d.

A version of *Abroad as I was Walking* (No. 1), *q.v.*, and of *Down by a River Side* (*IP* No. 28) with considerable differences. **B-G** printed an emasculated version in *SW*, 1st and 2nd editions.

125 *Strawberry Fair*

As I was agoing to Strawberry Fair,
Ri-tol-ri-tol, riddle-tol-de-lido,
I saw a fair maiden of beauty rare,
Tol-de-dee.
I saw a fair maid go selling her ware
As she went on to Strawberry Fair,
Ri-tol-ri-tol, riddle-tol-de-lido.

O pretty fair maiden, I prithee tell,
My pretty fair maid, what do you sell?
O come tell me truly, my sweet damsel,
As you go on to Strawberry Fair.

O I have a lock that doth lack a key,
O I have a lock, sir, she did say.
If you have a key then come this way
As we go on to Strawberry Fair.

Between us I reckon that when we met
The key to the lock it was well set,
The key to the lock it well did fit
As we went on to Strawberry Fair.

O would that my lock had been a gun,
I'd shoot the blacksmith, for I'm undone,
And wares to carry I now have none
That I should go to Strawberry Fair.

B-G J. Masters at Bradstone, 1891. Taken down by H. Fleetwood Shepherd

Chorus lines repeated throughout, as in stanza 1.

5.2 *blacksmith*: presumably locksmith

Our gratitude is due to **B-G** for preserving the original of this popular song, which I have not seen elsewhere; but so radically different is the 'buttercups and daisies' version, perpetrated by him and him alone, that to have popularized the song in this form must be considered a personal triumph of no mean order.

In his notes to *SW*, 1st and 2nd editions, **B-G** says: 'This song was certainly early, but unsuitable; and I have been constrained to re-write it. . . . The ballad is sung everywhere in Cornwall and Devon to the same melody. The words are certainly not later than the age of Charles II, and are probably older. They turn on a *double entendre* which is quite lost—and fortunately so—to half the old fellows who sing the song.'

This is interesting, as evidence that the metaphorical significance of the 'lock and key' was not lost on either **B-G** or *some* at least of his singers.

He also states that the song was a 'recast' of the sixteenth-century *Kytt hath lost her key*: but apart from the 'key' metaphor the two songs have nothing whatever in common.

Cf. the words of the children's singing game 'Betsy Bungay':

> Hi, Betsy Bungay, all day on Sunday;
> You're the lock and I'm the key,
> All day on Monday.
> (Gomme, *A Dictionary of British Folk-Lore*, Vol. I, 1894.)

See also Introduction, p. 22.

126 The Streams of Lovely Nancy

A

Come all you little streamers of these meadows so gay,
They are the highest mountains that ever was seen,
Fine fishing, eels and flowery fields and hunting also
And at the top all on this mountain there's a fine flower grows.

On the top all of this mountain my true love's castle stands.
It's surrounded all round with ivory from the top down to the sand,
Fine porches and fine orchards and diamond stones so bright,
It's a pilot for the sailors on a dark stormy night.

At the bottom of this mountain there runs a river clear
Where the ships all from the Indies, they all do anchor there,
With red flags a-flying and the beating of their drums,
Their sweet instruments of music and the firing of their guns.

If my Nancy had been true to me she might have been my bride
But her mind has been more changing just like the wind and tide,
Like a ship all on the ocean wide that's tossed to and fro,
Where an angel may direct us all and where shall we go.

So come all you little streamers wherever you might be,
Direct me to my own true love wherever she might be,
For her rosy cheeks enticed me and her tongue it tells me so,
Where an angel may direct us all and where shall we go.

B

Oh the streams of lovely Nancy was divided in three parts
Where young men and young maidens goes to meet their sweet-
hearts.
Drinking of strong liquors caused my heart to sing
And the noise of the valleys makes the rocks for to ring.

So in yonder high mountain there's a high castle stands,
Builded up with ivory near the black sand,
Builded up with ivory and diamonds so bright,
It's a pilot for the sailor on a dark winter's night.

And the sailor and his true love was a-walking along.
Said the sailor to his true love, I'll sing you a song.
You're a false-hearted woman, you makes me say no.
Fare you well, my dearest Nancy, and now I will go.

I never will get married nor yet made a wife,
I'll go down in some nunnery and there end my life.
Constant and true-hearted for ever I'll remain,
I never will get married till my sailor comes again.

C

O the sweet streams of Nancy
They divide in two parts
Where the young men in dancing
They do meet their sweethearts.
There in drinking strong liquor
It makes my heart sing
And the sound of the viol
It doth make my heart ring.

On yonder tall mountain
A castle doth stand,
It is built of white ivory
All above the black sand,
All of ivory builded
And of diamonds bright,
All with gold it is gilded
And it shines in the night.

On yonder high moorland
The wild fowl do fly.
There is one fair among them
Soars than others more high.
My heart is an eagle
With wings wide outspread,
It soareth and flieth
In pursuit of my maid.

Version A **G** Mrs Goodyear at Axford by Basingstoke, Hants, July 1907

Ms. gives title *Come, All You Little Streamers.*

Version B **G** Mr William Brown at Cheriton, Hants, n.d.

Version C **B-G** Matthew Baker (72), cripple, at Lew Down, July 1889
'This he says he learned when he was ten years old, that is 1827.'

Ms. gives title *The Streams of Nancy.*

B-G printed an altered version of C in *SW* under the title *The Streams of Nantsian*, with notes on broadside texts and on the Cornish word *Nant*, meaning a valley. A version appears in *English County Songs* (Broadwood and Fuller Maitland, 1893) under the title *Faithful Emma*. Other versions, including a Catnach broadside, are given in *FSJ* 3, 1901; 17, 1913; and 27, 1923.

In *FSJ* 17, 1913, Lucy Broadwood and A. G. Gilchrist contribute exhaustive notes on the many versions of this song, in which they venture the suggestion that a medieval mystical hymn to the Virgin Mary has been adapted by an unknown Cornish poet of later date. Lucy Broadwood, in one of her most brilliant annotations, identifies the 'little streamers' with the Cornish children who used to seek for traces of tin in the Cornish valleys. A returning sailor asks them for news of his lost sweetheart. The allegorical castle, with its luxuriant imagery, has been transmuted into some Cornish locality, either Falmouth or St Michael's Mount. The manner in which the words of the song apply to the topography of the area is most striking, and full details are given in the article referred to.

There is undoubtedly a tradition of religious mystical allegory in the background, but the extent to which such allegory incorporates sexual symbolism is perhaps not fully appreciated. What a contemporary reader cannot fail to notice is the strain of erotic metaphor running through the song: the 'fishing', 'flowery fields', 'hunting', the 'drums' and 'musical instruments' are commonplaces of the traditional *lingua franca*; while other references, notably to the 'ivory castle', recall the imagery of *The Song of Songs*.

127 *Sweet William*

A sailor's life is a merry life,
They rob young women of their heart's delight,
They leave them behind for to sithe and mourn
And never known when their love return.

Four and twenty sailors all in a row
And my sweet William cuts a nice show.
He's a proper sailor, genteel withal.
If I don't have him I'll have none at all.

Oh father, bring me a little boat
That I may on the ocean float
And every Queen's ship as I pass by
I may enquire for my sailor boy.

She had not sailed long on the deep
Before a Queen's ship she chanced to meet.
You sailors all, pray tell me true,
Does my sweet William sail along with you?

Oh no, fair lady, he is not here
For he is drowned, I greatly fear.
On yonders island as we passed by
There we lost sight of your sailor boy.

She wrung her hands, she tore her hair
Just like a woman in great despair.
Her little boat against the rocks did run
Saying, How can I live now my Billy's gone?

Then she sat down for to write a song,
She wrote it wide, she wrote it long.
At every line she dropped a tear
Saying at the bottom, I have lost my dear.

She wrung her hands, she tore her hair
Just like a woman in great despair.
She threw her body into the deep
In her William's arms to lie fast asleep.

B

A sailor's life is a merry life,
Which robs young girls of their heart's delight,
But where he's gone no tongue can tell.
I fear he's gone with some other girl.

I had not sailed far on the deep
Before a lofty Queen's ship we met.
Come jovial seamen, come tell me true,
Is my sweet William amongst your crew?

Oh no, fair lady, he is not here.
He is drowned, I greatly fear,
For the other night when the wind blowed high
That's when we lost our sailor boy.

Then she sat down and she wrote a song,
She wrote it wide and she wrote it long,
And every line she dropped a tear
Crying, That's the end, I've lost my dear.

G   Version A   Mr George Baldwin at Tichborne, Hants, n.d.
    Version B   Mr Job Read at Southampton Workhouse, n.d.

This is a typical ballad of a bereaved girl, and as such it has in some versions
attracted to itself certain extraneous stanzas belonging to the common stock.
The version in *English County Songs* (Broadwood and Fuller Maitland, 1893),
for instance, concludes with 'I wish, I wish, but it's all in vain', etc. In Frank
Kidson's version (*FSJ* 9, 1906) the girl's father returns home to find her hanging by a rope, with a farewell note in her bosom. A version collected by W. P.
Merrick in *FSJ* 3, 1901, is almost identical with A above, except for the
omission of stanza 7, in which the girl sits down to write a letter. This is
inappropriate enough, and is also part of the common stock; but it occurs both
in the Broadwood and in the Kidson version.

128 *The Tailor and the Crow*

There was an old crow and he sat upon an oak,
There he saw a tailor a-cutting out a coat.
Chorus With my heigh-ro and the old carrion crow cried 'Pork',
      Fol le rol le rol le rol le rido.

Oh wife, oh wife, bring my arrow and my bow
That I might shoot this old carrion crow.

The tailor he shot and he missed his mark,
He hit the old sow slap through the heart.

Oh wife, oh wife, bring me treacle and a spoon
That I may dress our old sow's wound.

The old sow died and the knell went toll.
The little pigs cried for the old sow's soul.

Never mind, said the tailor, I don't care a louse,
For we shall have black puddings, chitterlings and souse.

G Mr Henry Stansbridge at Lyndhurst, Hants, September 27, 1906

Chorus repeated after each stanza.

   6.2 *chitterlings and souse*: dishes made from pigs' offal.

This song, now frequently reprinted as a nursery rhyme, appears in a ms. of 1627 (BM Sloane 1489) and has been in print from at least the late eighteenth century. It has existed in oral tradition for over a hundred years and probably for much longer.

129 *Tailor and Louse*

It's of a tailor and a louse,
  Hey ho the weaver,
They lived together all in one house,
  Gentlemen the tailor.

He got so stout that he went out,
He caught the colic in his eye.

The louse was seen down in the street
With a pair of pattens on his feet.

The louse was seen upon the post
A-eating of a round of toast.

The louse was seen behind the pump
A-searching of his rub-a-dump.

The louse was sick and like to die.
They sent for Doctor Funny Eye.

They had six fleas dressed all in black
To carry the louse to Petty-back.

They had a bug to toll the bell
To carry the louse's soul to Hell.

H George Udal at Halstock, July 1906

Chorus lines repeated in each stanza.

Two jokes about tailors run through the popular tradition—first, that they have
no courage, and secondly, that they have unique opportunities with women.
They are accordingly spoken of with amused contempt. (See notes to *ODNR*
No. 496.) The traditional connection between tailors and lice is indicated in
the expression *to prick a louse*: i.e. to be a tailor, which goes back at least to the
seventeenth century. See also *Four and Twenty Fiddlers* (No. 45), stanza 4.

130 *There Goes a Man just Gone Along*

There goes a man just gone along,
He's gone to the prison that is built so strong,
He's gone to the prison that is built so strong
And so boldly they leads him along.
   Whack fol lol liddle lol le day
   Whack fol le dol lol liddle lol le day.

And when they came to the prison door
How they began to laugh and stare,
How they began to laugh and stare,
The prisoners all round him, I declare.

The very next day the turnkeys say,
Oh come, young man, you come this way,
Oh come, young man, you come this way
For I will iron you down this day.

Now the irons they are put on,
They are so heavy and so strong,
They are so heavy and so strong
That I can scarcely move along.

Now Salisbury assizes is drawing near,
Oh come, my lads, begin to cheer,
Oh come, my lads, begin to cheer
And wipe away all weeping tears.

G Mr George Blake at St Denys, Southampton, May 1906

Chorus repeated after each stanza.

I can throw no light on the origin of this probably incomplete local ballad, which I have not seen elsewhere.

131 *Three Maids a Milking*

Three pretty maidens a milking did go,
Three pretty maidens a milking did go.
When the wind it did blow high
And the wind it did blow low
And it tossed their milking pails to and fro.

Then she met with a man that she did know,
O she met with a man that she did know,
And she asked, Have you the skill,
And she asked, Have you the will
To catch me a small bird or two?

Here's a health to the blackbird in the bush,
Likewise to the merry ring-doo.
If you'll go along with me
Then in yonder greenwood tree
I will catch you a small bird or two.

So I went till we stayed at a bush,
We went till we stayed at two,
And the pretty birds flew in
O and you know what I mean
And I caught them by one and by two.

So whilst, boys, that we have our fun
And we all drink down the sun
We will tarry till we drink down the moon.
As birds of our feather
We will all flock together,
Let people say little or say none.

B-G   Roger Hannaford at Lower Widdecombe, May 1890

Ms. gives title *The Blackbird*.

IP No. 102.

   In *SW*, 1st and 2nd editions, **B-G** found it 'necessary' to write an entirely
different ballad, retaining only a slightly modified version of stanza 3 above.

He considered the original words 'not desirable'. In *SW*, 3rd edition, however he restored most of the original words, altering only 4.3–4, which reveal that the whole song is metaphorical and not to be taken literally. **B-G** was no doubt right in thinking that the public would be unaware of the *double entendre* if it was not pointed out.

For further discussion see notes in *IP*.

132 *Three Maids a Rushing*

A

Three pretty maidens a rushing they went,
A gathering rushes it was their intent.
Before that one came home she'd born a little son
And she rolled it up beneath her apron.

She went all home to her fine father's stairs
And her cheeks were pale and her eyes full of tears.
Says he, Where have you been, my pretty daughter Joan,
And what have you got there rolled up under your apron?

O it is nought, 'tis nought, my father, said she,
But an old lady's gown that is too long for me,
And I was sore afraid 'twould draggle in the dew,
So I rolled it up under my apron.

In the middle of the night when all were asleep
The pretty little baby O it began to weep.
O what and O what is that crying so shrill
In the chamber of the maidens that wakes me 'gainst my will?

O father, dear father, it's nothing, said she,
But a sweet little bird that is singing to me.
I'll handle it and dandle it and lull it to sleep,
That it shall not waken early in the May morning.

In the third part of the night when all were asleep
The pretty little baby O it began to weep.
O what and O what is that crying so clear
In the chamber of the maidens that I do hear?

O father, dear father, it's nothing to thee
But a pretty little baby that sleeps along with me.
O let it lie, O let it lie, 'twill never do thee harm.
I'll handle it and dandle it all night upon my arm.

O was it got of beggar man or gotten of a clown
Or was it got in luxury or gotten in a barn?

It was not got of a beggar man nor gotten of a clown
Nor was it got in luxury nor gotten in a barn.

'Twas gotten of as fine a squire as any up and down,
He gave to me a stomacher with my gay new gown to wear,
To wear so gay and gallant of a May morning.

B

A maiden sweet went forth in May
Nor sheet nor clout she bare,
She went abroad all on the hay
To breathe the fresh spring air.
Before that she came back again
The maiden bore a pretty son
And she rolled it all up in her apron.

She stood upon the drexil stone,
She stood within the door,
Then folded in her apron
The pretty babe she bore.
Her father spoke and shook his head,
Why come so late and what, he said,
Is rolled up in your apron?

O father dear, O father mine,
'Tis nothing unto thee,
But 'tis a pretty birdie fine
That's fluttered to my knee.
I'll lay the birdie to my breast,
I'll build for it a downy nest
And sing to it all in the May morning.

'Twas in the deep and dead of night
When all were fast asleep,
The pretty little baby bright
Began to wake and weep.
The father raised and thus did say,
What bird is this before the day
That sings so shrill in the May morning?

O father dear, O father mine,
'Tis nothing unto thee,
But 'tis a pretty baby fine
That's given unto me.
'Twill never hurt, 'twill never harm,
I'll dance my baby on my arm
And sing to it so sweet in the May morning.

O was it got of beggar man
Or got of shepherd swain
Or was it got of ploughing man
That ploughs the watery main?
I would a sword were in my han'
And I would slay that false young man
And leave him in the dew of a May morning.

It was not got of beggar man
Nor got of shepherd swain,
But it was got of a ploughing man
That ploughs the watery main.
He gave to me a stomacher
With my new gown of green to wear
So gay and gallant in a May morning.

262

Or was it in the kitchen got
Or gotten in the hall
Or was it in the shippen got
Or gotten in the stall?
I would a fire my hand had foun'
And I would burn that building down
Where you met with him on a May morning.

It was not got in kitchen
Nor gotten in the hall,
It was not got in the shippen
Nor gotten in the stall.
But down in yonder shady grove
Where willows bud and lovers rove
There I met him the dew of a May morning.

B-G   Version A   Samuel Fone, mason, at Mary Tavy, December 23, 1892
Version B   James Parsons, August 1890

Ms. gives title *The Maiden Sweet in May.*

B 2.1   *drexil*: threshold
8.3   *shippen*: cow-shed

IP No. 103.

B-G did not publish this song, which in both the above versions is fuller than the Sharp version. Version B may be earlier than A or the Sharp version, since it concerns a maying expedition by one girl, while the 'three maids' of the other versions do not quite seem to belong. However, it is clear that 'rushing' has exactly the same significance as 'maying'.

133 *Tinker, Tailor*

Come all pretty maids, some older, some younger,
In view of sweethearts I must not stop longer,
Some fourteen, some fifteen, some sixteen when they marry,
I'm five and twenty, I must no longer tarry.
   To my right fol the diddle, right fol the diddle,
   Whack fol the diddle lido.

My sister Susan she's crooked and mis-shapen,
Before she was sixteen, a bride she was taken,
Before she was eighteen, she'd a son and a daughter.
At my five and twenty I've never had an offer.

My sister Sarah she's younger than I am,
She's nine or ten sweethearts and still she deny 'em.
I wish I had one, I don't want so many,
I only want one if he would come to me.

I've often been told, 'tis by my old mother,
Going to one wedding soon brings on another.
Now if I thought so, I'd go without bidding,
So judge me now, young man, if I don't want wedding.

I'd make a good wife, nor scolding nor jealous,
I'd find him with money to spend at the alehouse.
While he was 'broad spending I'd be at home mending,
So judge me now, young man, if that isn't deserving.

Come shoemaker, sailor, come tinker, come tailor,
Come fiddler or fifer or drummer that's pretty,
Don't let me die an old maid but take me for pity.

H William Miller at Wootton Fitzpaine, April 1906

Ms. gives title: *Come all pretty maids.* Refrain indicated after stanza 2, but not subsequently.

I have not seen this elsewhere. I have adopted the present title to avoid confusion with many other songs beginning in much the same way.

134 *The Trees they are so High*

All the trees they are so high
And the leaves they are so green.
The day is past and gone, sweet love,
That you and I have seen.
It is cold winter's night,
You and I must lie alone,
Whilst my pretty lad is young and is growing.

O father, O father dear,
You've done to me great wrong,
That I should married be this day
Unto a lad so young.
It is cold winter's night
Here and I must make my moan
Whilst my pretty lad is young and is growing.

O daughter, daughter dear,
No wrong to thee is done,
For I have married thee this day
Unto a rich man's son.
It is cold winter's night
Here and I alone must weep
Whilst my pretty lad is young and is growing.

O father, father dear,
If that you think it fit,
Then send him to the school awhile
To be a year there yet.
At the buffle of the gale
Here I toss and cannot sleep
Whilst my pretty lad is young and is growing.

To let the lovely ladies know
They may not touch and taste
I'll bind a bunch of ribbons red
About his little waist,

265

And I'll wait another year
(O the roaring of the sea)
Whilst my pretty lad is young and is growing.

In a garden as I walked
I heard them laugh and call.
There were four and twenty playing there,
They played with bat and ball.
I must wait, awhile must wait
And then his bride will be.
O my pretty lad so young still is growing.

I listened in the garden,
I looked o'er the wall.
Of four and twenty scholars there
My love exceeded all.
O the snow, the snowflakes fall,
O I am chill and freeze,
But my pretty lad so young still is growing.

I'll cut my yellow hair,
I'll cut it 'cross my brow,
I'll go unto the college-ee
And none shall know me so.
O the clouds are driving by
And they shake the leafy trees
But my pretty lad so young still is growing.

To the college I did go,
I cut my yellow hair,
To be with him in sun and shower
His sports and studies share.
O the taller that he grew
The sweeter still grew he,
O my pretty lad so young still a-growing.

As it fell upon a day,
A bright and summer's day,
We went into the green wood
To frolic and to play.
O what did there befall
I tell not unto thee
But my pretty lad so young was still growing.

At thirteen he married was,
A father at fourteen,
And then his face was white as milk
And then his grave was green,
And the daisies were outspread
And the buttercups of gold
O'er my pretty lad so young now ceased growing.

I'll make my pretty love
A shroud of holland fine
And all the time I'm making it
My tears run down the twine,
And as the bell doth knell
I shiver as one cold
And weep o'er my pretty lad now done growing.

B-G   James Parsons and Mathew Baker at Lew Down, 1888

Ms. gives title *All the Trees they are so High*.

4.5   *buffle*: ms. gives huffle but a marginal note reads 'sung buffle'.
5.6   Line bracketed with initials SBG in margin as if the line had been supplied by **B-G**.

IP No. 96. See notes.
   B-G prints in *SW* an altered and abridged version. He substitutes 'seventeen' for 'thirteen' (stanza II), adding by way of explanation: 'In most versions, the age of the boy when married is 13, and he is a father at 14. I advanced his age a little, in deference to the opinion of those who like to sing the song in a drawing-room or at a public concert.'
   It seems, however, that not only has the boy's age been advanced, but the girl's age has been suppressed in most versions. According to one collected in Surrey by Lucy Broadwood (*FSJ* 4, 1902), the boy is 12 and the girl

'scarcely thirteen'. In another version collected by **B-G** from Roger Hannaford these ages are reversed:

> O father, father dear, you've done to me great wrong,
> You've wed me to a bonny lad who is far, is far too young,
> For I am only twelve, and he is scarce thirteen,
> But my bonny lad is young
> And is growing.

The Hannaford version also contains the stanza:

> I'll cut my gown of green, and cut it at the knee,
> I'll cut myself a pretty stick from out the greenwood tree,
> And all the world will think they have a bonny lad in me
> But my bonny lad so young
> Still is growing.

This connects the song, as **B-G** points out, with the ballad snatch sung by
the Gaoler's mad daughter in *The Two Noble Kinsmen* (1634), III.4.19:

> For I'll cut my green coat a foot above my knee;
> And I'll clip my yellow locks an inch below mine e'e:
> Hey, nonny, nonny, nonny.
> He s'buy me a white cut, forth for a ride,
> And I'll go seek him through the world that is so wide:
> Hey, nonny, nonny, nonny.

The text transcribed above from **B-G**'s mss. has, for a ballad in the oral
tradition, a strangely literary flavour in places. For comparison, I append the
following version from **B-G**'s own broadside collection (BM L.R. 271 a. 2,
Vol. VI, p. 33):

MY BONNY LAD IS YOUNG, BUT HE'S GROWING

1. O the trees that do grow high, and the leaves that do grow green.
   The days are gone and past, my love, that you and I have seen

2. On a cold winter's night when you and I alone have been,
   My bonny lad he's young, but he's growing.

   O father, dear father, you to me much harm have done
   You married me to a boy, you know he is too young,
   O daughter dear, if you will wait you'll quickly have a son,
   And a lady you'll be while he's growing.

3. I will send him to the college for one year or two,
   And perhaps in that time, my love, he may then do for you,
   We'll buy him some nice ribbons to tie round his bonny waist too,
   And let the ladies know he is married.

4. She went to the college and looked over the wall,
   Saw four and twenty gentlemen playing there at ball,
   They would not let her go through, for her true love she did call,
   Because he was a young man growing.

5. At the age of sixteen, oh he was a married man
   At the age of seventeen she brought him forth a son,
   At the age of eighteen the grass did grow over his gravestone,
   Cruel death put an end to his growing.

6. I will make my love a shroud of the fine holland brown
   And all the time I'm making it the tears they shall run down,
   Saying, once I had a sweetheart but now I have got none,
   Farewell to thee my bonny lad for evermore.

7. O now my love is dead and in his grave doth lie,
   The green grass grows over him so very high,
   There I can sit and mourn until the day I die,
   But I'll watch o'er his child while he's growing.

135 *Twankydillo*

A

Here's a health to the blacksmith,
The prince of good fellows,
Who works at the anvil
While the boy blows the bellows.
For it makes his bright hammers
To rise and to fall.
Says the old goat to the little goat
And the great goat of all,
Twankydillo, twankydillo,
Twanky-dil-dil-O-dillo,
And he that loves strong beer
Is a jolly good fellow.

B

The life of a shepherd is a life of great care,
With my crook and my dog Whitefoot I'll drive away all fear.
Twankydillo, twankydillo, dillo, dillo,
And he played on his merry bagpipes made of the green willow.
Green willow, green willow, willow, willow,
And he played on his merry bagpipes made of the green willow.

If ever my sheep should go astray on the plain O
I send my dog Whitefoot to fetch them back again O.
Twankydillo . . .

If ever I should meet with the old shepherd's horse O
I'll cut off his tail right close up to his erse O.
Twankydillo . . .

If ever I should meet with the old shepherd's wife O
I'll make him a cuckold all the days of his life O.
Twankydillo . . .

TWANKYDILLO

Version A **B-G** T. M. Snow, December 1889
'The usual words but with a slightly different refrain. First stanza only'. **B-G**
Version B **H** John Hallett at Mosterton, June 1906
'Final verse too indecent to write down.' **H**

What may be regarded as the standard version of this song is given in *English County Songs* (Broadwood and Fuller Maitland, 1893). Whether or not this is the original version, it is impossible to say. Version A is the first of the three stanzas of the standard version, with a refrain giving 'goat' instead of 'Cole'. Lucy Broadwood says in a note that 'foal' and 'colt' are also alternatives. This has led Margaret Dean-Smith to surmise that the song may have once been part of an animal mummery, like *Poor Old Horse* (No. 106). It appears to me as if the 'Twankydillo' refrain has a separate existence from the various stanzas to which it has been attached, and it may be older than any of these.

The Goose and the Gander (Mason, *Nursery Rhymes and Country Songs*, 1908) consists of two stanzas, of which the second (more or less unconnected with the first) is as follows:

> The blacksmith is black, but his silver is white,
> And he sits in the alehouse from morning till night.
> Tang dillo, tang dillo, tang dillo, tang dillo,
> And happy is the man that sits under the willow.

D'Urfey's *Pills* (Vol I, 1719) contains a ribald song about a rich farmer called Roger Twangdillo, not otherwise connected with the present song. This name and the form of the refrain as just quoted suggest that the trisyllabic form may be the older, and in this form there is a strong hint of an onomatopoeic representation of the noise of a hammer on an anvil. If so, the song must originally have concerned a blacksmith, and Version B, above, is a ribald parody.

A

Cold blows the wind tonight, sweetheart,
Cold are the drops of rain.
The very first love that ever I had
In greenwood he was slain.

I'll do as much for my true love
As any young woman may.
I'll sit and mourn above his grave
A twelvemonth and a day.

A twelvemonth and a day being up
The ghost began to speak.
Why sit you here by my graveside
And will not let me sleep?

O think upon the garden, love,
Where you and I did walk.
The fairest flower that blossomed there
Is withered on the stalk.

The stalk will bear no leaves, sweetheart,
The flowers will never return,
And my true love is dead, is dead,
And I do nought but mourn.

What is it that you want of me
And will not let me sleep?
Your salten tears they trickle down
And wet my winding sheet.

What is it that I want of thee,
O what of thee in thy grave?
A kiss from off thy clay cold lips,
And that is all I crave.

Cold are my lips in death, sweetheart,
My breath is earthy strong.
If you do touch my clay cold lips
Your time will not be long.

Cold though your lips in death, sweetheart,
One kiss is all I crave.
I care not, if I kiss but thee,
That I should share thy grave.

Go fetch me a light from dungeon deep,
Wring water from a stone,
And likewise milk from a maiden's breast
Which never babe had none.

She stroke a light from out a flint,
An ice-bell pressèd she,
She pressed the milk from a Johnnis wort
And so she did all three.

Now if you were not true in word
As now I know you be
I'd tear you as the withered leaves
Are torn from off the tree.

Now I have mourned upon his grave
A twelve month and a day,
I'll set my sail before the wind
To waft me far away.

B

So cold the wintry winds do blow
And down fell drops of rain.
I have had but one true love,
In greenwood she was slain.

I'll say as much for my true love
As any young man could say.
I'll sit and I'll weep on her cold grave
For a twelve month and a day.

When the twelve month and a day was up
The ghost began to weep.
Why do you sit here on my grave
And will not let me sleep?

There's one thing more that I do want
And that is all I crave,
And that is to kiss your lily-white lips
And I will go from your grave.

My lips they are as cold as clay,
My breath smells heavy and strong,
And if you kiss my lily-white lips
Your time will not be long.

Down in the garden of myrtle green
Where my true love and me did walk
The finest flower that ever was seen
Is withered unto the stalk.

The stalk is withered unto the root
And the root unto the ground.
That's why I mourn for the loss of my love
When she's not here to be found.

Version A **B-G** 'Sent first by Mrs Gibbons, daughter of late Sir W. P.
Trelawny Bart., as she remembered it sung to her by the nurse Elizabeth
Doidge, in about 1828. She did not recall verses 5, 6, 10, 11. These supplied
by [another source—illegible].' **B-G**

Ms. gives title *Cold Blows the Wind*. Four rows of dots between stanzas 12
and 13.

Version B **G** Mr Charles Bell at Andover, Hants, August 1906
Fourth line of stanza 1 repeated.

This ballad has been printed many times on broadsides and in folk song collections. Child (No. 78) gives four versions, only one of which is more than fragmentary. **B-G** gives in *SW* a garbled version, or perversion, partly of his own composition.

The many variants collected in the south and west of England, of which two are given here, agree as to the main lines of the story: a girl whose lover has died continues to weep for him beyond the prescribed term of one year. His ghost asks her what she wants. She asks for one kiss from his dead lips, and defies his warning that this would prove fatal to her. (In B, as in a minority of other versions, the sexes are reversed.) I am inclined to think that the 'lover's task' stanzas in A (10 and 11) are extraneous, and perhaps also stanzas 12 and 13; but it is possible that all the variants, where not actually confused, are fragments of a longer original, not yet discovered.

A version recovered by **H** is (apart from the reversal of the sexes) very similar to B, but contains an additional stanza of apparent authenticity which is not in other versions.

O! don't you see the fire, sweetheart, the fire that burns so blue,
Whilst my poor soul's tormented here, whilst I remain with you?

An article in *JEFDSS* 1941, enlarging on Child's notes, discusses the widespread diffusion in European folk-lore of the theme of *The Unquiet Grave*; this is based on the belief, held also throughout the East, that excessive grief on the part of the living disturbs the peace of the dead.

This strange and moving poem is a notable example of something far better preserved in the oral tradition than in ballad literature.

137 *The Wanton Seed*

As I walked out one morning fair
To view the fields and take the air
There I heard a pretty maid making her complain
And all she wanted was the chiefest grain
   Chiefest grain,
And all she wanted was the chiefest grain.

I said, My pretty maid, what do you stand in need.
Oh yes, kind sir, you're the man that can do my deed,
For to sow my meadow with the wanting seed
   Wanting seed,
For to sow my meadow with the wanting seed.

Then I sowèd high and I sowèd low,
And under her apron the seed did grow,
   Sprung up so accident-a-ly without e'er a weed,
And she always remembered the wanting seed
   Wanting seed,
And she always remembered the wanting seed.

H   J. Pomery at Bridport, May 1906

Ms. gives title *As I walked out one morning fair*.

  2 A space between lines 1 and 2 indicates a missing line.
  3.3 After *e'er* ms. gives *ary* in brackets, evidently the singer's pronunciation.

Ms. concludes with two stanzas described in a note as 'part of another song'.
I have not identified the song. The two additional stanzas are:

> The Cuckoo she sits on yonder tree
> She sang so sweet and she pleasèd me
> Oh! she sang so sweet and she pleased me well
> And 'tis Oh! my darling love farewell
>
> My mother she lives in Petticoat Hall
> If you come that way be sure to call
> For I make no doubt but she'll use you well
> And 'tis Oh! my darling love, farewell

I have not seen *The Wanton Seed* elsewhere.

276

138 *What did your Sailor Leave?*

What did your sailor leave you
When he went to sea?
He left me a sweet baby
In my arms as you see.
    Dear maid, how well she loved him.

How was your true love clothed,
What did he wear?
Blue was his pretty jacket,
White his trousers were.
    Dear maid, how well she loved him.

What if your sailor lover
Come ashore again?
Us shall the parson marry,
The clerk say Amen.
    Dear maid, how well she loved him.

What makes you weep and cry so?
He is far from I.
Home we shall be together
Until we die.
    Dear maid, how well she loved him.

Would that the wars were over,
Sailors back on shore.
Each would have a sweetheart
Who'd none before.
    Dear maid, how well she loved him.

B-G Robert Hard, November 1892

B-G did not publish this, and I have not seen it elsewhere.

139 *Willie O' Winsbury*

Oh it's of a merchant's daughter dear,
She was dressed all in green.
Oh and she looked over her father's castle wall
For to see the ships sail in.

Oh what's the matter with you, fair maid?
You do look so pale and wan.
I'm sure you've had some sore sickness
Or have you lain with some young man?

Oh no I've had no sore sickness,
No nor lain with no young man,
But it's all for the sake of my own father's ship
For she sails so long in Spain.

Now you pull off your gown of green
Oh and spread it on the plain
And declare unto me the very truth
Oh what you have undergone.

Oh is it by any lord or knight
Or by any noble man?
Oh no it's by nor lord nor knight
But it's by old Tom the Barber bold,
One of your 'prentice men.

Then he called down all his merry merry men
Oh by one, by two, by three.
Oh Tom the Barber used to come first
But the hinder one comes he.

Down then came Tom the Barber bold
All dressed all in silk.
Oh his eyes did change like the morning sun
And his hands so white as milk.

Oh will you wed my daughter dear
And take her by the hand?
And you shall dine and sup along with me
And be heir to all my land.

Oh yes, I'll wed your daughter dear
And take her by the hand
And I will dine and sup along with thee
And be heir of all thy land.

Now I have estate in fair Scotland,
I have gold and silver so free,
But where that you have got one guinea
There I have got thirty and three.

H   William Bartlett at Wimborne, September 1906

Last line of each stanza except 5 repeated.

For notes, see *IP* No. 59.

140 *Young Barnable*

Abroad as I was walking all in the month of May
I heard two lovers talking and thus to each other say.
'Twas of a mournful ditty and thus began their tale,
It filled my heart with pity, their grief for to bewail.

Samuel, Samuel, said Sarah, Samuel, Samuel, said she,
My friends and brother Barnable are so displeased with thee.
My friends and brother Barnable are so displeased with thee,
And here they mean to slay thee O all so cowardly.

Why is your brother Barnable so displeased with me?
Give me your hand, sweet lady, and I'll prove true to thee,
And I will fight young Barnable, though he a captain be,
And I will fight young Barnable, though he a captain be.

Yonder stood young Barnable a-bending of his bow,
Waiting for young Samuel, thinking to prove his woe,
Saying, I win you round, young Samuel, and unto me draw nigh
For here I mean to slay thee upon the mountain high.

Young Samuel stood amazèd, not knowing what to say.
At length he stepped up to him, his arrows he took away.
His arrows he took from him, his bow he broke in three
Saying, Where's the shot, young Barnable, you've got prepared
    for me?

Then on came Sarah Barnable a-tripping o'er the plain,
A-fearing lest young Samuel or her brother dear was slain,
A-wringing of her hands and a-wiping of her eyes,
At length she saw them coming down from the mountain high.

Young Barnable stepped up to her and took her by the hand
Saying, I do present my sister to be at your command,
I do present my sister to be your wedded wife.
God send you prosperation all the days of your life.

H   William Miller (85) at Wootton Fitzpaine, April 1906
For notes, see *IP* No. 115.

141 *Young Johnny was a Ploughboy*

Young Johnny was a ploughboy, a crafty young swain,
He went whistling and singing all over the plain,
Till he met with black-eyed Susan and her maiden head
And he valued her much more than the hairs on his head.

Good morning, pretty fair maid, you are in good time.
There's one thing I ask you, I think it no crime.
Will you go along with me, my love, to-morrow to the fair?
I will buy you some ribbons for to roll in your hair.

This girl seems uneasy, not willing for to go.
I wants no young man's ribbons, I would have you to know.
So don't trouble me nor tease me, it's more than you dare.
I wants no young man's ribbons to roll in my hair.

As they walked along together down by some shady grove
Where no one could see them but the angels above,
There he laid her down so softly before she was aware
And he gave to her some ribbons to roll in her hair.

When young girls are breeding they looks both pale and wan
And all they got to do is to please their young man.
So be constant and true-hearted wherever that you are,
You shall never want for ribbons to roll in your hair.

G Mr George Blake at St Denys, Southampton, June 6, 1906

1.4 *valued*: pronounced vallied (Note by **G**)

I have not seen this elsewhere. I think that 'ribbons' here implies an offer of marriage.

142 *Young Johnson*

Come all you lads and a warning, a warning take by me,
Never touch pen, ink or paper, for it's called forgery.
It was my wit and learning that brought me to this place,
Now at the bar I am arraigned, my parents to disgrace.

Young Johnson being a clever lad, well dressed from top to toe,
When the judge condemned him for to die, tears from his eyes did
  flow.
His uncle, he was standing by, reading a forgery will
Saying, We must hang young Johnson, though much it's against
  our will.

G Mr James Rampton at Whitchurch, Hants, May 1906

Evidently a fragment of a broadside which I have not discovered. Forgery was
made a capital offence in 1634, and a man was hung for it as late as 1824.

APPENDICES

APPENDIX I

FRAGMENTS

1.   *Flowers of the Valley*

There was a woman and she was a widow,
The flowers that were in the valley,
A daughter had she . . .
O the red, the green and the yellow,
The harp, the lute, the fife, the flute and the cymbal,
Sweet goes the treble violin,
The flowers that were in the valley.

No more remembered except these lines:

Three of them were seamen so brave,
The flowers that were in the valley,
Three of them were soldiers so bold,
O the red, the green and the yellow,
The harp . . .

and the end was:

There was an end of nine brave boys.

B-G 'Miss Gilbert of the Falcon Inn, Mawgan in Pyder, says that this was a song of one Thomas Williams, dead some years ago. Her brother William remembers another line: "Nine brave boys of her body were born".'

B-G prints in the *Garland* a fanciful lyric of his own composition based on this fragment, and says he tried in vain to recover the original ballad. Subsequent research has proved no more successful.

2.   *Little Miss Nancy*

It's little Miss Nancy, she's just in her teens,
She loves and she says, I know what it means.
The other day to her mother she said with a frown,
Indeed I must have a large flounce to my gown,
     Singing, fal le ral liddle oh laddle oh liddle oh
Fal le ral liddle oh laddle li day.

G   Mr Isaac Hobbes at Micheldever, Hants, June 1906

'The rest is wanting'—**G**

3.   *Oh Dickey, Oh Dickey*

   The parson sings:
   Oh Dickey, oh Dickey, how little dost thou think
   I'm here eating thy meat and drinking thy drink.
   If God spare my life I'll lie with thy wife
   And sing oh for a tankard of ale,
      O' more ale,
   And sing oh for a tankard of ale,
      O' more ale.

   Dickey's wife:
   Oh Dickey, oh Dickey, since thou art from home
   God send thee fair journey and never come home.
   If I ever do lack I've a priest at my back
   And sing . . .

   Oh Dickey, oh Dickey, since thou art so near
   Then out of my hop-bag thy head shall appear.
   If a friend getteth lack I'll stand at thy back
   And sing . . .

H   William Miller at Wootton, April 1906

Described in ms. as 'Fragment'. 'We could not get the recitation in which the song occurs'—**H**

4.   *The Virgin's Wreath*

I am a maiden sad and lonely,
Courted I was by a nice young man.
Early and late he waited only
Until my innocent heart he won.

Easterly winds why are they blowing
And tear the green leaves from the tree?
The lilies tall in gardens growing
And all abroken down like me.

O hearken to the cocks a crowing

B-G Fragment from Henry Langdon at Penrose, St Eval: also Peter Sandry

Ms. gives three lines of dots after the last line.

The lines about 'easterly winds' are a commonplace in ballads of deserted maidens. See notes to *Died of Love* (No. 34).

APPENDIX II

THE KEEPER

The Keeper was recovered by Sharp and **B-G**, both of whom published expurgated texts. For Sharp's version and notes on the song see *IP* No. 52. **H** took down the following chorus from Mrs Gulliver in May 1905:

O down, derram down, down and amongst the green leaves that
    do grow
Jacky; master; singing well, very well
O down derram down, down and amongst the green leaves that
    do grow.

To this he appended the following note: 'The tune of the verses is the same as that of the chorus, but Mrs Gulliver cannot remember any of them.'

B-G's mss. contain no words for this song, but in *SW* 1906 he refers to a 'Garland' text (BM 11621. c. 2). This text is No. 3 in a chapbook entitled *The Ewie wi' the crooked Horn's Garland containing four excellent new songs.* Licensed and entered according to order (n.d.).

> There was a keeper a shooting did go
> And under his cloak he carried a bow,
> 'Twas all for to shot the merry doe,
> Among yon leaves so green O,
> Jacky, master, sing you well,
> Very well, with my hey down, down,
> With my how down, down, etc.
>
> The first doe he shot at he miss'd,
> The second doe he hugged and kiss'd,
> The third doe he went where nobody wist,
> 'Twas among yon leaves so green O,
> Jacky, master, sing you well, etc.

The fourth doe jump'd over a brook,
The keeper catched her fast with his hook,
What he did there you may go and look
'Twas among the leaves so green O,
Jacky, master, sing you well, etc.

The fifth doe jump'd over the stile,
The keeper catched her fast by the heel;
There I believe he did both see and feel,
'Twas among the leaves so green O,
Jacky, master, sing you well, etc.

The sixth doe ran over the plain,
But he with his hounds did turn her again
It's there he did tickle her all in the merry vain,
'Twas among the leaves so green O,
Jacky, master, sing you well, etc.

APPENDIX III

BARING-GOULD'S SINGERS

[Taken from *Old Country Life* by S. Baring-Gould (Methuen 1890) Chapter XI.]

One, James Parsons, a very infirm man, over seventy, asthmatic and failing, has been a labourer all his life, and for the greater part of it on one farm. His father was famed through the whole country side as 'The Singing Machine', he was considered to be inexhaustible. Alas! he is no more, and his old son shakes his head and professes to have but half the ability, memory, and musical faculty that were possessed by his father. He can neither read nor write. From him I have obtained some of the earliest melodies and most archaic forms of ballads. Indeed the majority of his airs are in the old church modes, and generally end on the dominant. At one time his master sent him to Lydford on the edge of Dartmoor, to look after a farm he had bought. Whilst there, Parsons went every pay-day to a little moorland tavern, where the miners met to drink, and there he invariably got his 'entertainment' for his singing.

'I'd been zinging there,' said he, 'one evening till I got a bit fresh, and I thought 'twere time for me to be off. So I stood up to go, and then one chap, he said to me, "Got to the end o' your zongs, old man?" "Not I," said I, "not by a long ways; but I reckon it be time for me to be going." "Looky here, Jim," said he. "I'll give you a quart of ale for every fresh song you zing us to-night." Well, your honour, I sat down again, and I zinged on—I zinged sixteen fresh songs, and that chap had to pay for sixteen quarts.'

'Pints, surely,' I said.

'No, zur!' bridling up. 'No, zur—not pints, good English quarts. And then—I hadn't come to the end o' my zongs, only I were that fuddled, I couldn't remember no more.'

'Sixteen quarts between feeling fresh and getting fuddled!'

'Sixteen. Ask Voysey; he paid for 'n.'

Now this Voysey is a man working for me, so I did ask him. He laughed and said, 'Sure enough, I had to pay for sixteen quarts that evening.'

Another of my old singers is James Olver, a fine, hale old man, with a face fresh as a rose, and silver hair, a grand old patriarchal man, who has been all his life a tanner. He is a Cornishman, a native of St Kewe. His father was musical, but a Methodist, and so strict that he would never allow his children to sing a ballad or any profane song in his hearing, and fondly fancied that they grew up in ignorance of such things. But the very fact that they were tabooed gave young Olver and his sister a great thirst to learn, digest, and sing them. He acquired them from itinerant ballad-singers, from miners, and from the village song-men . . .

At Halwell, in North Devon, lives a fine old man named Roger Luxton, aged seventy-six, a great-grandfather, with bright eyes and an intelligent face. He stays about among his grandchildren, but is usually found at the picturesque farmhouse of a daughter at Halwell, called Croft. This old man was once very famous as a song-man, but his memory fails him as to a good number of the ballads he was wont to sing. 'Ah, your honour,' said he, 'in old times us used to be welcome in every farm house, at all shearing and haysel and harvest feasts; but, bless'y! now the farmers' da'ters all learn the pianny, and zing nort but twittery sort of pieces that have nother music nor sense in them; and they don't care to hear us, and any decent sort of music. And there be now no more shearing and haysel and harvest feasts. All them things be given up. 'Tain't the same world as used to be—'tain't so cheerful. Folks don't zing over their work, and laugh after it. There be no dances for the youngsters as there used to was. The farmers be too grand to care to talk to us old chaps, and for certain don't care to hear us zing. Why for nigh on forty years us old zinging-fellows have been drove to the public-houses to zing, and to a different quality of hearers too. And now I reckon the labouring folk be so tree-mendous edicated that they don't care to hear our old songs nother. 'Tis all *Pop goes the Weasel* and *Ehren on the Rhine* now. I reckon folks now have got different ears from what they used to have, and different hearts too. More's the pity.'

In the very heart of Dartmoor lives a very aged blind man, by name Jonas Coaker, himself a poet, after an illiterate fashion. He is only able to leave his bed for a few hours in the day. He has a retentive memory, and recalls many very old ballads. From being blind he is thrown in on himself, and works on his memory till he digs out some of the old treasures buried there long ago. Unhappily his voice is completely gone, so that melodies cannot be recovered through him.

There is a Cornishman whose name I will give as Elias Keate— a pseudonym—a thatcher, a very fine, big-built, florid man, with big, sturdy sons. This man goes round to all sheep-shearings, harvest homes, fairs, etc., and sings. He has a round, rich voice, a splendid pair of bellows; but he has an infirmity, he is liable to become the worse for the liquor he freely imbibes, and to be quarrelsome over his cups. He belongs to a family of hereditary singers and drinkers. In his possession is a pewter spirit-bottle—a pint bottle—that belonged to his great-grandfather in the latter part of the last century. That old fellow used to drink his pint of raw spirit every day; so did the grandfather of Elias; so did the father of Elias; so would Elias—if he had it; but so do not his sons, for they are teetotalers.

Another minstrel is a little blacksmith; he is a younger man than the others, but he is, to me, a valuable man. He was one of fourteen children, and so his mother sent him, when he was four years old, to his grandmother, and he remained with his grandmother till he was ten. From his grandmother he acquired a considerable number of old dames' songs and ballads. His father was a singer; he had inherited both the hereditary faculty and the stock-in-trade. Thus my little blacksmith learned a whole series which were different from those acquired from the grandmother. At the age of sixteen he left home, finding he was a burden, and since that age has shifted for himself. This man tells me that he can generally pick up a melody and retain it, if he has heard it sung once; that of a song twice sung, he knows words and music, and rarely, if ever, requires to have it sung a third time to perfect him.

On the south of Dartmoor live two men also remarkable in their way—Richard Hard and John Helmore. The latter is an old miller, with a fine intelligent face and a retentive memory. He can read, and his songs have to be accepted with caution. Some are very old, others have been picked up from song-books. Hard is a poor cripple, walking only with the aid of two sticks, with sharply-chiselled features,—he must have been a handsome man in his youth, —bright eyes, a gentle, courteous manner, and a marvellous store of old words and tunes in his head. He is now past stone-breaking on

John Helmore

the roadside, and lives on £4 per annum. He has a charming old wife; and he and the old woman sing together in parts their quaint ancient ballads. That man has yielded up something like eighty distinct melodies. His memory, however, is failing; for when the first lines of a ballad in some published collection is read to him, he will sometimes say, 'I did know that some forty years ago, but I can't sing it through now'. However, he can very generally 'put the tune to it'.

The day of these old singers is over. What festive gatherings there are now are altered in character. The harvest home is no more.

Richard Hard

We have instead harvest festivals, tea and cake at sixpence a head in the school-room, and a choral service and a sermon in the church. Village weddings are now quiet enough, no feasting, no dancing. There are no more shearing feasts; what remain are shorn of all their festive character. Instead, we have cottage garden produce shows. The old village 'revels' linger on in the most emaciated and expiring semblance of the old feast. The old ballad-seller no more appears in the fair. I wrote to a famous broadside house in the west the other day, to ask if they still produced sheet-ballads, and the answer was, 'We abandoned that line thirty years ago'; and no one else took it up.

APPENDIX IV

116 The Seeds of Love
117 Seventeen Come Sunday *I'm Seventeen Come Sunday*
131 Three Maids a Milking
132 Three Maids a Rushing
134 The Trees they are so High *Still Growing*
139 Willie o' Winsbury *Lord Thomas of Winesbury*
140 Young Barnable *Young Barnswell*

INDEX OF FIRST LINES